One Family's Journey

ONE FAMILY'S

PETER BENTLEY

As told to **Robin Fowler**

JOURNEY

CANFOR AND THE TRANSFORMATION
OF B.C.'S FOREST INDUSTRY

Douglas & McIntyre

D&M PUBLISHERS INC.

Vancouver/Toronto/Berkeley

Douglas & McIntyre
An imprint of D&M Publishers Inc.
2323 Quebec Street, Suite 201
Vancouver BC Canada V5T 4S7
www.douglas-mcintyre.com

Cataloguing data available from Library and Archives Canada
ISBN 978-1-55365-868-9 (cloth)
ISBN 978-1-55365-869-6 (ebook)

Jacket and text design by Peter Cocking
Jacket photographs courtesy Canfor Forest Products Ltd.
Printed and bound in Canada by Friesens
Text printed on acid-free, 100% post-consumer paper
Distributed in the U.S. by Publishers Group West

We gratefully acknowledge the financial support of the Canada
Council for the Arts, the British Columbia Arts Council, the
Province of British Columbia through the Book Publishing Tax
Credit, and the Government of Canada through the Canada
Book Fund for our publishing activities.

I WOULD LIKE TO DEDICATE this book first to all of the employees of the Canfor Group of Companies, in appreciation for their service.

I would also like to dedicate these stories to my fifteen grandchildren. I want each of them to be proud of the role their family has played in the development and growth of Canfor, and the benefits that have flowed to the communities in which we have been located.

Contents

Introduction

ALL MY LIFE I have been steeped in British Columbia's forest culture. I was raised in it and loved every aspect of it—the forests, the manufacturing, the relationships with customers and suppliers, and the business economics.

In past years, friends and colleagues often asked why I hadn't yet written a book about Canadian Forest Products, the company founded more than seventy years ago by my father, Poldi Bentley, and my uncle, John Prentice. My answer was always the same: I felt that such an account would be of interest to only a few. Over time, however, I became convinced of this project because I saw that it would allow me to describe my views of an industry that has changed so dramatically in the past century, and more important, it would permit me to thank the many first-rate people on our team—people who helped Canfor grow and prosper.

What follows is a business memoir that gives my perspective on the most interesting aspects of and turning points in Canfor's evolution.

PETER BENTLEY, *October 2011*

1

A Long Journey
Vienna to Vancouver

I T WAS GOOD fortune and a love of hunting that first brought my father, Leopold Bloch-Bauer, to Canada in 1937. A friend from Germany had invited him along on a big-game hunting trip in the Rocky Mountains. He immediately fell in love with Canada. When he returned home, he enchanted us with stories about the beauty of British Columbia's Elk Valley, close to the Alberta border. He was complimentary about Canadians and impressed that nobody complained as they slowly recovered from the Great Depression. He admired the positive attitude of the people he met and remarked on how genuine they were.

Fresh from the wilds of Canada, my father joined my mother, Antoinette ("Toni"), and her parents for a tour of Chicago, San Francisco, Los Angeles, Houston, and New York. That journey left my father with the impression of the United States as "artificial" and assured of his preference for Canada. I remember him pondering how things weren't looking good in Europe with the continuing emergence of the Nazi movement in Germany. He kept talking about how we should consider starting a business in North America. It seemed certain that, if ever we were to settle anywhere other than in Austria, it would be in western Canada.

A year later, in 1938, we became newcomers to this immense country. I was eight years old, fluent in German and Czech, with some French but no English, and had only started to digest the drastic changes imposed on our family and so many others in recent months. We had abruptly left a luxurious, privileged, and peaceful life in Austria.

Memories of my earliest years are few but vivid. I can see myself as a toddler, pedalling my silver Arrow push-car through the large rooms of our third-floor apartment on Strohgasse in Vienna. I was awed by the height of our rooms and recall one occasion when I tried in vain (but with some consequence) to spit my spinach in the air in an effort to reach the ceiling. We passed idyllic summer months playing in my grandparents' gardens at their home near Salzburg, or with my cousins in Oberleutensdorf, in the Sudetenland of Czechoslovakia. It was a happy, sheltered, and very European life. But it was fleeting.

Our family was technically Jewish, though we never thought of ourselves as such. We didn't practise religion, and it was my impression that my parents and relations identified far more as Austrian. I attended a synagogue only once, for a wedding.

The late thirties were confusing times for a small child. I didn't understand why machine-gun nests began appearing at intersections in Vienna in about 1936. Nor could I escape the embarrassing fact that I was suddenly being walked to and from school when I was perfectly capable of making my own way. But my parents insisted, saying, "No, you must never be outside alone."

Our life as we had known it in Vienna changed on March 12, 1938. History books refer to what happened that day as the *Anschluss*, a German word that translates as "link up." It was, of course, Hitler's terrifying invasion of our country. I had just crawled into bed after dinner and was still awake when my father came in and told me to get dressed. Within hours, my mother, my cousins, and I were being driven with both our nannies to the Czech border. My father had little trust in my grandparents' chauffeur, so he followed behind to ensure we got through. Our car was the last vehicle to cross the border that night, and we were probably permitted to leave because my nanny and I spoke fluent Czech. My father saw us pass and then returned to Vienna, where he hoped to put his business affairs in order. Instead, he was arrested by the Gestapo and put in jail.

We waited in the temporary safety of our family home in Oberleutensdorf, where my mother's family owned a spinning mill. My maternal grandparents, Otto and Käthe Pick, and my aunt and uncle, Hans and Evi Pick (my mother's brother and sister-in-law), soon joined us. They had been at a cotton convention in Egypt when the Nazis marched into Vienna. It was clear that Czechoslovakia wouldn't be secure for long. Within days, the family chartered a three-engine Junkers German aircraft to take us from Prague to Zurich. A normal scheduled flight might have landed somewhere we didn't want to go.

I attended grade two in Zurich for a couple of months and struggled with handwriting because it was very different from what I already knew. Instead of the rounded Austrian script, I was expected to change my hand to create narrower, more vertical letters.

A particular thrill for me was living at the magical Dolder Grand Hotel, a magnificent structure that sat on a hill overlooking Zurich. I remember enjoying the footpaths around the hotel, the skating rink, and the swimming pool.

Many decades later, I would take my family for a tour of central Europe. We arrived the week before the 1972 Summer

Olympics began in Munich. Because we had once owned the Canadian distributorship, Mercedes-Benz generously made available a twelve-passenger minibus for the journey. When the seven of us arrived at the Stuttgart airport, three buses were waiting—one white, one blue, and one red. A Mercedes-uniformed driver greeted me, saying "Herr Director, you did not specify a colour, so we brought you a choice." My children chose the white bus and I drove up to the familiar front entrance of the Dolder Grand to let everyone off and unload our luggage. The hotel had kept its original beauty and elegance, just as I had known it at the age of eight. Assuming I was a hired hand, the doorman suggested I go to the servants' entrance. I told him if I could not come in, our rooms would not be paid for.

While in Zurich in 1938, my family continued to shelter my cousins and me from all details related to the crisis that was rapidly unfolding in Europe. Little did I know that my mother was not only worried about my father's imprisonment in Vienna, but also about his fractured ribs, an injury he had sustained several days before the *Anschluss* while playing international field hockey for the Austrian national team. I certainly didn't understand the danger my father was facing, and had no idea how close he would come to being sent to a concentration camp. I had no reason to believe he would not be with us again.

I remained in the dark about what was happening as my family anxiously hoped for my dad's release from jail. A stroke of fortune allowed that to happen when Mrs. Herta Strohschneider, one of our family's closest friends and a devout Catholic, intervened. When she heard that my father had been arrested, she went directly to the chief of the Gestapo with a strategy in mind. She knew that the man had competed with my mother, an internationally renowned equestrian, in dressage shows.

"Are you aware," Mrs. Strohschneider asked, "that Mrs. Bloch-Bauer's husband is in jail?"

The man sent immediately for my father and invited him for lunch, during which he announced that a car was waiting to take him home. "If you are not out of the country by midnight, I cannot guarantee your safety," he warned.

When Dad did join us in Zurich, it was a happy reunion, though it would be a long while before I would truly understand how joyful the event was for our family.

At the time, there was a lot of excitement about the pending championship fight between world heavyweight champion Max Schmeling from Germany and Joe Louis from the United States. Schmeling had won against Louis two years earlier. I was curious why that 1938 fight was so significant, not knowing that it would become one of the most famous boxing matches in history. I later realized that Hitler's statements about the "super race" had generated propaganda on both sides. Everybody we knew celebrated Joe Louis's victory at Yankee Stadium that June.

Several months after my father's happy arrival, we left Zurich for London, where we stayed in an apartment on Grosvenor Square while waiting for our official documents. We had been granted immigrant status to the United States. Instead of joining us in London, my grandparents, Otto and Käthe Pick, chose to head for Paris, an apparently safe haven that was closer to home. They could not foresee that most of Europe would end up besieged, and they would not leave until the Germans started to move into France.

Despite our U.S. immigrant status, my father had his heart set on Canada. He was determined to find a way in. As he went about trying to find one, the agent general for British Columbia in London introduced him to the local manager of the Bank of Montreal, a meeting that would prove most helpful in the months to come.

My father had another important task while he searched for a means to move us to Canada. Otto Pick was an industrial visionary and ahead of his time. He had built the first windowless, air-conditioned plant in central Europe on a large piece of land that had once housed the Daimler auto factory in Wiener Neustadt, Austria. Other companies had established modern plants on the site as well. As tensions rose under Hitler, my father and grandfather became suspicious about how some areas of the site were being used. By the time we left Austria, they had confirmed that the Germans were building a Messerschmitt aircraft plant there and using the former auto test track as an airport. Dad's self-assigned mission in London was to visit the British Air Ministry and deliver the plans for the plant, which he had brought with him from Austria. Many years later, at a Palm Springs golf club, retired U.S. Air Force General Keith Compton told me the story of how he successfully led an attack from North Africa and bombed the plant.

It was difficult in 1938 to immigrate to Canada. But as still more luck—and perhaps a little strategy—would have it, my father played a fortuitous game of golf in England with Beverley Baxter, a Canadian-born journalist and member of the British Parliament. My father and Baxter were partners in a foursome, and my dad birdied the last hole to win the match one up. After the game, he asked Baxter for help in getting landed immigrant status. Baxter was leaving on a ship for Canada the following day, but he quickly wrote a reference note and handed it to my father. That was a crucial turning point in all of our lives. The note was short and to the point: "We need people like this in Canada." Some time after that, we were granted immigrant status in Canada.

Both my mother and I had contracted the mumps in London, a fact that fortunately was not picked up by the medical examiner.

After getting medical approval, we made our way with Canadian papers in hand to Southampton, where we boarded the *Empress of Britain,* bound for Quebec. The 42,000-ton vessel was Canadian Pacific's flagship, built in 1930. It was the finest and largest of the Canadian Pacific fleet, carving an alternate northerly passage from Europe to Quebec, instead of following the usual route across the Atlantic to New York.

We were a large family group on board the *Empress*—my parents; my nanny, and me; my Uncle Hans and Aunt Evi; their two daughters, Elizabeth and Marietta; and their nanny. I remember thinking how funny my two cousins looked during the ship's safety drills with their life vests reaching from their necks to their feet, as though they were wearing evening dresses.

Throughout our halting escape from Europe, I was secure only in the comfort of being surrounded by my immediate family. I had no idea where we were going, but I knew that North America was gigantic compared with Europe. We were just more than four days at sea, and as exciting as it was for me, for my parents my first trans-Atlantic journey was a mix of anticipation and sadness. Our extended family had spun off in many directions to escape what had become a tragic and brutal reality in Europe, where Jews and many others were being rounded up.

We disembarked in Quebec City and travelled by train to Montreal, where we checked into the Windsor Hotel. I was impressed by the cannons in the park where I played opposite the Sun Life Building, which was then famous as the largest building in the British Empire.

I loved cars and was pleased when my dad bought the Cadillac that carried him, my mother, my nanny, and me on our long transcontinental journey to the West Coast. My dad had never been to Vancouver, but he had heard it was a beautiful city with a temperate climate. Before his hurried escape from Vienna, he had identified Vancouver as our final destination and optimistically arranged for our belongings to be shipped there.

With no direct route across Canada at the time, we headed to the U.S. border and on to the Ambassador Bridge from Windsor to Detroit. As we drove through the northern states, we had to stop and buy bug screens for the radiator grill at the front of the car. It was a terrible year for grasshoppers and they quickly clogged the cooling system. We were witnessing the end of the "Dirty Thirties"; there was little rain and grasshoppers swarmed around everything the dust didn't cover.

My dad was a fast driver and a good one, and it was inevitable that at one point we would be stopped by the highway patrol. The uniformed man approaching our car from behind set my parents' nerves on edge. He asked where we were from and where we were going.

"Vienna and Vancouver," my dad answered cheerfully.

"If you have come so far and have so far to go, keep going!" the officer said and waved us on our way.

We arrived in Vancouver on a grey day in August and checked into the Hotel Vancouver at its old site on Granville at Georgia. The city's beauty at the time was far from obvious. It was a dry summer on the coast as well, and one of the worst forest fires in B.C. history raged out of control for thirty days, burning 35,000 hectares. The smoke from Vancouver Island obscured the North Shore Mountains for weeks. Oak Street was a narrow, two-lane road with a streetcar that led to the gun club. Beyond West 41st Avenue, you left the houses behind and headed into the bush.

We stayed at the Hotel Vancouver until the academic year began. I recall my father saying that we couldn't afford that level of accommodation for much longer. Aunt Evi and Uncle Hans had joined us in Vancouver and with my parents went looking for a home large enough to accommodate our two families. They found a typical 1920 Shaughnessy house to lease from the Canadian Pacific Railway (CPR) at the corner of Balfour and Cartier. Our neighbours across the street and the first people I met in the city were the Bloedels, an American family that we came to know well. At the time, they were part of the forest company Bloedel, Stewart, and Welch, which was later bought by MacMillan to become MacMillan Bloedel. The two Bloedel daughters, Virginia and Eulalie, were close to my age and on several occasions I would spend a week with them at their summer home on Bainbridge Island. We have remained lifelong friends.

Within a few months, we had moved again, this time to a home on Matthews with the rest of the family. In 1941, my father would buy our own family home at 1402 McRae, which we would keep at my father's request until my mother died in 2004. The railway owned a great deal of the neighbourhood at one time. The house on McRae, known as the Nichol Mansion after its first owner, was one of the first distinguished homes built after the CPR decided to create a community called Shaughnessy. I loved the house, which closely resembled the home that Sheila and I have lived in for many years. The same architect designed both houses.

I was struck by the beauty of Vancouver's residential neighbourhoods. Living amidst large green gardens within a city was new to me after my early childhood in our Vienna apartment. Like my father before me, I also noticed that Canadian people were very friendly. Members of the community invited my parents out soon after we arrived, and my dad was quick to establish friendships grounded in golf and tennis at the Jericho Golf and Country Club at Spanish Banks.

Soon I noticed the city's dramatic Marine Building and the new Hotel Vancouver, both towering over a small downtown core. The following spring, we heard the exciting news that King

George VI and Queen Elizabeth would be coming to Vancouver in time to officially open the Lions Gate Bridge and the Hotel Vancouver, then the city's tallest building. It was a special day when I carried my stepladder to the corner of West 16th Avenue and Granville, climbed to the top rung, and watched the royal motorcade pass on its way downtown.

SEVERAL MONTHS AFTER arriving in Canada, my father adopted a new family name and became Leopold Lionel Garrick Bentley. He changed our surname from Bloch-Bauer because in his mind our new beginning required a more pronounceable and anglicized name. He also felt that, with the war pending, it might be easier on me to have an English name. He later said he was unsure if that had been a wise decision. My uncle also changed his name from Hans to John, and from Pick to Prentice.

It was a time of enormous adjustment for all of us, and we had a great deal to learn about our new home. My entire family had the advantage of being fluent in English—except for me. Austrian business people spoke English but I had not had time to learn it. In the fall of 1938, I attended Prince of Wales School for a few weeks while my parents arranged for me to transfer, on the recommendation of Butch Keeling, the reverend at St. John's Shaughnessy Church. He suggested that I would benefit from the smaller classes at St. George's School. Before too long, I was baptized in the Anglican Church and subsequently confirmed. That was the only religious training I ever had.

My experience at St. George's was generally positive from the start. I was placed in grade four and picked up the language quickly, though a few boys occasionally teased me about my accent. I adapted readily; however, it would always be the case that I just didn't like studying. I was proficient at math and not very good at most other subjects. The full mental transition to

English didn't happen until grade six or seven, when I finally found myself no longer doing arithmetic in my head in German. English became my primary language, though my family spoke German to me at home so I would maintain it. I used to resent that because we were at war with Germany. I will always be indebted to St. George's for what the school did for me.

As a newcomer, I was certainly intimidated by the teasing I endured because of my accent, but I was less sensitive to signs of overt discrimination that might have affected my parents at the time. One such occasion arose when my father was considering submitting an application to the Vancouver Club. Many of his friends were members and some had offered to sponsor him. One thoughtful friend feared my father would be rejected and took him aside to advise that he might be better off if he didn't submit an application. I did not join the Vancouver Club myself because of that incident. Decades later, the club president and the membership chair came to see me and asked why I had not applied.

"Well, I understand that my dad wasn't good enough to make it," I explained. "If you want me to join, I would love to, but I have a condition. I would like you to invite my father as a precleared member, so that when you call on him you can tell him that, if he wants to join, he's in."

The club complied with my request, but as it turned out, by then my dad preferred playing golf and bridge with his friends at the Marine Drive Golf Club. After all those years, he chose not to join, but he called me and said, "Go ahead. Thank you." As far as I know, that's about as close as we got to discrimination.

We never forgot how fortunate we were to be granted immigration status; it's no secret that Canada closed its doors to Europeans needing to escape Hitler's gruesome regime. News of the war was foremost on our minds. We heard in 1939 that the Allies had sunk the heavily gunned German battleship the *Graf*

Spee off the coast of South America. I recall two years later, when the HMS *Hood*, supposedly an indestructible battle cruiser, was sunk. After Japan entered the war in 1941 with the bombing of Pearl Harbor, the West Coast initiated blackouts. My father and I would walk around the neighbourhood on patrol to ensure that people had their lights turned off or their curtains drawn tight.

Our family gathered regularly around the radio at home to listen to news of the war. The German attacks on England were severe. We would cheer when we learned of any small Allied victories.

We were deeply concerned about my father's sister Luise, her husband, Viktor Guttman, and their two children, who had fled to Yugoslavia. Even though Tito was hailed as a hero in the United States, we knew he was an evil man. My uncle Viktor was thrown in jail by the Nazis during the war. After the war, he was rearrested by Tito and executed. The excuse we received was that during the war, his company continued to produce lumber for the Germans. The real reason for his execution, of course, was that he was a capitalist. We were all stricken with grief. My aunt Luise, her second husband, Beppo Gattin, and the children eventually joined us in Canada.

The thought of the war ending never crossed my mind. I had been a Cub, and rather than going into Scouts next, I joined the St. George's cadet corps. I took it for granted that, when I was old enough, I would become a fighter pilot, a far better prospect than spending days and nights in a cold, wet, muddy trench somewhere.

AT A YOUNG AGE, you don't think about your parents' relationship, but in hindsight, I see that my mother and father had a close, though rather pragmatic marriage. They had a great mutual admiration, but I never got the impression that there was any love or warmth between them. Naturally, that affected me in a significant way. If it hadn't been for my Czech governess, "Frauli," who came to Canada with us, I don't think I would have experienced any affection at all as a child. She married a Croatian man in Canada called Mr. Jurak, and they lived in the attic of my mother's house until they both died.

My father wasn't an affectionate man, but I remember him teasing me. When I went to bed, he used to tickle my feet. I was very ticklish and it drove me crazy. As a child in Vienna, I would wait with great anticipation to do things—anything—with my dad. I loved being in his company and found it particularly exciting to watch him shoot pheasants on a private estate just outside the city. It was all driven birds (whereby beaters are used to make the birds fly over a line of shooters) and he was a very good shot. At one point in Hungary, I remember he set a record of 398 cock pheasants in a day. You did not keep any birds from those shoots. The estate would sell them to restaurants. Dad also did a lot of big-game hunting.

Later, I would occasionally accompany my father across the north arm of the Fraser River on the old Marpole swing bridge, to the fields on Sea Island, near the airport. Anyone who owned land or foreshore rights there could legally shoot ducks. Later, the family company also owned Douglas Island, at the confluence of the Fraser and Pitt rivers, a booming ground we used to store logs upriver from the mill during the spring freshets. We went duck hunting there, too, with our springer spaniels or Labradors. In my adult years, my father and I enjoyed shooting together in Spain and we had a shared passion for golf. Dad passed along to me his love of sports and cars. I was always keen on his cars. I remember my excitement as a boy in Vienna when he bought an American 1936 Cord that was way ahead of its time.

My father had a wonderful spirit and he generally enjoyed life. He had a strong personality and made friends easily. Everybody liked him. One of the best descriptions I ever heard of him was that he was equally comfortable with royalty and the cleanup man. He was also a generous and giving person, and he often said he got much more joy from giving than receiving gifts.

I did not have much contact with my Uncle John in Austria, though we naturally grew to know each other after we immigrated. I always had great admiration and respect for him as a bright, well-educated, and thoughtful person. He had been "Dr. Pick" in Europe because he had a law degree, and he dropped that formality when we came to Canada. He enjoyed sports, and although he wasn't as athletic as my dad, he played tennis and enjoyed horseback riding, as did my mother. John had a passion for professional sports that my father and I shared.

John's wife, my Aunt Evi, was always a central member of our family. I worshipped her; she was always Sheila's and my favourite. Evi was a warm, outgoing person and she adjusted readily to life in Canada. In contrast, my mother never did adapt to this new world. From 1938 on, she was not unhappy here, but it was obvious to us all that she blossomed during her visits home to Austria after the war.

2

Pacific Veneer
A Solid Beginning

I WAS A BOY of eleven when I started attending family business meetings. We would gather on Tuesday evenings in my grandparents' living room. I loved being a part of the business, even then, quietly listening and absorbing all that went on. Never a child relegated to the periphery, I was welcomed to sit with my father, my uncle, and my grandfather, often with their wives, privy to their discussions about how they planned to build a new life for us all with a company that eventually would realize their hopes. My grandparents Otto and Käthe Pick arrived in Vancouver three years after we did, so my father and uncle were on their own in deciding the direction they would take in 1938.

I was not too young to recognize the difficult task these two men had ahead of them. They were new immigrants with a relatively small amount of capital to invest and not a lot of room for error. Still, they were more fortunate than many newcomers in having some limited wealth to invest, even if that precious capital was a fraction of what my family had been forced to leave behind in Europe. What they had in their favour was a strong family foundation, a particularly European brand of confidence, a good education, and the fact that they were still young men.

Our two families, the Bloch-Bauers and the Picks (now the Bentleys and the Prentices), weren't as close in Europe as they became in Canada, though they had been gradually building toward a special working relationship. After a traditional European upbringing and schooling, my father had attended university in Vienna and then studied textile engineering in Germany. He had decided not to follow his brothers, Charles and Robert, in their decision to join their uncle Ferdinand's sugar business. Instead, he chose to work with my mother's father, Otto Pick, and her brother, Hans (John), running their cotton-spinning venture.

With our move to the safety and promise of Canada's West Coast, my father and Uncle John wanted to create a successful business and a decent standard of living. In all the years we were a private company, from when we started until 1983, we never took a dividend; the company reinvested its entire cash flow. Both men always wanted a good reputation. Dad was a people person and a visionary; Uncle John loved numbers and technology. Together they held a strong belief in the principles of integrity, family, and safety. They had an amazing partnership in which they shared core values and respected each other's strengths. They both had excellent business sense and they worked well together. With the eventual and ongoing support of my grandfather, they stood a good chance of succeeding in whatever they put their minds and ambitions to.

THE TENSION IN EUROPE was escalating as my father and uncle went about searching for a means to make a good living in Canada. They were fortunate from the start to have a pair of invaluable connections in Vancouver. One had been made months before in London when the agent general for British Columbia had introduced my father to the Bank of Montreal. The second was the prominent Rogers family, known to us through my great-uncle Ferdinand's sugar enterprise. The fact that they also dealt with the Bank of Montreal was both encouraging and convenient.

My father and Uncle John enjoyed their early meetings with the Rogers family about possible opportunities. They had an idea involving two other newcomers to Vancouver who had an appealing business plan. In short order, a meeting was arranged.

John Bene, born in Austria and raised in Hungary, had a broad education in engineering and forest operations, with recent experience working in his family's plywood factory. When Bene arrived in Canada in 1938, he quickly noticed that no companies in British Columbia were manufacturing his family specialty, hardwood furniture veneers. Together with his colleague, Leslie Schaeffer, he had been looking for business partners. Thanks to the Rogers family, they found them in my father and uncle. The four men must have sensed right away that it was a good match. My family lacked any practical knowledge of wood, but my dad and uncle both had a strong business acumen that would contribute to any new venture.

Fortunately, a small portion of our family's textile wealth was held beyond the reach of currency controls in Europe. With foresight, my dad, uncle, and grandfather had grasped the opportunity in 1937 to overpay for the machinery from England and the United States bound for their new mill being built in Wiener Neustadt, outside Vienna. In the same way, they paid above the invoice price for cotton purchased in the safe haven of the United States, instead of continuing to purchase cotton in Egypt. All of this was handled through the financial firm Morgan Stanley, and money was put aside from each transaction and placed into our account.

During their early days in Canada, they had completely open minds and no fixed idea of what they would do. They said that they had wanted to look around and they weren't in a great hurry. They were prepared to start a business for themselves, but the unexpected opportunity to join Bene and Schaeffer seemed timely, especially because, at that time, no other veneer companies operated in western Canada. Our family ended up taking 60 percent equity and the Rogers family backed our Hungarian partners for their 40 percent.

On the north bank of the Fraser River in New Westminster, a sizeable piece of swampy land, serviced by railroad tracks at the foot of Braid Street, was up for sale. Because the site required a lot of work, the cost of the property was next to nothing, but still a little steep from the perspective of new immigrants. Bene and Schaeffer went with my dad and uncle to see Fred Hume, then mayor of New Westminster, to see if they could strike some sort of deal. Hume would later become Vancouver's mayor, known as "Friendly Fred" and admired for donating his salary to charity. But in 1938, times were tough, with unemployment still plaguing Canadians in the wake of the Depression. Hume wanted a brighter future for his municipality's population of twenty thousand, and he was willing to negotiate. If the mill my dad and his colleagues were proposing guaranteed the hiring of twenty-five people or more, then Hume would promise a tax advantage over three years.

New Westminster, the oldest city in western Canada, was an ideal place to launch a business on the coast. I remember watching the dredge, which was already working for the harbour boards on the Fraser at the time in an effort to make the river more navigable. By September 1938, the partners were ready to start creating a piece of dry land from the ready supply of sand available from the riverbed. It was important to ensure that the site was built up with enough sand to bring the new surface higher above the moody Fraser than any recorded floods in the area. A couple of months later, my father and his three partners signed the documents incorporating Pacific Veneer Company Ltd., affectionately known as "PV."

By the following spring, the site was ready and they erected a small building that housed a sixteen-foot slicer, a dryer, a clipper, hog conveyors, and auxiliary equipment. Then there was my uncle's favourite—the boiler house, where boilers burned waste and generated steam. He had found a man to do the brickwork and, in an understated ceremony, Aunt Evi lit the first fire.

John Bene and Leslie Schaeffer were capable men who led the way for my dad and uncle when it came to designing the new plant. I didn't have a lot of contact with them, of course, but I recall that Schaeffer had great problems learning English. Once, when he was negotiating with one of the equipment companies, he was getting hot under the collar. In his frustrated efforts to tell the man that the worsening conflict might develop into a lawsuit, he declared, "If you don't watch out, this will turn into a suitcase!"

As promised in the deal with Mayor Hume, the plant employed twenty-five people in addition to the four owners, and my father's brother Robert became the company's first accountant. He had arrived in Canada shortly after we did, with his wife, Thea, and their son George. Eventually, Robert looked after municipal taxes for all of our company operations throughout British Columbia. According to employment records, a William Johnson started hourly work at the plant on March 15, 1939, and Sigrid Sovik was the first woman to begin hourly work in July of the following year.

In the early summer of 1939, the plant began to produce veneer used for panelling walls in expensive homes and for making furniture surfaces. As British Columbia does not have any exotic hardwood to speak of, many of the logs were imported from tropical countries in Africa, and from the Philippines and Honduras.

The exotic species included zebrawood, teak, and mahogany, but we also brought in bird's-eye maple from eastern Canada.

Through those initial months, my father and uncle learned a great deal about handling wood and conducting business in Canada. Years later, my dad admitted that he had not been at all optimistic about the new venture. He had seen it as a modest operation with little growth potential because we were selling to the Canadian furniture industry.

As he worked with my father to develop the business, Uncle John continued to show a great love for boiler houses—in fact, anything to do with steam and boilers. Aunt Evi wasn't as close to the business as my mother was, though it was never clear to me whether my mother asked about the business as much as she did because she was indeed interested or because she was raised in a family that simply expected one to know what was going on.

THE INITIAL COST of decorative wood from the Pacific Veneer plant appears on a now-yellowed invoice delivered in 1939 with materials to our home on Matthews Avenue. The walnut panelling was a grand four cents per square foot and planks of the same wood ran at ten cents per board foot (twelve by twelve inches by one inch thick). Characteristic of my father's efficiency, a note on the invoice shows that he paid the bill within twenty-four hours.

The new business was going well that year. What no one at Pacific Veneer realized was that everything was about to change, and the world was going to need a very different kind of product—in a hurry. With their narrow escape from Europe barely behind them, my family would have a chance to contribute more than they could have ever imagined to the war against Germany. Once Hitler's army marched into Poland in September, launching declarations of war from Britain and France, the British were immediately cut off from their supplies of aircraft plywood, which had previously come from Finland and Sweden. Someone from the British Ministry of Aircraft Production, an agency formed to mobilize civilians in the production of military equipment, contacted my dad through our agent in England. He asked if Pacific Veneer could be converted quickly into an operation capable of producing specialized birch plywood for British war aircraft. My father and his partners discussed the possibility and agreed that John Bene was qualified to design the layout and the manufacture of this new product, and they went ahead.

Pacific Veneer's new contract demanded that the mill's total production consist of specialized three-ply birch material, with each ply measuring one-hundredth of an inch in thickness. My uncle used to say that the product was so fragile it had to be "babied all the way." They would never use a forklift to lift a load for fear of damaging its corners. The plywood was manufactured by alternating the direction of four-by-eight-foot veneer sheets and, between the layers, placing film glue that resembled carbon paper. The glue would melt in the hot press and the result was incredibly strong yet flexible plywood that could withstand the stress of flight. Before long, all shipping was dedicated to goods necessary for the war effort.

My father and uncle scrambled to find suitable material for the aircraft plywood. Some of it came from as far away as Slave Lake, Alberta. They obtained the birch locally at first and then extended their sources farther afield—up the Fraser Valley to the Chilliwack area, then to Quesnel and Prince George, and even to Ontario and Quebec. As the search continued, they even wrote to local postmasters, saying, "Do you know of any stands of birch in your area?" They actually got a couple of leads.

The company began to produce materials for use in the construction of Anson and Oxford training planes. New plywood also went into the building of the de Havilland Mosquito bomber, reputedly one of the finest aircraft in the war. The plane was affectionately known as the "Timber Terror" or the "Wooden Wonder" for its speed, versatility, and durability, all of which related to the fact that the bulk of the plane was constructed from a very light, specialized plywood.

New improvements to the glue made it more water- and fungus-proof. They switched from birch to spruce, a very light wood from the Queen Charlotte Islands (now Haida Gwaii), that they used to make the plywood for the British Air Ministry. Spruce plywood ended up on the leading edges of the wings for every Mosquito that ever flew, as did birch that we got from other sources. The Mosquito was described as fast, beautiful, and dangerous. It also became popular during the war because it could be made from materials that weren't considered strategic. Various versions of four basic models performed much better than even their designers had anticipated, and some remained active into the 1960s.

In addition to the highly specialized aircraft material, we produced thirteen-ply Douglas fir plywood for the U.S. military's motor torpedo boats. We made a variety of other products, too, and became known for making the thickest available plywood as well as the thinnest. The high quality of the material we were producing was proved in a later report from the Ministry of Aircraft Production describing how a shipload of Pacific Veneer aircraft veneer had been sunk in the North Sea. It was salvaged eight months later and, after it dried, not a single piece failed.

My father may have been right about the future of the new veneer business, but with the developments that transformed it into a plywood company, the business was off to a good start. Looking back at the early days of Pacific Veneer, Uncle John later confirmed that the market for fine furniture veneer had been nothing like what the founders had hoped at the outset. Simply put, the demand here was nothing like it had been in Europe.

Vancouver had struggled through the years following the Depression, when the mild climate drew thousands of unemployed to the West Coast. But with the advent of war, Pacific Veneer, like many other plants in the region, was running full tilt. Vancouver was buzzing with new jobs that could not be filled fast enough by workers who streamed in from the B.C. Interior and from other provinces. Traditionally male occupations were suddenly open to women at the Pacific Veneer mill and also in the city's shipyards and at munitions and aircraft plants. When the plant's production rose dramatically during the war, they needed more people. Before long, Pacific Veneer had a work force of close to a thousand, with women accounting for about 60 percent.

There were other reasons, however, to welcome women into the world of delicate veneers. "There were a few in the green end," Uncle John said, referring to the feeding of veneer to the driers. "But certainly there were mostly women from the dryers on and in the plywood operation. It wasn't entirely because of wartime circumstances. You have to remember that veneer was rather fragile before it was glued and so the female touch was welcome in this type of work."

The production superintendent at the Pacific Veneer mill, Jack Zilm, was an instinctively brilliant man. He smoked strong cigars, as did my uncle. When they sat together in the same office on either end of the desk, you could not see across the room for the blue clouds of smoke hanging in the air above them. Norman Springate was the maintenance supervisor, and he developed a lot of the mill's specialized equipment. He later moved on to launch his own machinery company. Another man I remember was a French Canadian nicknamed "Frenchie," who was a forklift driver and by far the star player on our company hockey team. I played on the team with him and was on the same line as another employee, Jimmy Robinson, though I had to lie about my age. Players were supposed to be twenty-one and I was only sixteen. We played in the industry league against Alaska Pine, the Salmon-bellies (a lacrosse team that also played hockey), Heaps Machinery, and occasionally the University of British Columbia (UBC).

My uncle wrote a detailed report to the Inspector of Income Tax in 1943 that included Pacific Veneer's administrative sala-ries. At the time, Uncle John was president and general manager and my dad was vice-president and secretary. Both of them drew an annual salary of $12,000 or less. My grandfather Otto Pick, never big on titles, was named as a director and earned $6,000. The report describes the company enjoying "phenomenal growth" complicated by "significant management issues" having to do with operating three shifts a day to fill the war orders "on which the company is almost entirely engaged." What is also clear in this document is how proud they were of becoming the largest aircraft plywood factory in the British Empire and one of the two biggest industrial operations in New Westminster. By this time, the roles of the other two partners as specialists in veneer had diminished as the mill got further into the manufacture of plywood. Leslie Schaeffer was in charge of the research lab and John Bene was plant manager.

The war offered interesting challenges and a few unusual events. My dad remembered a time when Pacific Veneer products were briefly tainted by a sinister message from the enemy. One day, two RCMP officers arrived at the office in New Westminster and asked if the plant was having any difficulty with the glue they were using in the plywood. "I was absolutely flabbergasted," my father said. "We bought our glue from a company in Philadel-phia, which had German connections. We *had* had difficulties. We tested every piece and we had to reject seven days' production at that time. I found out that they had two guys in Philadelphia suspected of sabotaging the glue because they knew it was going into the production of aircraft plywood."

My dad and uncle must have been gratified at the end of the war to know that their plant had helped build aircraft that shot down something like six hundred enemy planes by the end of 1945.

With the end of the war in view, the British Air Ministry wrote to Pacific Veneer to say that their orders would soon cease and the demand for military plywood was subsiding. Then came the inevitable discussion about what to do next. Pacific Veneer's owners tossed around ideas for new markets. When they looked at the postwar hunger for materials to rebuild five years' worth of damage, they saw a looming need for Douglas fir plywood, which was being spoken of in the industry as "a product for the future in B.C." The Air Ministry suggested that the timber controller in England would provide Pacific Veneer with orders for our entire production of Douglas fir for some time to come. It was a big decision for Pacific Veneer to switch to a completely new line because almost none of the plant's specialized machinery could be used in its production. The change required more new installations and machinery, but it was worth it. By 1944, all production was Douglas fir plywood and Pacific Veneer had a contract for 100 percent of our supply to the U.K. for two years. After the war, we hired returning veterans and the number of women employed dropped, though many stayed on to patch plywood or to feed and unload the veneer dryers.

From the beginning of my family's Canadian career, my father and uncle had ideas about new ventures, inspired by their entrepreneurial spirit. It was clear that furniture veneers were not going to provide any useful long-term revenue and, by 1940, all remaining stocks of the hardwood veneer had been liquidated.

Early on, they had decided that it was crucial to gradually integrate their operations by purchasing manufacturing plants as well as timber holdings. An integrated company, in my dad's words, "has to do everything at the same time." And so, in 1940, they saw value and potential in the purchase of an inexpensive sawmill in Vancouver known as the Eburne mill. Before the end of the war, they would also go on to acquire a number of logging operations in the Fraser Valley and on Vancouver Island, starting the family on its course toward integration.

I WENT TO WORK for the family company for the first time at the age of fourteen. It was exciting to pass the summer of 1944 at the camp at Spring Creek Logging, a small operation set on the northern end of Harrison Lake. The family sent me there as a "fire watcher." Rex South, a logger's logger and a tough guy, was my boss and the supervisor at the camp during the two summers I spent there.

I usually worked with someone else as a fire watcher and we were taken to high ground to scan the landscape for smoke. As it turned out, we had a very serious fire that year, so before I knew it, I was fighting the flames instead of looking for smoke. The sirens sounded in the dark of night and we had to wait until dawn before attacking the fire with shovels, hoses, and portable water pumps. Caterpillar operators tried to build fire trails around it, but fire travels from above and from below. It can spread underground through tree roots and it can also hop from treetop to treetop with the wind.

Although the fire was exciting for a youngster like me, fighting the blaze proved difficult. The majority of workers at the camp were from the Tipella Reserve of the Douglas First Nation, and at the time many of them interpreted the fire to be part of the natural renewal process, and therefore they would not fight it. Only a handful of us battled the flames and I worked with the small crew sixteen hours a day, earning twenty-five cents an hour. I was thrilled about how much money I made that summer.

I loved the idea that I was working and I liked being with the men even though life in the bunkhouses could be a little on the rough side with language and the odd knife fight. Small things would trigger disagreement. It was a growing-up experience. I stayed on the sidelines for the most part, but occasionally I would offer up an opinion.

The following summer, I returned to the same camp. By then I had a driver's licence and could be a lot more use to them. I was the youngest in camp by a long shot, but my dad wanted me to learn how to drive properly, and what better way to do so than in a gravel truck? My job was to deliver the gravel from a nearby pit to the logging road construction. One of the two gravel trucks at camp was a relatively modern Fargo and the other was an old Leyland. The gearshift was outside the cab and I had to double clutch while shifting both up and down. Now *that's* how you learn to drive. I made sixty cents an hour that summer, and if I happened to be waiting in the truck and unable to load or unload immediately, I would say to myself, "I've already made one or two cents!" I cherished my breakfast at the camp and I usually ended up with the Leyland because I was last to get there. My favourite in those days was one hotcake and two eggs over easy with bacon and sausages.

Meanwhile, during the winter months, I was getting through my years at St. George's and focusing for the most part on sports. I loved playing cricket and rugby, and was captain of the ice hockey team. My good friend Austin Taylor and I took boxing lessons together at the Western Gym, where we delighted in watching professional wrestlers rehearse for their next match.

I was surrounded at St. George's by men I came to greatly admire. I particularly remember the headmaster, John Harker, and his younger brother Douglas who succeeded him. Mr. Harker was more of a character builder than an educator. He had a vision that he stuck to, as did his staff, most of whom were from the U.K. like he was. Athletics and deportment, not academics, were their priorities, and Harker led by example, insisting that we all get involved in athletics and give our best. He also expected us to be properly dressed—ties straight and hair combed.

I was also grateful for the contact I had with the sports coaches, Captain Basil Robinson and Nip Parker. Both men were not only characters in their own right, but they brought out the best in all the students. Butch Keeling, a great scholar who studied at Cambridge and a particularly gentle and thoughtful person, was by far the most influential and helpful among my teachers. Some time after he recommended that I attend St. George's, he left St. John's Shaughnessy Church to join the school as the chaplain and Latin teacher. I spent many Saturday afternoons at Reverend Keeling's home, where he tutored me in English.

PACIFIC VENEER WAS doing well despite minor setbacks. In 1939, my dad and uncle had been sure to build up the land on Braid Street to guard against flooding. They knew that New Westminster was within flood boundaries and that the impressive Lower Fraser was likely to show its force again at some point or other. The highest freshet reported in 1894 had caused massive flooding. But in 1948, the river rebelled in a memorable way. I recall the water rising to waist level and the mill having to shut down for a time.

Whatever damage the river inflicted did little to impact the mill's success. Stan Burke wrote an article in the January 8, 1949 edition of *British Columbia* magazine titled "The World Knows the PV Label." It was Pacific Veneer's tenth year in operation and Burke described it as "one of the most remarkable developments of the sort in the B.C. lumber industry." The company employed 850 people at the time and wasted very little of its by-products. They used as much of the log as possible for plywood, and cut the cores into railroad ties. Waste materials were converted to hardboard in a brand-new plant that was one of the first of its kind in North America. Anything that remained was burned in the power plant.

They started using the waste from the veneer plant to make hardboard, with products that ranged from standard plywood to exotic and decorative panels manufactured in the plywood and hardboard mills. The mill would go on to manufacture a unique material called Ecofibre, a solution sprayed on steep inclines where roads were being built to seed the soil and grow grass, which provided stability. In hindsight, that was something we should have marketed widely, but we became too focused on the core business of lumber and pulp to see the opportunity.

Pacific Veneer evolved through different phases and several name changes, from Pacific Veneer Ltd. to the Pacific Veneer and Plywood Division of what would evolve as a single entity—Canadian Forest Products Ltd. Other changes were under way. One of our competitors had started to give volume discounts on plywood, which led to retailers forming buying groups to get an optimal discount. In response to this, and in order to protect ourselves against this discounting getting out of hand, in the early 1950s, we created a wholly owned subsidiary called Canfor Building Materials, internally known as our Building Materials Division (BMD). Through BMD we purchased several companies across the country with numerous warehouses to service retailers. We carried some very well known lines—Armstrong Floor Coverings, Olympic Stain, and Weiser Locks, to name just a few. It was a tough but reasonably successful part of our business.

By the 1960s, we were boasting our status as the "largest plywood plant under one roof in Canada," with eleven hundred employees and an annual payroll of $6 million. Pacific Veneer had research-and-development and quality-control departments in addition to testing labs, all of which added to its reputation as a global producer of quality materials.

The community of Pacific Veneer employees was a tight one, and they all looked out for one another. Like many other divisions in the company, they launched a social club and published monthly newsletters called the *Pacific Veneer Vox-Pop* (*PVVP*). Safety was naturally a big issue for the staff, and the newsletters regularly referred to injury prevention. The New Westminster people were in a world of their own and always seemed more inward-looking than the other divisions we developed over time. We would send out newsletters to all divisions, reporting the company's progress. We also went out to the various divisions and held question-and-answer meetings. It was at these events that I recognized how many operations did not want to engage in the wider story of the company. In hindsight, I should not have been surprised. Although I felt it was my responsibility to offer a corporate overview, the employees' well-being was naturally more tied to their immediate workplace than to the overall company.

PACIFIC VENEER was the key starting point of the company and the division that for many years had the most employees. As time passed, however, the demand would drop for clear plywood (wood without knots) manufactured from high-quality logs, and we saw that making clear lumber from those logs would offer a better return. The plywood plant had to go. It was a sad day for us all when we accepted that Pacific Veneer's products were no longer in demand. We closed that mill in 1985 and I wrote one of those letters I hate to write, explaining to our employees that after examining all the alternatives we had decided that our losses were too great. A small sample of our very last thin piece of plywood ever made at the mill in October of that year sits in a rarely opened manila envelope in the Canfor archives.

The hardboard mill on the Pacific Veneer site would continue for some time, using urban waste—beams or lumber—from demolished buildings or construction sites as raw material. Like most aspects of our business, the panel industry would change over the years. Our first panelling product was plywood, made largely from Douglas fir. Later, we made sheathing plywood for construction, and this gradually led to using less costly spruce, pine, and fir (SPF) from the Interior.

I intended to keep the company out of the oriented strand board (OSB) business because its manufacture involved having to log whole timber, an idea I never liked when we could make hardboard with recovered waste. Despite my preferences, OSB (used for nonweight-bearing structures like subfloors and walls) became an increasingly popular panel product and, in many instances, where structural strength wasn't needed, OSB replaced plywood. Much later, we would in fact end up in the OSB business for a time when we purchased an operation that included an OSB mill and a plywood plant in Fort Nelson, both of which are now indefinitely closed.

The company acquired a half-interest in a second plywood mill in 1956 in Grande Prairie, Alberta, and it ran until we built a new larger capacity sawmill. North Central Plywood in Prince George came with a more recent purchase in 1999. A fire completely destroyed that operation in 2008 and in the face of a reduced annual allowable cut because of the pine beetle, we chose not to rebuild.

We always wanted to be at the forefront of new product development. Canadian Forest Products was one of very few companies in the Canadian industry that conducted its own research in addition to the research done through the industrial associations. In recent years, we are the only Canadian forest company to have our own research department. From the outset, it was headed by Dr. Suezone Chow. The department moved from Pacific Veneer to Marpole and then to the UBC campus. Currently, it is known as the Canfor Pulp Innovation Centre, located in South Burnaby under the direction of Dr. Paul Watson. It's a joint venture of Canfor, UBC, and the University of Northern B.C.

EARLY ON in my father and uncle's partnership, it was obvious that despite their complementarity, they had markedly different approaches to business. My dad was more gung-ho, "Let's get on with it," and more impulsive. In contrast, Uncle John was very thoughtful and slower moving in every respect. He was a thinker. As the head of the World Chess Association, he did a lot to promote the game in Canada. Although the two men showed a strong mutual respect, outside of business they did not share much except an interest in bridge, which they played together regularly.

I would go on to learn a great deal from my father's and my uncle's individual styles. My dad was more apt to give me hell if he thought I had made a mistake. He might say, "What the hell do you think you're doing?" whereas Uncle John was more reserved and would want to discuss the situation at length. We often reviewed what I had done, and he sometimes guided me into considering another way.

I became particularly attached to my uncle the year after my dad died, which was only a year before he himself passed away in 1987. We had some of the same contacts back east, and we developed a real bond over time.

My father and uncle's leadership and vision were well rewarded. The Canadian Business Hall of Fame honoured my dad in 1982. He and other B.C. residents who had been inducted into the Canadian

Business Hall were the initial inductees when the B.C. Business Hall of Fame was started. My father also received an honorary doctorate of laws from UBC. Uncle John enjoyed similar distinctions, including becoming an Officer of the Order of Canada and being nominated chair of the Canada Council. Both men were excellent leaders and devoted from the beginning to their newfound community. They saw honour and responsibility in the privilege of becoming Canadian citizens, and each had an ability to spot possibilities and make the right decisions. Dad played a big role in creating the Council of Forest Industries and in promoting business overseas.

As I would become more familiar with the business, my dad and Uncle John were supportive in allowing me to strategize in ways that were new to the industry at the time. I was and continue to be inspired by these two mentors who built a business out of nothing. I look back with enormous admiration on what they achieved with so little. I never claimed that I could have done as well as they did with such a modest start. They clearly brought an unusual business sense to British Columbia and actively promoted the growth of western Canada. Through my daily contact with these two great men over several decades, I learned to make my own decisions and saw that I, too, could make a difference.

3

Eburne
Moving toward Integration

B EING AN OPPORTUNIST, my father was the driving force behind most of the purchases the family went on to make. My uncle was considerably more conservative. I remember my dad saying, "We didn't know very much about business conditions here, but let me tell you that business is the same all over the world. Regardless of what business you are in, the principles are the same. If you produce a good product cheaper than your competitors and sell it possibly for a little more, then you are doing all right."

My dad and my uncle believed in total cash reinvestment. As the company grew, we were able to access more credit, which allowed us to reinvest not only our cash flow but also the additional borrowing to accelerate growth. In late 1940, two years after launching Pacific Veneer, we entered the lumber business, which was more of an opportunistic move than a strategic decision.

My father and his partners had received word in 1940 of an active but faltering sawmill for sale near the mouth of the Fraser

River in south Vancouver's Marpole neighbourhood. Eburne Saw Mills was advertised as being in receivership, which made it all the more attractive. It would be our first acquisition, and all the partners were comfortable with the purchase because it filled two basic requirements: it was industrial and it was land.

My dad remembered seeing many operations up for sale at the time. He was specifically attracted to Eburne because of the mill's excellent location and good labour supply—even if the facility was an eyesore that was running at only 50 percent capacity. "It was more of a museum than a mill," my father said. "It was a horrible mill physically and we knew we could buy the mill very cheap and then rebuild the whole thing completely from scratch to get an efficient operation." At a low cost of $50,000, it seemed like a good risk.

A mill had existed at that site since the last decade of the nineteenth century. The dilapidated plant occupied an ideal spot on the Fraser River, close to Georgia Strait, where a town centre had grown up around the successful dealings of Harry Eburne, who had settled there in 1875. Fishing and logging developed naturally in the area, and several logging camps sat to the northwest of the mill around the current neighbourhood of Kerrisdale. Prior to 1890, timber was sent to New Westminster or Vancouver for milling, but as soon as foreign markets learned about the impressive durability of Douglas fir, the demand picked up and sawmilling became an obvious fit for the area. In 1908, the site, then known as the Manitoba Sawmill, was bought by new owners, who changed the name to Eburne and increased the workforce from forty to eighty. Within four short years, the mill increased its production to about 100,000 feet board measure (FBM) per day.

The town of Eburne boomed in 1911 when the Canadian Pacific Railway reached it, and with that essential link in place, what had been a separate municipality was soon absorbed by the city of Vancouver. In 1913, two hundred employees worked two shifts at the mill, and its advertisements guaranteed "prompt delivery by tram, wagon, or scow." The company struggled in the years that followed, and then the Depression hit and the bank took it over. It was during this phase, with 150 employees working at the mill for a base rate of thirty cents an hour, that our family took over the operation. Our new mill would later become the Eburne Saw Mills Division of Canadian Forest Products.

With the purchase of Eburne, our company became members of Seaboard Lumber Sales, a lumber company cooperative formed in 1936 that then comprised two companies—one for sales and one for shipping. The war slowed things down, but soon after the conflict ended, Seaboard perfected the shipping of packaged lumber in sophisticated vessels and continued to improve the services they offered to the industry. A large part of our coastal production was shipped out by water and sold to overseas markets—and that was Seaboard's job. Our own staff took care of rail and domestic sales. Seaboard offices opened in London, New York, and Australia, and each member company's ownership share was adjusted from time to time based on throughput. The bigger players in Seaboard would eventually include Crown Zellerbach, Canadian Forest Products, Weldwood, and Interfor, with many smaller outfits joining as well. As our Interior sales increased, our throughput in the cooperative dropped because those deliveries were done by rail and truck. Both my dad and I served as chair of Seaboard over a number of years. Its sales arm shut down some time ago, but the shipping operation continues to this day, now owned by Interfor.

The rail siding at Eburne made it easy to send out boxcars of lumber across Canada and the United States, whereas more distant shipments of mostly green lumber were carried by scow from the Fraser to Vancouver Harbour, where Seaboard organized the loading of deep-sea vessels bound for the Atlantic coast or overseas. Higher-grade shipments went by rail to the United States, and local sales were delivered by truck.

When our company took over Eburne, even my young eyes could see that the mill was a real clunker by coastal standards. At the time, most of the coastal lumber industry, which accounted for the bulk of British Columbia's production, consisted of relatively modern and well-equipped plants. In contrast, the Interior industry was less sophisticated, with the bulk of production coming from small bush mills that delivered lumber to planing mills situated on the railroads. Materials from those mills were very crude with poor sizes and unbelievable waste. The Interior lumber was SPF, which can be processed by the same equipment. The coastal lumber was Douglas fir, hemlock, cedar, and yellow cedar, requiring a variety of mills, some specializing in single species.

The purchase of Eburne was a practical move at an opportune time, but it was during the operation's rapid growth that my father really showed his strength in making wise decisions. Dad could see the importance of using the whole tree. When you have a handle on each level of manufacture, you can make deals by trading chips for logs, logs for logs, and all the rest of it. As the company upgraded the mill, all the waste from Eburne went to one of several chippers, and the chips were used as raw material for pulp. Any waste beyond that, in the form of bark or small particles and shavings, went into hog fuel for the steam-generating plant and the surplus was loaded on scows bound for pulp and newsprint mills, where it was used as fuel for their steam plants. They used the entire log and did not waste a scrap.

The B.C. forest industry was very different from operations in eastern Canada, where there was a significant pulp and paper industry and very little lumber manufacturing. The trees there were comparatively small and the early technology was not good enough to make lumber on a cost-effective basis. In British

Columbia, we had the reverse situation—a well-established saw-mill industry and an insignificant pulp and paper industry that used the residuals from the mills and low-grade logs from the woods for pulp.

MY FATHER MOVED to Eburne and took on the management of the mill. Uncle John maintained his office at Pacific Veneer in New Westminster, overseeing operations there for decades to come, while taking on responsibilities such as overseeing the wholesale Building Materials Division.

Although they worked as equals, Uncle John was president and my father vice-president, and each had his areas of direct responsibility. John spent less time with our employees beyond New Westminster, which meant that he had a lower profile. He represented us as a director with the Pulp and Paper Association, and my father did the same with other industry organizations. The two of them worked independently on a day-to-day basis, but they always put their heads together on matters of developing strategy or deciding on acquisitions. They worked closely until the end of their careers, invariably reaching a compromise whenever they disagreed. Both of them were analytic in different ways and neither panicked when faced with a crisis. They would sit down and calmly discuss the pros and cons, and ways to solve the situation. They focused on looking ahead and not regretting what had passed. My dad was perhaps a little quicker to come to conclusions, but they both had an excellent overview of the total scene.

In my dad's early days of overseeing the Eburne plant, neither he nor the other partners really knew anything about lumber, so they went in search of guidance. Bill McMahan came on board with a wealth of experience in logging operations. He joined the head office and later became vice-president and a director. My dad and uncle gave him a lot of credit for the success of our business and our strong position within the industry.

Early on, the Eburne property covered fifteen acres at the foot of Hudson Street near the swing bridge leading to Sea Island. The sawmill was big compared with others at the time. It dealt with large logs purchased on the open market. At first, different species were all being cut in the same mill, which was a remarkably inefficient way of doing things. One of the first decisions we made was to abandon the manufacture of fir lumber. We added a second mill for medium-sized trees, and a third mill followed for cutting small hemlock logs.

In the first five years, the Eburne plant grew quickly through the building of those two additional mills, plus new kilns, blacktop roadways, and a refurbished machine shop. To load the scows moving our lumber to Seaboard's deep-sea dock more efficiently, we added a large overhead crane.

The company's progress depended on finding logs to feed both Eburne and Pacific Veneer. In the early years of Pacific Veneer, we had accessed a hardwood supply from foreign sources before getting into plywood production during the war, when we began to use B.C. logs. But the opportunity to acquire timberlands in the province was ever decreasing, because most of the available forests had been allocated. It was essential for us to control a significant portion of our raw material base, so the firm decided to make timber acquisitions.

The first purchase was a small private operation at Vedder Crossing near Chilliwack in the Fraser Valley. It was a rustic outfit with ancient equipment, including a steam-fired "donkey"—a machine with a long cable that attached to a log and reeled it in. Continuing with our efforts to integrate, we moved on to purchase two more operations, Spring Creek and Consolidated Timber, at the north end of Harrison Lake. More significant in terms of scale was Chehalis Logging at Harrison Bay, with private timber rights coming to us from a company called Rat Portage. That large acquisition came to us through Fred Brown, a friend of the family and the father-in-law of my close friend Ron Cliff, who later became a director of the company.

The final operation and timber rights the company secured in the Fraser Valley was Suicide Creek, and with that deal came Stave Lake Cedar, a shingle mill that we did not want to buy. But buy it we did, at the insistence of the seller, who did not want to be left with a mill and no timber. As luck would have it, this mill ended up paying for itself within the first year because the shingle market took off.

The Stave Lake mill sat on the Nicomen Slough and was one of the operations hit by the 1948 flood. In fact, it was one of the first plants to feel the full force of the rising Fraser in the late spring. The mill came to a standstill for a number of weeks, and the Public Works Department requisitioned our staff to work on the dykes.

In 1948, we acquired another shingle operation just west of Eburne called Huntting-Merritt, the largest of its kind in the province. After not being in the business at all before our purchase of Stave Lake, we were suddenly the largest producer of red-cedar shingles and shakes in the world. With that purchase we also gained a number of valuable people.

The game plan for these logging operations on private land was to clean up small volumes of timber in an orderly fashion. But you did not go through it too quickly; you wanted to make it last and provide employment. In time, almost all the logs feeding the Eburne mill came from our various logging operations. The most impressive of these acquisitions was Englewood, which deserves a chapter of its own.

Of course, when you're bringing in a reasonably sized log supply, you also need transportation and storage facilities, which also served as real estate investments. As a part of our strategic growth, we acquired Douglas Island and Iona Island to get the foreshore rights, which served as booming grounds. The company would go on to buy more companies and wholesale distributorships farther afield: Ottawa Valley Lumber, with operations in Quebec and the Maritimes; Regent Plywood in Ontario; and Steamer Maxwell in Winnipeg. We developed our own warehouse system instead of buying from others in the rest of Canada.

I BENEFITED FROM my father's planning when it came to real work experience. In addition to jobs I had as a teenager in the logging camps, I went to work at Eburne for the summer of 1949, in the machine shop under the watchful eye of Len McDonald, which taught me metalwork and how the shop supported the mill. From there I moved to the number-two greenchain as a lumber puller under the supervisor, Bob Murphy. As the different lengths and widths of lumber came by me on the conveyor, I would pull off the pieces and put them in the appropriate loads. In recent times, drop sorters have replaced greenchains, with sensors and cameras determining the bin into which each piece is dropped.

I had taken a grading course at night school and I moved on to a grading job. Working with a lumber grader named Johnny, I would look at each piece and inspect both sides, and then mark it with chalk, indicating whether it had to be remanufactured or identifying the proper grade if it was a finished product. I did a reasonably good job and he did not have to correct me very often. I was like a sidekick to him and made his job easier.

The chains moved slowly and the mill workers managed to keep the mill clean. The trim table moved a lot faster. As the technology improved, we went from having to manually saw each end to having a fellow sit there with a keyboard, operating a series of circular saws positioned at every foot to make cuts or trim the ends. He played it just like a piano.

I also worked in the railcar-loading shed, where we manually filled the boxcars with kiln-dried lumber, mostly high-end products. I enjoyed working with the guys at Eburne. I loved the work and the people and learned quickly that there were many ways to cut and produce lumber. I may not have appreciated it at the time, but I came to love the smell of the wood and the sawdust. I found it exciting.

I WENT BACK to Eburne as an adult trainee and eventually as manager. There may have been some thoughts in the early days about nepotism, since I was the boss's son, but I tried to overcome any sense of that by working as hard as I could. I was intent on finishing loading my railcars before others finished theirs. Being a competitive person, that extra effort came naturally to me, and it also meant that they couldn't criticize me. It was not in my nature to lag behind, but if I had, I would have sent the wrong signals. From the beginning, I sensed an obligation to lead by example and I had to do everything as well as possible.

I never felt alienated by the guys. The closest I ever came to that was when my grandfather, Otto Pick, would ride around the lumberyard in his chauffeur-driven car. If I was working on the greenchain, he would get out and come and talk to me. I found it a little embarrassing, but of course he meant no harm.

I was lucky to have that kind of work experience. It was important for me as a young man to learn what was going on in the industry and in our operations. I don't think anyone, including me, assumed that I would end up anywhere other than in the family business, even if that looked doubtful for a few years later on. My early exposure to our business "on the ground" was in timber cruising, surveying, timekeeping, and twice working on the booming grounds. I did it all. These jobs taught me the importance of understanding the attitudes and thought processes of hourly workers, whether in logging camps or in mills. It was a matter of getting close to the man on the job and becoming one myself. I began to really appreciate what these workers were up against. I had and still have great admiration for the fallers and buckers, and for the chokermen who set chokers on steep hills, running up and down the felled and bucked timber. I was amazed at how they did that and did it safely. Logging on the coast is a high-risk business, more so than milling or Interior logging. My father and uncle always impressed upon me the importance of safety. It was always on their minds; it would always be on mine and it remains a major Canadian Forest Products principle.

I became and still am a believer in summer jobs because they show the value of a dollar. Most importantly, these jobs bring you in contact with people. My son, Michael, spent time at Fleetwood Logging on the Sechelt Peninsula one year, and another summer at our mill in Chetwynd. My four daughters, Barbara, Susie, Joanie, and Lisa, all had summer jobs ranging from retail to working as bank tellers to office work and even serving coffee at the office.

As I did, all my five children benefited enormously from their early work experience. I don't think my kids are spoiled in any way; they are all down-to-earth. I attribute a lot of that to the fact that they had to go out and work during their summer holidays, which gave them a better understanding of the value of a dollar as well as a feeling for their fellow workers.

ONE TIME DURING the Cold War, the Soviet minister of forests was scheduled to visit our Eburne mill. I was concerned about that visit because I knew we had some communist literature floating around the lunchroom and I didn't want any disruption, whatever that might be. So I went to the RCMP to advise them that there may be a problem. The officer thanked me for the heads-up and in return gave me the names of three Eburne employees the RCMP knew to be communist. I also learned from him that every radio transmitter in the area was staffed on night shifts by communists. The RCMP were concerned that the whole community was at risk because all communications could be cut off if the Communist Party so decided, but they couldn't do anything about it.

We avoided any incident at the mill during that official visit, though I quickly saw that nobody was going to get near the minister anyway, as he was surrounded by KGB (the then Soviet Union's Committee for State Security). I remember the minister being very critical about how many conveyors we were using to move sawdust and waste. He thought it would be much better for us to employ as many as two hundred women with wheelbarrows to do the job. That short exchange told me that the main function of mills in the Soviet Union at the time was to employ people. I knew then that, although the Soviets had a great timber base, they would not pose a threat in the marketplace for many years to come.

Some of us in the industry hosted a farewell dinner for the minister. At the event, H.R. MacMillan, Aird Flavelle (the founder and head of Flavelle Cedar) and I each received a Russian friendship medal, which I interpreted to mean, "Shoot this man on sight—he's a capitalist!"

I have never worn my medal.

WE BECAME IMMENSELY proud of the Eburne mill, which some described as an iconic industrial site in Vancouver. It was certainly a landmark for many and a good employer. A number of heads of state and other dignitaries visited because of its proximity to the city and the airport. A wonderful, active group of people worked at that mill. Some of the foremen may not have been great managers, but they excelled on the people side of things.

My dad was close to the employees because he was based at Eburne and his personal style made it easy and pleasurable for him to be a part of what was going on. Whether he was visiting the logging camps or the shingle mill, wherever he went he made eye contact and had a solid rapport with the people. He enjoyed that part of the business. One of the disadvantages of our moving to head office in downtown Vancouver was losing that close personal contact.

In later years, I also enjoyed going down to the mill in the evening after work and wandering around. My wife, Sheila, would come with me on occasion. By then we had catwalks, so we could navigate our way around safely without interfering. I loved the smell of the freshly cut wood and the sawdust. I would watch the lumber being cut and wonder what the edger man was going to do when he set the levers. It was all done by eye and intuition. It was a pleasure to be there and I often had a chance to talk to the guys on the job. They accepted me; I was not a distant part of management because I had worked with them on the floor.

By the mid-1960s, Eburne was one of the most modern sawmills in the Pacific Northwest, with six hundred employees producing 180 million FBM of hemlock annually. The plant had grown from a single-line, low-production unit to a highly efficient mill that was top tier, along with Crown Zellerbach's Fraser Mills; MacMillan Bloedel's Canadian White Pine; and Rayonier's Alaska Pine and Universal Box.

A decade passed and we launched into a new era by opening a long-awaited, computerized planer mill. As I remember it, we were the first in Canada to introduce a computerized system. In 1979, the leader of the federal New Democratic Party, Ed Broadbent, came to visit Eburne. At the time, his party was castigating the forest industry as well as the federal government for their investment policies, but Broadbent praised our company for investing our profits in Canada and for keeping our operations up to date. We were always on top of improvements at the mill, and in 1990 won an award for Eburne's energy efficiency.

When we made our decision in 1997 to close Eburne, we were under a great deal of pressure. It seemed inevitable that we would be accused of thinking only of profits, but if that had been the case, we would have shut that operation down long before we did. We knew that our personnel did not want to hear about the increasingly "competitive environment," though it was just that. The situation in the forest products industry had been dire for a few years with evaporating Asian markets, quotas on U.S. exports, and a significant reduction of 24 percent to the allowable timber cut on the coast. The coastal harvest had dropped 40 percent in the previous ten years.

The fact was that our fibre sources were dwindling. The sawmill industry on the coast was shrinking yet the pulp industry remained constant and in need of chips. We were one of the three largest forest companies in the province and we were all in trouble. Everyone—the public, the government, the International Woodworkers of America (IWA), our industry—needed educating about the changes at play.

It was an emotional time for us and for more than two hundred Eburne employees. We had looked at all sorts of solutions to deal with the diminished fibre supply for our pulp mill as well as our operating losses, and we could not find another way around these problems. Some of the staff wrote me to say that we did not care about the people, which could not have been further from the truth. We hated the idea of closing the mill. We offered first-class severance packages for those who wished to take them, and we made every attempt to find jobs for others who wanted to stay on.

Before announcing Eburne's closure in March 1998, we of course notified the government and the minister so they would not be blindsided by the news. I also went to see Ken Georgetti, who at that time was the head of the B.C. Federation of Labour. I wanted him to know the shape of the package and the opportunities we were offering people. We were short of personnel in our Northern operations, so we were prepared to help with moving expenses to transfer people if they wanted to go. Most of the Eburne employees were residents of Richmond and Surrey and, understandably, many of them wanted to stay in the Lower Mainland. I also pointed out to Georgetti that whatever took place at the site after we sold it would probably provide more jobs than the sawmill had at the time, and I believe that to be true to this day.

It was not a complete surprise when some employees protesting the closure showed up at head office along with some media people. They were demonstrating at the Bentall Centre, where our head office was located, and I was warned not to go outside. I chose to do the opposite. I went down and spoke to them. It was only then that many of them understood the magnitude of Eburne's losses and the gravity of the situation.

Close to six decades after we bought Eburne I was terribly saddened by the demise of a plant that had become very special to me.

4

Englewood
Canfor's Backbone

MY FATHER AND uncle made a new purchase in 1944 that would change my life a few years later by influencing my commitment to our family business.

Six years after arriving in Canada, my family was immersed in the forest business, owning and running the Pacific Veneer plant, the Eburne sawmill, and several smaller coastal logging operations. My father and uncle had learned a great deal about the industry. One important aspect they had come to understand was the difference in timber holdings across the border. In the United States many lumber manufacturers were not landowners; they bought logs from the federal and state governments and from private timber holders. Each of these groups owned roughly one-third of the available forests, though the proportions varied by state. The situation was very different in British Columbia, where there was little private timber and the government owned (and still owns) 95 percent of the forests. One simply could not exist here by logging private lands. If we were to grow—and you cannot stand still in this business—it was essential for us to access Crown timber.

As my father and uncle looked for ways to secure a larger log supply, the partnership with John Bene and Leslie Schaeffer began to falter. Bene had a curious aversion to timber and logging operations, and he was adamant about not wanting to invest in that type of enterprise. He was mistakenly convinced that we could source raw materials for Pacific Veneer without securing a stable reserve, as we had been doing with our smaller operations. He and Schaeffer also objected strongly to my father's and uncle's decision to borrow and spend on new acquisitions what for us was very big money. Specifically, Bene and Schaeffer insisted they were industrialists and not "farmers," and did not want the company's biggest investment to be in timber rather than manufacturing. My family could not talk them out of their position. Just as my dad and uncle finished negotiating with the Bank of Montreal about the purchase of a major logging operation, they had to go right back to the bank to finance a buyout. The new purchase put us into significant debt, but it was the right thing to do. Bene saw the error of his ways much later, when he admitted having been "a hundred percent wrong."

Bene and Schaeffer left together and, unfortunately for us, they chose to carry on in the Douglas fir plywood business, launching Western Plywood at the foot of Fraser Street in Vancouver. That was the forerunner of Weldwood (founded by Bene in 1964), which would become a major forest products company. At first, the parting of ways was amicable. To our family's regret, however, the former partners took with them a good 25 percent of our people from Pacific Veneer and things became very unfriendly. My father, and my uncle to an even greater degree, resented their taking our employees far more than their decision not to go along with the significant acquisition of timber. Bene and my parents and the Prentices never spoke again. I would get along with him myself much later as we sat together on an industry committee when he headed Weldwood. I admired the work he did and we had a good rapport.

That was the situation in 1944 when my father and uncle said good-bye to their original partners and stepped deeper into their commitment to create an integrated company. They purchased timber rights and a complete, existing logging outfit called Englewood in Vancouver Island's Nimpkish Valley, where western hemlock, Douglas fir, western red cedar, and Sitka spruce had been modestly harvested since 1908. Once again, they had learned of this opportunity from our family friend Fred Brown.

Dad and Uncle John may not have realized at the time that Englewood would become the backbone of our company. Pacific Veneer had been a good start and Eburne had helped us begin to grow, but the purchase of Englewood would be our biggest single move toward integration.

Two men by the names of English and Wood (Engle-Wood) had founded the Nimpkish Valley operation, and various companies had since owned it and the rights to log the land. Our family acquired Englewood from the Puget Sound Pulp and Timber Company of Bellingham, Washington. I don't think they knew what an excellent asset they were selling. They had been doing some logging, but the timber was of far better quality than that required for their pulp mill. I believe we bought the entire operation—including the roads, the tugboats, the logging equipment, and the original railroad—for $4.2 million, an incredible sum for us at the time.

Decades after our purchase of Englewood, an ironic situation arose. John Bene, who had rejected our initial move toward timber investment and walked away, had to change his tune when he needed peeler logs for Weldwood. To meet this need,

Bene acquired one of the licences that we had not bought in the Nimpkish Valley. Those many years later, he paid $6 million for a single licence. To make matters more complex, Bene was forced to give us the contract to log the timber because no other access was available. Furthermore, once logged, the land reverted to our tree farm licence.

THE NIMPKISH VALLEY was a magical place for me as a seventeen-year-old. I had seen a fair bit of British Columbia by then, but I had never encountered anything like it. It was an immense valley, filled with majestic timber, with no public access. Since that summer of 1947, I have travelled the world in many directions and have yet to see a place with so much natural beauty.

The valley lies in the heart of northern Vancouver Island and runs diagonally, northwest to southeast, for more than a hundred kilometres. The Maquilla, Shoen, Pinder, and Sebalhall mountains surround the Kla-anch (Upper Nimpkish) River's headwaters. The water starts flowing in these mountains near Gold River, passing through the larger lakes—Vernon, Woss, and Nimpkish—and continuing to its end in Broughton Strait on the Pacific Ocean near Alert Bay. The timber in the valley was and is the best I've seen anywhere. It was tall, it was straight—it was absolutely magnificent.

From our earliest years, Canfor had outstanding forestry support. Tom Wright was our first chief forester and we were lucky to get him. Like John Liersch after him, Tom had been head of the forestry school before it became a faculty member at UBC. Tom left us later to return to university life, but only briefly, as my father somehow convinced him to return to Canfor. He was a superb forester with great vision, and he attracted first-rate people. One of those was Glen Patterson, who became his fire protection officer at Englewood before moving through management and heading first our Alberta operations and then northern British Columbia.

Wright set out in 1947 to understand why a certain stand of Nimpkish timber was so remarkable. With the help of Patterson and a UBC student, he concluded that the fir, hemlock, and cedar in the stand dated back to 1550. It had thrived on a gentle slope surrounded by higher grounds that provided year-round seepage and outstanding productivity.

With Englewood came a vast expanse of that virgin timberland, mostly Douglas fir, hemlock, and red cedar. The forests stretching over the valley's length would supply our mills. With this purchase, we had acquired the daunting responsibility of managing an enormous forest. As we grew into our new role as caretakers, research into the flora and fauna of the valley would become a priority that more than matched our attention to replanting the timber we were cutting.

When we bought Englewood, only Camp 'A' existed as a production unit on Anutz Lake, a small body of water off the west end of Nimpkish Lake, known for its stiff northwest winds. Included in the new operation was a small subsidiary mill at Beaver Cove called Canadian Forest Products, a name that immediately appealed to my father and uncle. Within a few years, they had organized all our operations under that corporate name, with several divisions, including Pacific Veneer and Plywood, Eburne Saw Mills, Harrison Mills Logging, and Englewood Logging. (Canfor, the company's abbreviated name, would not become our popular name until the 1980s, though it appeared on our logo and the Canfor Building Materials Division long before.)

The well-known industrialist and horse breeder E.P. Taylor was intending to start up a forest products business in 1946 and was in search of a name for his new company. Our family ran into Taylor while we were vacationing in Jasper, Alberta. He asked my dad if Canadian Forest Products or the name of the company might be for sale.

"Absolutely not," my father said without hesitating.

"Well, I really like your company's name," Mr. Taylor continued. "Can you not sell it to me? I'm putting together a forest company and there isn't a better name out there."

I was still a teenager but it was no surprise to me that my father didn't budge, and Taylor went on to name his company B.C. Forest Products.

IN THE FIRST half of the twentieth century, the government of British Columbia had no firm policies to regulate harvesting, and forestry officials granted timber sale licences according to demand. Commercial harvesting in the province had begun in the late 1900s, and the impact of logging at the time was small. For a long time, reforestation was not an issue, and tree planting was deemed unnecessary because of the seemingly endless supply of trees. Reforestation began in earnest in the 1930s and further improved after Chief Justice Gordon McGregor Sloan produced reports from two Royal Commissions he chaired in the 1940s and '50s. Justice Sloan was a brilliant man who asked incisive questions. His investigation into forestry practices transformed the industry and helped move it toward area-based management instead of a quota system. Eventually, that change led to reforestation becoming mandatory.

The quota system required the licence holder to reforest the area after completing the harvest. Rather than having future long-term rights to the timber, the licence holder only had annual rights to cut within that "working circle." Money spent on reforesting was not an assured benefit because the holder did not control the land.

In contrast, a tree farm licence (TFL, known as a forest management agreement or FMA in Alberta) makes the licence recipient responsible over many years for the management of a designated geographic area. Subject only to performance, the rights are renewable. This system encourages the spending of more capital on fertilizing, thinning, pruning, and generally enhancing the future value and volume of the forests in the area. If a company has a TFL and does a good job at tending the forest, the licence will be renewed, which is an incentive for better forest practice.

Before we purchased Englewood in 1944, it was a relatively modest operation limited to one part of the valley. Our opening up the valley had changed the logistics of logging there. Justice Sloan asked my dad at the commission hearing why we did not have a TFL for the self-contained Nimpkish Valley, which he felt should have been managed as a unit, combining private and Crown timberlands—and that was a very good question. My father explained to me, and undoubtedly to the commission, that the reason we did not have a licence was that the minister of forests from 1952 to 1956, Robert E. Sommers, had been allegedly corrupt and expected bribes. My family would not do business that way.

I heard from my father that when he had expressed interest in a TFL a few years earlier, Sommers had said that it was not "doable." Tahsis was awarded a licence in 1954 even though we felt we deserved one as much or more than they did because, as I remember it, the Nimpkish was more self-contained and we had a higher percentage of private timber relative to adjacent Crown timber. I and others have always suspected that money changed hands. In 1958, Robert Sommers was convicted of bribery and conspiracy.

So much of the Nimpkish Valley cried out for a TFL once we had bought the majority of the private timber in the valley and had the rights to surrounding Crown timber. With the access there, it made sense that it be designated as a licensed area, which it was in December 1960 when TFL 37 was finally awarded to us under the auspices of the new minister, Ray Williston.

CECIL SALMON WAS in charge of our Fraser Valley operations before moving with his wife, Diane, to become general manager of Englewood and subsequently general manager of Coastal Logging. It was a lot to ask of the Salmons to leave their prominent status and their farm in the Fraser Valley, and they sacrificed a lot to do so. We were very lucky to have them.

Initially, we were one of a few companies that continued some railroad logging, whereby trees were taken down and put straight onto railcars. The Englewood Logging Division had impressively high production with numerous logging units throughout the valley. They were all truck-logged, and the loads were delivered to one of several reload points, where the whole truck was transferred to railcars. All of this fed into one new rail system that ran the length of the valley. Building the new railway involved extensive blasting, excavation, and the building of nine major bridges. It terminated at Beaver Cove, where the logs were sorted on a dry-land sort, bundled, and then put in booms for the journey to wherever they were converted to end products. This system replaced the old one of dumping the logs into Nimpkish Lake, reloading them onto a railroad that delivered them to Englewood, and then dumping them into the salt chuck to be boomed for the long haul down the inland waterway.

In preparing the logs for transport you moved them around in the water using a long pike pole with a sharp, spiral spike and a hook on one end. Standing on one log, you had to use all your weight on that pole to get the other logs moving one at a time. The Camp 'A' foreman was a tough guy, and one day I saw him watching a worker who was stabbing away with his pike pole at a log that wasn't budging.

"Son, how long have you been doing this job?" the foreman asked.

"Two weeks, sir," the fellow answered.

"That's just perfect," the foreman snapped. "Go in and pick up your time."

That foreman had a way about him.

The man in charge of booming at Englewood was Cliff Bentley (not related to us) who worked with his son Ray. Cliff and Ray were a wonderful pair. Cliff always had his dog along. On one memorable afternoon, a cougar attacked the dog. Without missing a beat, Cliff picked up the cougar by the tail and hurled it around until he got near enough to a cliff to swing it against the rock wall. The cat dropped the dog on impact and Cliff finished the cougar off with a rock.

MY APPRECIATION FOR the valley grew during the summers I spent there, surveying, working on the booming grounds, timber cruising, and timekeeping. It was fabulous. I loved it—I was working outdoors and I was learning. We had extended the railroad as far as Vernon Lake, which lies in a deep trough between the steep valley slopes. I got to know the rail equipment and in my off-duty hours I would enjoy taking a speeder—a small, self-propelled railcar for moving people—out for a trip down the valley, or wandering up to the camp's garbage dump to shoot crows.

We built up the Englewood operation quickly. Our family constructed a guest house in the family area at Camp 'N'—Nimpkish—at the far end of the lake, where we all stayed. Other families also settled there and opened a school that later moved with the office to Camp 'W'—Woss, which became the heart of the operation.

Over time, camps were set up at each of the lakes, with a very small one at Beaver Cove since most workers there lived in nearby Port McNeill or Port Hardy. We had family housing and bunk-houses at each camp. At Englewood's peak three hundred people worked there, and the community in total comprised about six hundred. I remember being inspired by how many families threw their hearts and souls into that valley. They had an absolute love for it, and they would not have thought about working or liv-ing anywhere else. It was their life and many of them had been there for two or three generations. They were wonderful people, a tight-knit community that loved the outdoors and they were unbelievably loyal to the company and to each other.

One of the summers I worked at Englewood, we were timber cruising way down the valley, and we packed our supplies in on our backs for a week at a time. Seven of us—two professional for-esters, a cook, three other students, and I—worked in two units. We were working in rough terrain, and crossing streams was chal-lenging. Depending on how steep the hillsides were, we might wade through the water or fell a tree and walk across it while bal-ancing a heavy backpack—doing our best to avoid looking down.

The company had a policy that encouraged injured workers to do light work rather than collect compensation, and an injured truck driver by the name of King came along as our cook. We lived in a tent camp, which was a great experience for me. Every meal we ate at bush camp that summer was "à la King" and very basic, quite a contrast to the main camp's cookhouse meals, which I loved.

At first, I was surprised and curious to discover that everyone was silent during our meals. I quickly learned that this was just part of the culture. You were there to eat and not talk. They had marvellous food. Breakfast was my favourite, with any kind of egg you wanted, hot cakes, bacon, ham, and sausage. It was delicious and a growing young man's dream. The men at camp got charged $2.50 per day for room and board, though the meals cost much more than that. That fee never changed over the years. To keep the men and have the manpower, the company significantly subsidized those costs.

THE VALLEY HAD a rich folklore, with one true story that I remember well. One summer the Englewood Logging Division was the site of a series of unfortunate deaths that shocked us all. I was at my family's home at Camp 'N' when we got disturbing word of a cook who had been shot dead at Camp Woss. Shortly after the shooting, another cook from Camp Woss called for a plane to pick him up at Camp 'N,' then the operation's headquarters. He was waiting on the dock when an RCMP aircraft landed, bringing officers in to investigate the murder. Well, the cook who was waiting for the plane panicked and shot himself, making the police investigation a lot easier. It was not hard for them to conclude that he had been the person who had committed the murder.

We had a lot of mouths to feed, so we sent for a replacement cook right away. It was the new cook's terrible misfortune that he had been drinking heavily before his arrival. As he was getting off the boat, somebody shouted to him, "You must be a brave guy! Two cooks have died and you're coming to replace them!" Well, he lost his balance, fell off the gangplank, and got crushed between the boat and the wharf. He did not survive. It happened very quickly and nobody could do anything. We had lost three cooks in forty-eight hours: the first a murder at Camp Woss, the second a suicide at Camp 'N,' and the third a drowning at Beaver Cove.

A LATER TURN of events at Englewood unexpectedly led to my first meeting with Bill Vander Zalm. I was in charge of the company when a new public highway cut its way through the valley. We had known it would only be a matter of time before that would happen, and, of course, the highway changed everything. Our operation had enjoyed a good reputation in the area as a place to work, but getting in and out had been challenging. Once the highway was in, employees could commute from Courtenay or Campbell River, spending their weeks at camp and their weekends at home.

To service the new highway, a gas station went in at Woss and we leased it to an operator. He had wanted to buy the small piece of property, but we could not be seen selling private lands in the forest management area, so we decided to lease the land to him for a dollar a year in return for the service he provided. Well, to my surprise I was called to Victoria one day because it turned out that this fellow was complaining to the government about the company's "lack of cooperation." Vander Zalm was then minister of municipal affairs, and in that role he had to deal with land matters. We were summoned to his office, and as we waited outside his door, this fellow was calling me all manner of names. When we finally met with the minister, Vander Zalm said he wanted to understand the situation.

"What's the problem?" he asked.

"Well," said the fellow, "the company won't sell me the land my station is on."

The minister turned to me. "You lease the land?" he asked.

"Yes," I replied.

"You own the land?" he queried.

"Yes," I repeated.

"Why won't you sell it?"

"We're reluctant to sell any private land that is part of our contribution to the TFL," I explained.

"That makes sense," he said. "I think this meeting is over."

"But I want the government to intervene!" the fellow insisted.

"I don't need to," the minister concluded. "When somebody owns private land and they have a reason for not selling it, there's nothing I will do on behalf of the government to compel them to sell it."

So that was the first time I met Vander Zalm. It was a short meeting and he made the right decision.

ENGLEWOOD WAS THE SOURCE of another drama that unfolded, in 1950 when I was still at university. Michael Cudahy, of the U.S. meat-packing family, sued our company for improper logging practices—an absurd accusation. It was an extremely lengthy trial. Cudahy owned some of the private timber that our family had not bought in the Nimpkish Valley, and because we logged his licences annually, the U.S. income tax people deemed Cudahy's timber revenue to be income rather than capital gains. A report that Cudahy commissioned from a local forest company came back as favourable to our practices, so Cudahy sent them back to write another one that supported his point of view.

The second report was devastating. It accused us of leaving behind too much timber because its wood measurement unfairly included spar trees. A "spar" tree (usually a Douglas fir, chosen for its strength) is used for yarding logs in. Spikes were hammered into it and wires attached. Under a strict Workers' Compensation Board requirement, we could not remove spar trees after using them because the spikes would endanger mill workers if the saws hit them. Leaving spar trees behind was all part of a logging company's normal practice.

The mood got tense in the courtroom when one of our supervisors, Ollie Jurnberg, was asked to describe what they did with a spar tree. Well, Ollie decided to go into great detail, saying, "After I put in the spikes, I climb higher and put in more spikes... and then more spikes..." He went on and on.

The whole argument was long and drawn-out, with many more witnesses called to testify. After a while, it became glaringly obvious that the issue for Cudahy had little to do with our logging practices and everything to do with his taxes. My father said as much when he took the stand.

"Well, Mr. Bentley, why do you think we're here?" the judge asked.

"That's simple," my dad answered. "We're here because Mr. Cudahy doesn't want us to log on a regular basis because it affects his income tax."

That point had not come up before that moment in the trial, and though the proceedings continued as if nothing had happened, my father's statement turned the tide. The judge finally understood that there had been two reports and that the second was manufactured to satisfy the client.

In the end, Cudahy lost the suit and had to pay the court's cost, our costs, and his own costs—close to $3.5 million, as I recall.

It was a big waste of time.

THE COMPANY was extremely responsible in its logging practices, and from the outset we replanted every acre that we harvested. It was obvious, however, that we needed expertise, so we engaged excellent professional foresters to help us manage the timberland. I came to admire many of the people who helped us grow Englewood into an impressive operation. Our logging manager Bill McMahan had joined us four years earlier, just after we bought Eburne in 1940. The entire site was under the care of Russell Mills and his wife, Estella, an outstanding married couple, both professors—he in forestry and she in soils—at the University

of Washington. Russell was way ahead of the times in his understanding of the field and management of the valley.

I remember both Bill McMahan and Russell Mills as men of
remarkably few words. On a trip Bill and I made to Englewood one
year, I prepared a list of all the things we needed to accomplish.
When we got back to the house that evening, we were reviewing
our day.

"I think we did all but one on my list," I said to Bill.

"What was that?" he asked.

"We didn't discuss a certain siding."

"Oh, that's done," he said. "I pointed my cigar at it and Russell
nodded."

IT HAD BEEN my hope and my father's, too, that I would join the
business in earnest after completing university. I remember my
wife, Sheila, telling me about a conversation she had with my dad
after we were married. She had mentioned how lucky they were
that I so loved the business and wanted to carry on. "Naturally,"
my father replied, a statement that confirmed for me that he had
always assumed my continued involvement.

I never discussed my future with anyone until I finished high
school, but the family made it clear that they wanted me to take
forest engineering. I, on the other hand, was firmly oriented
toward law, with commerce as my second choice. The last faculty
I wanted to be in was forestry, because I did not like the sciences. I
took my senior matriculation at the end of high school, which put
me into second year at the university, but St. George's did not offer
the prerequisite courses for forestry. Anyway, I did not want to go.

In the end, I surrendered and signed up at UBC for all the pre-
requisites, which included chemistry, physics, biology, botany, and
geography. The only course I managed to enjoy was Economics 200.
Predictably, I ended up doing less and less work and developing my

passion for sports. In the end, I was doing a whole lot of athletics with a fair bit of gambling and running raffles thrown in for good measure. Those extracurricular activities earned me $64 a day on average—tax-free—for the entire time I attended UBC. That was big money in those days. I did not want my parents to know, so I became secretive. I was rebelling in a big way.

In the fall of 1947, I enrolled in forestry according to my father's expectations, and my studies lasted through the beginning of 1950, when I dropped out. Or should I say, when I was asked to leave. I was not at all surprised that my parents were upset.

It was a bad mistake, but I was going to correct it. I was a self-made outcast when I left university, and it was plain luck that John Hecht of Bridge Lumber took me in. In fact, I could not have been more fortunate, as the training I got there was some of the best I ever had in office and mill management. Hecht ran a very tight ship and had an unusual business. His was a good sawmill that had no raw materials; they custom cut logs that customers brought to them. They also made chips that the log supplier might keep or that Bridge could sell. In 1950, I did their bookkeeping, ran the office, and supervised the mill. The owners, who had never gone away at the same time before, were thrilled when they returned from a month in Europe to find that the mill had had its best month in the company's history under my supervision. They offered me a permanent job, but I wanted to move on and get experience that was more practical.

A man from Chicago by the name of Overton Chambers had impressed me when he came as a dinner guest to our family home in Vancouver. A bright, well-spoken man of good taste, he and his two brothers operated a reputable lumber wholesaler operation with just the three of them and one secretary. I contacted Chambers and asked if I could go and work for him for no pay, just commissions. It was a low-risk deal for him, so off I went in 1951.

He sponsored me as a guest member at the Union League Club in Chicago, where I stayed, just across the back alley from the office. With little to lose, Chambers turned me loose on a couple of accounts and I got busy developing a sales strategy that I thought would work. I was playing a solid game of golf at the time. I went to one of the best clubs in town, where I knew the head pro, and explained to him that I did not want to hustle, I just wanted to meet important people.

The first weekend at the club I played with Phil Swift of meat-packing fame and who was also chair and CEO of the Continental Bank of Illinois—then the biggest bank in Chicago. He had two daughters and no sons, so he took me under his wing and introduced me to his business. I spent a week in the stockyards and then made my way to purchasing to see how things were done. Before long I asked him where he got his wood for his pallets, crates, and fencing. When I learned that he was buying it from a yard down the road, I explained that he could get it wholesale through an industrial account with Chambers, and I signed him up.

My marketing strategy had worked well; these clients needed an industrial volume of wood, and I was able to give it to them for a great price. I went on to use the same approach with Inland Steel, Caterpillar Tractor, Budd Body, and both the Ford company and the Pontiac division of General Motors. By the time I left Chicago at the end of 1951, I was bringing in as much money in commissions as Chamber's company was from all its other sales.

WORD SOON SPREAD back home that I was doing very well in the United States, and the family asked me to join the business. They had just purchased the Port Mellon mill in Howe Sound and they contacted me along with Harry Macdonald, a former night watchman at Eburne who had just returned from his studies at Oxford as a UBC Rhodes Scholar. The story goes that after reading about

Harry's award in the newspaper in the late 1940s, my father had called him into his office and congratulated him. He had also given him a cheque, saying that he hoped it would help him while he was at Oxford. Dad only asked one thing in return: before Harry accepted a job elsewhere, he wanted him to come and talk to us.

Neither Harry nor I had a regular job with the company, but Dad and Uncle John wanted to talk to us about what needed to be done, and who might do what. According to the plan devised by my father and uncle, one of us would do the hiring and the start-up at Port Mellon, and the other would go to New York to work with our sales agent, finding out who used pulp, and what they did with it. So they called us in to discuss who went where.

Harry was a few years older and far more experienced, so it was logical that he go to Port Mellon and help start up the operation. I was happy to go to the eastern United States. None of us knew the market there and I wanted still more experience. New York did not end up being as fruitful as I had hoped, but I carried on from there to Savannah, Georgia, to see how Union Camp managed to manufacture a million paper bags a day, which struck me at the time as an astronomical number. From there I made my way to Texas to see Southland's method of making newsprint from southern pine, which nobody thought they could do. All along, I worked out of the office of the sales agent Perkins-Goodwin. My mission was to identify the players who used pulp and what they were looking for in terms of quality.

DURING MY TIME in the United States, I came to another important turning point in my life, though the person involved had made a brief appearance a few years before. I remember well the evening during a family ski trip at a Sunshine ski lodge when my mother and I went to see a movie in Banff. A very attractive girl in ski clothes was sitting in front of me at the theatre. I knew the girl's name was Sheila McGiverin, but we had not been introduced.

We both had attended UBC, and when a mutual friend, Jean Cochrane, later asked Sheila if she knew me, she said no. When Jean asked me if I knew Sheila, I fibbed and said that I had taken her to a movie in Banff. When we were finally introduced, Sheila very politely said, "It's nice to see you again."

"What the hell are you talking about?" I replied. "You just told Jean you didn't know me!"

Sheila, of course, was quite right. We had never met and she had no idea that I had sat behind her in the theatre that night, nor who I was.

Soon after that second meeting, Sheila bought one of my lunchtime raffle tickets at the university, which varied in price from a penny to a dollar. She was not pleased when she paid ninety-eight cents, and she accused me of having only high-priced tickets. In any event, that interaction led to our first date. We went to the Palomar nightclub, a low-rise, one-and-a-half-storey shack located where the Burrard Building now stands at Georgia and Burrard. The Palomar was then *the* place to go to see live entertainment like the Ink Spots, Louis Armstrong, and Duke Ellington.

At the Palomar on another night, when I was there with my closest friend, Austin Taylor, some guys at the next table were yakking and carrying on during the national anthem at the close of the evening. Austin, who was a big man, told them to shut up. When the anthem was over, one of the guys took a beer bottle, broke it on the table, and came straight for Austin. The Palomar had lightweight wooden chairs with rounded backs and discs for seats. I grabbed my chair and broke it over the guy's head. It was

the biggest mess. I think we broke everything in the place bury-
ing those guys. But the Palomar was tame the evening Sheila and I
went there for our first date.

Sheila and I went out a few times after that but then things
fizzled for a while. I ran into her again during an impromptu visit
to the home of the youngest Bloedel daughter, Eulalie. As I was
leaving, Sheila ran out to the driveway and asked if I would be her
escort for her sorority party. She was president of the sorority and
her date had fallen ill. I did not like being asked to fill in for someone else, so I acted cool and drove off, spinning my tires.

"I'll call you in the morning," I shouted.

It was not very nice of me to do that, so I called her the next
day to say I would be happy to escort her to the party, and I asked
whether it was white or black tie. Well, Sheila was eager to get me
back at me for my behaviour the day before. She intentionally lied
to me, saying it would be a white-tie event, probably because I had
told her a story of how I almost choked once because of my white
tie's tight collar.

When I arrived with Sheila at the party, I was the only fellow in
white tie. We went out together for a while and enjoyed each other's company, but then we both moved on from UBC and went in
different directions. Sheila travelled in Europe that summer with
three of her friends while I focused on my golf game, and then I
was off to gain some experience in the United States.

When I came home after my stint in Chicago, I was best man
at my friend Philip Strike's wedding in late December 1952, and
Sheila was a bridesmaid. That was when we really hit it off. By the
time I had rented my room in the Gotham Hotel in New York in
early January, I was keeping pretty much to myself and writing a
letter home to Sheila almost every day. My room was tiny, with a
bed, a desk, and an armchair for a negotiated rate of $12.50 a day. I
would pass the hours when I wasn't working or writing letters by

chipping golf balls into the chair. One evening, the ball bypassed the armchair and went straight out of my open window onto Fifth Avenue. I quickly closed the blinds and was relieved not to hear any news about an accident below.

When I returned to Vancouver from the United States, I asked Sheila to marry me, and lucky for me she agreed. We got engaged in December 1952 and married the following May.

AFTER THE WEDDING and our honeymoon that took us from California to Mexico City, where I was best man for my friend Austin Taylor, and on to Europe, it was time to consider my career options. It was both a honeymoon and an educational trip for me.

I had proved myself in the United States and it was time to see what was happening overseas. For a number of months, Sheila and I lived in London, where I continued my education in timber and pulp and paper. I divided my time working with our agent, Seaboard Lumber Sales, in the office and calling on their customers. I needed to learn about who they were and discuss a problem regarding wormholes in hemlock that was affecting our industry at the time. Our worm issue in Canada was minimal: the worms had long gone and the wood was not compromised in any way. The South American Paraná pine, on the other hand, contained worms that were active and would eat up the wood on an ongoing basis. That U.K. problem was giving our Canadian hemlock a bad name and that—in addition to significant pricing challenges—had caused our sales to drop for the first time since the war. I spent a lot of time explaining to customers that our wood was sound.

While I was in the United Kingdom, I travelled extensively to Scandinavia, particularly to Sweden and Finland, to explore what they were doing in the forest industry. Those trips were interesting and thoroughly enjoyable. Although all my hosts were hospitable, the Finns were most open and eager to offer blueprints and suppliers' names, whereas the Swedes were very secretive. On one occasion, they said they could not explain a technical detail because all their engineers were German. When I told them I was fluent in German, they were uncomfortably surprised, but we did go on to have a discussion.

I was pleased to return to Vancouver in the mid-1950s with some international experience and very ready to be a part of the family business. My father and Uncle John had made significant strides in my absence and were well into integrating further with new markets and products.

I WAS TWENTY-SIX when I attended one of the first classes of the Banff School of Advanced Management in 1956. Seventy-two attended our six-week class, including Henry Hansen, the manager of our Englewood Logging Division. Bud McCaig, who subsequently made quite a name for himself in Calgary, and Jerry Kramer of Kramer Tractor (the Finning equivalent for the Prairies) were the other young students in the program. Sheila and I were expecting our second daughter, Susie, at the time.

I enjoyed the program very much. It was located at the Banff School of Fine Arts and was a cooperative effort involving the Harvard Business School and the three western Canadian universities. The head of the school was Senator Donald Cameron, and UBC's head of commerce, Dean Earle MacPhee, was the program director.

Some of the students, particularly the older fellows from the oil industry, appeared to have been sent to the class as time off for good behaviour. Their management level or their attitude (or both) made it difficult for them to take policy issues seriously, and they did not contribute to group discussions. I later wrote a strong report saying that, if the class was to survive, they had to do more screening instead of just taking warm bodies. In time, the school went the other way and started offering two courses a year, which meant they would have to lower their standard and risk killing the program. With such a small business community in western Canada, no suitable candidates would be left in the market to take their courses.

With the introduction of in-house MBA–type classes for executives at UBC and the University of Alberta, the Banff program started to lose its appeal. But it had been a great experience for me because I wanted to excel in every way I could, having messed up my own university career.

TEN YEARS AFTER my departure from UBC, I was invited back to talk to the forestry graduating class. The irony of that invitation was obvious to anyone who chose to take note of it, but I was keen on the idea. In preparing for the event, I reflected on how I was well on the way to making something of myself, yet it was obvious how misguided it had been for me to waste those earlier years. In my speech, I offered my views on the industry as it was then, and made it clear to the class how stupid I had been for not doing my work. I did not want to cover up my conduct at the university, which must have horrified the people who had invited me to speak. I made it clear that I had made the wrong choice, and that I admired them for their perseverance and success—something I had lacked, but had since rediscovered.

5

Grande Prairie
The Alberta Advantage

CANADIAN FOREST PRODUCTS (CFP) headed into the late 1950s, ready for further expansion. We were fully integrated on the lumber side of things, and successful in our production of plywood, hardboard, lumber, shingles, and shakes. Lumber was our basic product, but we also had a lot of leftover waste materials or residuals, otherwise known as hog fuel, comprising bark, sawdust, and shavings. We used it in various ways to create steam or electricity and sold it to pulp mills as fuel. We also sold chips, which were used to produce pulp.

I HAD LEARNED many lessons in the United States, Europe, and at Banff, where I found that only a handful of my fellow students genuinely understood corporate responsibility. I did not agree with most of my classmates who thought that Dean Earle MacPhee's focus on social values was bunk. I was happy to get back to work and apply his sage advice.

My father and Uncle John were supportive and ready to give me rein to make certain changes I felt were necessary. One of these was combining into one department all the groups responsible for the buying, selling, and transporting of raw materials, including logs, chips, and hog fuel. These functions had been disjointed, and we had lost opportunities to trade effectively for what we really required. In my new role as coordinator of raw materials, I not only merged these functions into one department, but also oversaw the negotiation of all contracts for residuals as well as contracts for services we had never offered before—towing and transportation.

Before this change, no transportation contracts were available in the industry, though they were sorely needed for companies like ours that were becoming fully integrated. Integration meant that residual waste materials needed to be shipped out, and on a continual basis. I wanted to ensure that we always had scows waiting at the sawmills because, unless you hauled away waste materials as they were produced, the mill would have to shut down. There was nowhere to store more than two hours' worth of chips on our dock. We were the first company ever to sign a chip-towing agreement, which was far more effective than transporting materials on a quote basis. This was a new idea in the local industry and it briefly gave us a competitive advantage.

In our log department at head office, the two men I worked with were Hank Burnett and his able right-hand man, Elmer Boyes. Hank was moody but capable. Elmer was a character. He organized social events at head office and was constantly on the go and full of beans—a very happy fellow who always had something nice to say about everyone. The raw material staff included Joe Jetter from Czechoslovakia and Lorne Frame, two individuals popular in the industry who supervised the daily flow of chips for Howe Sound Pulp. I took care of the chip-contract negotiations, but they were the people who made it all run smoothly with the towing companies and our external chip suppliers.

I WAS FINALLY getting my feet wet at CFP and developing my own management style. Looking back, I see that I was somewhat impulsive—perhaps because of my father's influence—and quick to reach decisions. For better or worse, I am still inclined to act that way. From the start, I was determined to get things done and I have enjoyed working with good people who could help me achieve my goals. When it came time to take my turn at hiring, I always aimed to get the best. Some people I brought on board may not have shared my view of the growth I wanted to see, but many of them were a lot smarter than I and a lot more skilled in their various specialties.

After a few years of solid management experience, I encouraged what was known as "skunk works," where the managers were somewhat autonomous and didn't have to preclear all decisions with me. I did insist, however, on order when it came to the management of capital. Each division manager reported in and participated in decisions on how and where our money would be spent. CFP's divisions competed for discretionary capital, both by mill and by product line. It was important for us to spend where the company's bottom line would receive the most benefit. However, sometimes we made a purchase that initially might have had a lower payback than an internal investment. Such decisions allowed us to grow, and we could not pick our own timing for these opportunities.

PLYWOOD STILL REPRESENTED one of our major commodities in the 1950s. Pat Burns was our sales manager for plywood and a genuine character. He was a likeable, fun-loving fellow and one of our first plywood employees. At one point he came to us to say that, if we were going to continue being competitive, we should be manufacturing poplar (cottonwood) plywood. Other companies were producing it and we were not. That was something about which I knew very little, but we followed Burns's hunch.

For the first time, we turned our attention away from the coast and set out in search of poplar. We found Northern Plywood Ltd., located in Grande Prairie, Alberta, a relatively new birch and poplar plywood mill that held promise, and in 1956 purchased a 50 percent interest in it from the Bickell family. That close relationship began with marketing support and would gradually grow into technical assistance and our supply of capital funds for expansion. Five years later, we secured the remaining 50 percent.

I had not visited Grande Prairie before, but I made my way up there soon after negotiations were finalized. The connecting flight on a DC3 from Fort St. John to Grande Prairie is forever etched in my memory as the most dramatic turbulence I have ever experienced. We were barely a thousand feet above ground the whole way, and the combination of heat and wind made it seem that the aircraft's wings would fall off. One of the pilots was a fraternity brother of mine and, as we stumbled off the plane, I told him it was the worst flight I had ever been on. "Me, too," he answered, looking a little green himself. Once I recovered from the experience, I realized that for the entire bumpy ride the only landscape below us had been agricultural fields. I had not seen one tree. "What the hell have we got ourselves into here?" I wondered.

We did get to the forests eventually that day and I found the Bickells top-rate in every way. John Bickell, a marvellous storyteller, was in charge as the founder of the business. Of his three sons, Roy was the eldest and in charge of our Alberta operations from the day we joined them until he moved to the coast as vice-president, wood products, which included logging and all our lumber, plywood, and shingle mills. Roy worked for us for thirty-seven years and spent several of those as Canfor president—and a damn good one. He stepped down in 1991 and moved back to Alberta, where he and his wife, Noreen, could once again enjoy four seasons instead of two. In latter years, Roy's brother, Bob, became vice-president, northern wood products. Both men were highly capable.

WHAT WE HAD found in northwestern Alberta, in the low foothills east of the Rocky Mountains and the surrounding farmlands, were large forests of white spruce and lodgepole pine. The poplar and birch that we used at Northern Plywood were brought in from Slave Lake.

Grande Prairie was entirely engaged in winter logging, which was new to me. We had to bring in all the wood from early November to the end of March, because frozen roads were essential to the trucks and the heavy loads they carried. Once the frost was out of the ground, the roads were impassable. The winter haul averaged more than 150 kilometres, with logs coming by truck from south of Grande Prairie.

The Alberta government was markedly more sympathetic to the industry than the B.C. ministry was. We always had an excellent relationship with the Alberta government. The deputy minister at the time, Fred McDougall, was consistently straightforward and professional with us.

When Don Getty was minister of energy and natural resources for Alberta, and when John Zaozirny later became minister, we held individual, off-the-record meetings in Vancouver about forest policy. The Alberta forest industry was still new and the sawmills were mostly small bush operations; there was no need for chips because no pulp industry existed there at the time. The ministers had little experience in our area and, when they were appointed, everyone in the Alberta government seemed desperate for the province to get into the pulp and paper industry. We thought we could be of assistance in helping them sort out what policies would make the most sense. We offered to meet with the ministers on different occasions. Doug Rickson, our chief forester, joined me and Glen Patterson, our man in charge of Alberta, in walking them through various approaches based on what was happening in other jurisdictions. They respected what we had to say because we gave them a list of available options even though some were not as favourable to CFP. I enjoyed the high-level rapport and mutual respect we developed with our Alberta landlords.

By the time we owned 100 percent of the Grande Prairie operation in the early 1960s, we had made a number of changes. The first was to switch from cottonwood in the plywood mill to SPF, which was more economical. The cottonwood from Slave Lake came a good distance—nearly three hundred kilometres—and, contrary to Pat Burns's opinion, it offered no advantage in the marketplace. The second was to develop a free-standing stud mill on the south side of Grande Prairie to process the peeler cores and small logs.

Eventually, we converted the stud mill to a full-fledged sawmill and we had to close down the plywood mill. Plywood was not selling well, and we were able to get better value putting high-quality logs through the sawmill and ending up with optimal products. Furthermore, there was not enough suitable timber available to run both mills at capacity.

CFP never went into the manufacture of OSB (oriented strand board) for good reason. To build OSB, you have to use a whole log to create flakes, which are glued together to form the board. If you have low-grade logs and if you are close to the market, say in the Carolinas or in Georgia, and if you have low transportation costs, then manufacturing OSB is fine. But being a long way from major population centres, it did not make sense. So despite a number of studies we conducted about OSB, we elected not to go into it and favoured products made from our existing waste. Putting our waste to good use has always been a priority. We went into hardboard in New Westminster so we could use our waste. The same was true in our later manufacture of pulp from chips, and also in our burning hog fuel instead of fossil fuel to make power and steam.

CFP also investigated the possibility of establishing a pulp mill in Grande Prairie, which seemed a promising idea in 1960, before we delved into the implications. The Alberta government was willing to give us a forest management agreement (FMA), which would have given us permission to proceed. We negotiated an agreement but never signed it. When we explored the U.S. markets in depth, we saw that most of the major companies were integrated and would have used our pulp only on an incremental basis, when their supply was lacking. We also recognized that, with the modernization of paper machines, the days of small, nonintegrated independent companies were numbered.

We woke up to the important fact that, if we were going to build a world-class pulp mill in Alberta, the U.S. market was essential. We knew that Canada did not consume much pulp and most of the demand was in the East. It made no sense to compete with eastern mills because hauling would eat up all our revenues; transportation costs are very important in our industry. For a pulp mill to be successful in Grande Prairie, its sales had to be in North America. In the case of our Howe Sound pulp mill, which was on tidewater, we had a freight advantage in transporting product mostly to overseas customers and shipping significantly less to our small U.S. customer base. The lesson was simple: you can't change geography.

That realization led to one of the most difficult conversations I ever had with government. After putting everything in place to build a pulp mill in Grand Prairie and asking the Alberta ministry to do the same, we were cancelling our bid. I had done all the preparatory work until John Liersch joined us as executive vice-president. We planned to travel together to deliver the bad news but, unfortunately, John fell ill and was unable to accompany me.

I flew to Edmonton on my own to tell the minister and the premier that, even though they had done everything necessary to launch a pulp mill, we could not deliver. The minister asked if we would reconsider if he gave us another thousand square miles. Management leases didn't exist at the time, so nothing was allocated and he could do whatever he wanted.

"I don't think I will ever live long enough to turn down a thousand square miles again," I replied. "You have already offered us enough timber to do what we intended, but we simply cannot deliver. It would be foolish to build a mill without a market to take the product."

I explained that we wanted to expand in Alberta and really liked doing business there, but we had been unsuccessful in locating U.S. partners to help us open a mill. If they could find U.S. people interested in building a pulp mill, we would cooperate. As a safeguard, I added that we hoped that, in exchange for our support for their pulp mill, they would not permit any such U.S. company to enter the Alberta lumber or plywood business.

JOHN LIERSCH had come on board in the fall of 1960 as executive vice-president. My father had wanted to appoint me to the position, but I had reservations. I explained that I wasn't yet ready and that John was the person I most wanted to work with and learn from. We could see that he had been frustrated as the former executive vice-president at the Powell River Company, which MacMillan Bloedel had purchased the year before. He and I had worked together on our failed merger with the Powell River Company.

By 1961, we had bought the remaining shares of Northern Plywood as well as the Grande Prairie Lumber Company and combined all the operations into North Canadian Forest Industries (NCFI). John Liersch decided to send Glen Patterson to Grande Prairie as general manager for Alberta, where he did a wonderful job of leading and developing the company. He was an excellent communicator and did well with both the Forest Service and the Alberta government.

When we first moved in to Alberta, we had accessed our timber south of Grande Prairie on a quota basis. In 1964, under Glen Patterson's leadership, NCFI was granted an FMA, the first to be awarded to a mill other than a pulp operation. With it came long-term tenure for twenty years and an assured supply of timber based on the forest growing capacity of 1,110 square miles of timberland.

A year later, we became the first company in Alberta to centralize our sawmills in Grande Prairie, thereby doing away with the relatively crude bush mills and reducing excess by establishing waste wood chipping. We were doing a much better job using almost all of the forest resource instead of leaving it on the ground. By the end of the decade, we had bought out the smaller bush mills and timber quotas in the area and had built a new stud mill in Hines Creek, ninety miles north of Grande Prairie.

During those early days operating in Alberta and British Columbia, we saw significant differences in stumpage systems— the fees paid to provincial governments to cut timber. In Alberta, the companies tended to be small, and most could not pay stumpage when delivering logs because they had to bring in the year's inventory over a short winter season and therefore didn't have much cash built up. Consequently, they had established a logical system of paying stumpage on a monthly basis according to the amount of lumber leaving the mill. That way, companies paid stumpage fees at the same time they were paid for their product.

In British Columbia, it worked differently then, as it still does today. When the truck delivers the logs over the weigh scales, companies are billed for what they have brought in on a weight basis, and that is their stumpage fee. But that system causes problems. In British Columbia's northern Interior, more timber is harvested in the winter (as it is in Alberta) when operations can build up quite a lot of inventory and stumpage can lag behind the market by one to three months. In a poor lumber market, when you are bringing in your wood, the stumpage may be down, but by the time you process the logs, it may be up. Companies could make a larger than normal profit on that wood, but the reverse can also happen. I have never fully understood why none of our politicians have allowed us to switch to the far more sensible system used in Alberta.

AS OUR GRANDE Prairie operation grew in the early 1960s, our coastal operations in British Columbia were running smoothly and we were looking at the northern Interior for opportunities. November 22, 1963, is etched in the minds of many North Americans—the day John F. Kennedy was assassinated in Dallas. It was also the day we bought our first sawmill in the B.C. Interior.

The Fort St. John Lumber Company (a misleading name as the operation was located in Chetwynd) was owned jointly by Gordon Moore of Chetwynd and the Broderick family, well-known lumber wholesalers from Pittsburgh. As we sat in our old boardroom finalizing the purchase, we heard a knock at the door. It was Arnold Smith, our human resources manager.

"President Kennedy has been shot," he said.

We closed the deal and I took the group for a sombre lunch at Trader Vic's. My fortune cookie offered up a message that matched the mood of that unnerving November afternoon: "This is a day to be brave."

"I don't know if this is because your president has been shot," I said to my colleagues, "or because we have bought your company."

The Fort St. John Lumber Company had a planing mill in Dawson Creek, a small sawmill at Little Stewart Lake, and its main sawmill in Chetwynd. The planing mill was not on the same site as the sawmill because the Pacific Great Eastern Railway had not yet completed its line to Chetwynd. The lumber had to be trucked in to Dawson Creek and from there hauled east by rail.

A year later, these mills and other timber quotas we purchased in the Peace River District were consolidated into CFP's Chetwynd Division. In the late 1980s, Glen Patterson would use our position there to secure tenure in the region through Tree Farm Licence 48, known as the Chetwynd TFL.

WE KNEW from our homework, years before, that any company with an established market in the United States could build a pulp operation in the Grande Prairie region. Consequently, it was no surprise in 1967 when two corporations—Buckeye Cellulose (a subsidiary of Proctor and Gamble) and a Canadian mining company—applied to the Alberta government for permission to build a pulp mill. At a public hearing in Grande Prairie, we supported the Proctor and Gamble pulp lease application because they said all the right things about us working with them and about only being interested in the pulp side of things. Their market in the United States comprised only their own operations, which required large volumes of pulp for paper packaging.

At the same hearing, NCFI also presented a case for more timberland based on our significant growth over the previous decade as well as the community's related expansion and prosperity. From the time our Alberta FMA was granted in 1964, our foresters had diligently surveyed the lease area, and their research confirmed our need for an additional ten-year forest reserve to sustain our operations. We gave evidence at the hearing, requesting that our needs be given priority, and reassuring those present that we would be complementing and not competing with pulp operations in the area. We also recommended that the pulp lease applicant be restricted to pulp mill development because we did not feel that the Grande Prairie district had the capacity for additional production of sawlogs and peelers without jeopardizing our future growth. We were proud of NCFI, which had pioneered the concept of centralization and integration of forest operations in Alberta. We could happily co-exist with a pulp mill, but we could not afford to welcome a company that would infringe on our line of business.

Proctor and Gamble won the agreement and went ahead with the pulp mill in 1972. Subsequently, however, they built a sawmill, which was very upsetting. It did not take away any of our business, but it did limit our opportunity to expand. I highlighted a copy of the transcript from the public hearings and sent it to the government, asking why they would allow that to happen.

Proctor and Gamble were also difficult to deal with on chip prices because they were the only game in town and they were tough. Our senior management and their management tended to get confrontational instead of working cooperatively. That changed when Weyerhaeuser bought the operation in 1992 and George Weyerhaeuser Jr. and I went to Grande Prairie. There we spent time with both management teams, always in each other's company, explaining that we wanted them to work cooperatively for our mutual benefit. Those meetings significantly changed the relationship for the better.

Years later, the Alberta government approached us about opening a sawmill to offer employment in Grande Cache. A coal mine was closing there, and they wanted the community to survive. We prepared ourselves for the public hearing, and B.C. Forest Products (BCFP) joined in with a competing bid to open a paper mill. Horst Schmid was an associate minister of economic development at the time, and he appeared to like BCFP's idea of a paper mill. We were sure a paper mill would be a nonstarter because the geography was all wrong; freight rates are higher for paper products than pulp. We thought we had a good chance of winning the bid.

I did not want to appear at the hearing on the company jet, so we travelled on a small charter aircraft. I recall another independent applicant, Nelson Skalbania, arriving in a DH-125 and pulling up to the hotel in a taxi he did not have the cash to pay for. There he was, representing himself at the hearing, bidding to build a mill, and I had to loan him the money for his cab!

Skalbania did not have much grounding in the forest industry, and it was a little unusual that he was submitting an application entirely on his own. He made a number of mistakes while giving rather impractical evidence at the hearing. When he was asked about his business experience, he mentioned his involvement in the submarine business. During the proceedings, I was seated in the audience behind Dr. Joseph Ross, the minister of forests, who turned to me after Skalbania spoke.

"That's the first time I've seen someone torpedo his own application with his own submarine," he said with a wink.

The week before the hearing results were made public, I was at a dinner in Calgary for the executive of the Business Council on National Issues. Our guest, Premier Peter Lougheed, was seated in an awkward position at the table—between me and Alfred Powis of Noranda, the company that controlled BCFP. Given that the premier would soon be delivering the good news to only one of us, he must have felt a little uncomfortable.

A week later, Lougheed announced that the contract had been awarded to BCFP. The ministry was complimentary about our integrity, but they preferred the idea of bringing in another major player. BCFP never delivered on their promise to build a paper mill, though that was the main reason they were chosen over us. Instead, they built a sawmill, but they built the wrong kind of sawmill for small timber, and they lost a lot of money. It would have been easier for us since we knew the area. Knowing what we did about Alberta timber, we would have built a small wood mill, and any larger timber could have been redirected to our Grande Prairie mill.

ONCE ALL OUR MILLS were up and running in Grande Prairie, Hines Creek, and High Level, we reached our peak production in Alberta of roughly 50 percent of the province's annual allowable cut at the time. We had become a major player in the provincial forest industry.

As far as our continuing interest in pulp was concerned, our early plan to bring pulp to Grande Prairie was a forerunner of important changes to come. Soon after we pulled out of the pulp plan in Alberta, we had gone looking for a different location—where we could export to a global market, where we had an existing customer base, and where we could have partners. We hoped that we could make it work a little closer to home, in the northern Interior of British Columbia.

6

Prince George
Going Global

CANADIAN FOREST PRODUCTS (CFP) was about to transform itself and a good part of British Columbia in the early 1960s, but we didn't know it yet.

In 1961, Garvin Dezell, the mayor of Prince George, invited me as CFP's coordinator of raw materials to talk to the city's Industrial Development Commission, chaired by Harold Moffat. The commission wanted to know why no pulp mills existed in the north-central Interior of British Columbia when such good wood was available, and why it was that no usable chips—pulp's lifeblood—were being produced in the region. I jumped at the opportunity.

The questions were good ones, and it took me a while to paint the whole picture for my audience. Much of my talk reflected the problems we had discovered and our lessons learned in Grande Prairie. I explained to the commission that only two central sawmills in the Prince George area—Eagle Lake and Shelly—were big enough to consider installing barking and chipping equipment. I

also told them that the cost of hauling chips to the coast was prohibitive and just about matched the value of the chips themselves.
With those obstacles, I asked the audience, did it make any sense
to manufacture chips?

Moving on to the pulp mill issue, I proposed that indeed such
an operation in the Interior would do well, but it was unlikely to
materialize since all the timber there was already allocated to the
sawmill industry. I concluded my talk with an inescapable fact:
the government could do very little to induce someone to build a
pulp mill under those circumstances.

I delivered my speech without knowing that, within a year,
those explanations would lead to our development in Prince
George and to the creation of all that I was explaining as unlikely,
if not impossible. The mayor's enthusiasm took us a long way, as
did the eagerness of Harold Moffat and Ray Williston, a former
schoolteacher turned Social Credit minister of lands and forests
from Fort George.

Moffat was the owner of Northern Hardware and a citizen
with an inspirational plan for his community's economic development. As mayor of Prince George a decade later, he is quoted as
saying: "We must have Vision, Faith, and Will... the vision to see
the future, the faith to see the vision, and then the will to carry
on." Politically, Moffat was the man behind Williston. The two
men were close and each positively influenced the other.

Ray Williston was a completely honest man with a pleasant
personality. As British Columbia's education minister, he had
promoted the new concept of university education for teachers, but as minister of lands and forests he had a far greater
impact. From power projects to forestry practices, he introduced innovative changes throughout the 1950s and '60s. Ray
was a passionate advocate for major development in the Interior
and in northern British Columbia, and a long-time supporter

of maximum utilization of the wood supply. With that type of person rooting for us—along with most of Prince George—and a geography that allowed the backhauling of pulp to the coast, everything became achievable. We were ready to move forward with building a mill that produced high-quality pulp. It was exactly what our European customers wanted, accustomed as they were to producing printing and writing papers with Scandinavian pulp made from long-fibred wood similar to what we have in the northern Interior.

Ray never lost his passion for education. He decided early in his tenure to reserve the top of Prince George's biggest hill as a potential university campus and not let the government sell any of the land for real estate even though it had the best views in town. No university was even contemplated at that time, yet Ray set that site aside.

Ray Williston was a very generous donor, not only of his time but also his money for the University of Northern British Columbia (UNBC). It was appropriate for him to receive an honorary degree from UNBC in 1997. When we celebrated the university's tenth anniversary in 2004, it was an honour for me as chancellor to bestow a number of degrees, including those given to Mike Harcourt and Bill Vander Zalm, whose cooperation regarding education in Prince George was greatly appreciated; when it looked like the government may change, the two of them agreed that, regardless of who won the election, certain commitments to UNBC would be honoured.

AS WE HAD DONE in northern Alberta, our first move was to send our chief forester to do detailed research in the area. Tom Wright had already noted the astonishing fact that, of the trees cut in the northern Interior, by volume, only 25 percent wound up as lumber in the boxcar. With the exception of the two larger operations, the rest of the area's lumber was cut in small bush mills (numbering close to six hundred) and delivered to planing mills located along the railroad line. None of them was big enough to install barking and chipping equipment to recover the waste when it was still in its usable form. A research study funded by the Prince George Chamber of Commerce confirmed that residual waste might be employed as the foundation for a pulp industry in the region.

Tom Wright took Ray Williston on a tour of a selection of those crude bush mills, explaining how most of them butchered the timber and how, with no pulp mills in the area, the wood residue had no market. It was important for Williston to see it all first-hand and to understand that there was a limited future in Interior operations with the situation as it was. He would soon recognize the importance of competing with the coast, where mills were utilizing all their waste.

Soon our research was complete and we were convinced. With John Liersch having recently joined us, CFP was in a strong position. We were optimistic that the Interior pulp would be competitive with the coastal pulp while offering a quality advantage. We also concluded that, if we could work something out with the B.C. government to get access to timber, all of which was then allocated through quotas to the sawmill industry, the chips would be cheap enough to ship the superior quality pulp back to the coast.

At the time, the sawmill industry standard was a ten-inch DBH (diameter at breast height) and a six-inch top, compared with today's standard of a six-inch DBH and a four-inch top. For the pulp mills, we were prepared to accept wood below that standard if we could apply for stands of small or defective timber. Gradually, a concept evolved for allocating timberlands for pulpwood. After considerable discussion, the provincial government passed legislation to establish Pulpwood Harvesting Areas (PHA, now

shortened to PA) to promote the integrated use of all the softwood in the region, primarily lodgepole pine and spruce, and
lesser amounts of balsam and Douglas fir. The initial PHA concept
was twofold: first, all chip-producing sawmills within the PHA
boundaries were obligated to offer the designated pulp mill first
refusal on their chips (though this would change over time). Second, the pulp mill, if it was lacking the necessary chip supply or if
the residual chips were too expensive, was allowed to harvest timber below the sawmill utilization standard.

The assurance of an adequate wood supply was critical to
our obtaining financing for the pulp mill. With the additional
allowance of smaller trees, we were convinced that CFP and our
partners would have enough volume to support a pulp mill. We
were aware that some sawmill operators might resist the idea,
but we felt the more visionary ones would welcome the change
because it would create more revenue than ever as well as an outlet for waste that they would otherwise burn or leave behind. The
challenge for all concerned was to support a new pulp industry
while safeguarding the production of traditional lumber.

JOHN LIERSCH WORKED HARD in the fall of 1961 to keep CFP's
cards close to his chest despite rumours that were spreading
quickly around the province about our building a pulp mill near
Prince George. One day, the editor of the *Prince George Citizen*
called John and pumped him for information. John told him yes,
we were investigating a few sites in the area and Noranda Mines
Ltd. was doing the same. He also made it clear that both CFP and
Noranda were keeping clear of each other's "sphere of interest." He
even took the time to explain that, if the idea materialized, we
would be getting our wood supply in the form of waste material
from various sources, including the sawmilling business, logging operations, and the cutting of pulpwood stands. Finally, John

added, we were particularly interested in the area because of legislation passed earlier in the year wherein the government was prepared to assure a pulp operation of a supply of raw materials. At the end of his conversation with the editor, he insisted that no conclusions were to be drawn, because we still had to work out details such as the cost of transportation, market availability, the market price of pulp, and capital costs.

WE HAD STARTED to turn our attention away from the coast and toward Alberta's and British Columbia's northern Interior for many reasons. An important one was the fact that all the available coastal timberlands and agreements had been granted. Another was the negative image of cutting old-growth timber. In the Interior, the trees are much smaller and cutting them down does not leave the same impression. Advances in technology were making it possible to saw those smaller logs more effectively and other developments like the chip-saw and new logging equipment made it cost-effective.

It had long seemed clear to us that the B.C. government was often overly optimistic in calculating logging quotas. In our opinion, part of the coast was over-cut. Our foresters saw that the growth rate in the Interior on average was significantly higher than the government had calculated it to be. This presented a significant problem in a region where much of the timber was older and should have been harvested at an earlier age. The trees were dried out and subject to attack by the pine beetle and fire—and we all know what transpired on both those fronts. In the future, with careful restocking of the lands, we hoped to have better and younger timber with less likelihood of attack.

The introduction of pulp mills in the Interior would also create an instant market for wood waste and lead to a brand-new saw-mill industry to replace the bush mills. We wanted to develop the pulp industry so all of that could happen. We also wanted to help the sawmill operators centralize their facilities and create or purchase more operations. We made the business case to show them the advantages they would enjoy and, in some cases, we helped finance the improvements.

A pretty good sawmill in the early 1960s cost somewhere in the range of $6 to $10 million. To put an energy system into the current sawmills now would cost about $14 million. Optimizers and the new computerized systems included in some of the sawmills' rebuilding range from $30 to $100 million. Improvement costs have also increased in the pulp industry, and the projects are much more expensive. A new power boiler at the pulp mills today would cost more than the mill itself when we first built it.

BEFORE A PHA or another form of tenure was granted, the public was always given an opportunity to speak for or against it. Accordingly, the next step for us was a public hearing chaired by Ray Williston in June 1962 at which CFP submitted an application for an exclusive PHA in the Prince George area. It was important for CFP to reassure the minister, the hundred or so people present, and especially the district lumbermen, that our proposed mill would not harm the existing industry in any way.

As expected, we enjoyed considerable support at the proceedings from many local sawmillers who saw our new operation as an opportunity to centralize and upgrade their mills while also receiving revenue for the wood waste that they were accustomed to burning. There was opposition, however, from Cooper-Widman Ltd., a wholesale lumber company, and particularly from Noranda. Each company had shown up at the hearing to share its own plans for pulp. As I remember it, they argued that Canadian Forest Products was too small a company to be able to afford a new, world-class mill, and that Noranda had better means to finance one. They asked that the hearing be adjourned for six months to allow them time to prepare formal applications. Adam Zimmerman, comptroller of Noranda, led those attacks. He told the hearing that his company planned to build a pulp mill just south of Prince George.

My father was on his feet and ready to respond. He delivered a heated rebuttal, saying that he resented the suggestion that CFP was not making a firm proposal. He was fierce in his defence of our excellent record, explaining that the company employed more than three thousand people at the time and had made a far bigger investment in British Columbia than Noranda. Without any discussion, he turned to the minister and said that CFP would put up a million-dollar bond, which the government could take if we did not build at least a five-hundred-ton-per-day mill within the required period.

Dad continued: "We have done our homework, a lot more than was told here today. I am not willing to disclose our partners, who they are, how much they are putting up—I would be crazy to do so... We are willing to go ahead. I think it's unfair, in view of our negotiations with partners and customers, to put off a decision."

That seemed enough to satisfy Minister Williston, who announced that he could find no reason to postpone the decision when CFP had indeed presented a firm proposal. The other companies' statements at the hearing would be treated as objections rather than proposals. He went on to explain that the final decision would be made in light of whether the creation of a pulpwood harvesting area would be in the public's best interest. If that turned out to be so, the proposed area would be established under the B.C. Forest Act, giving our company the rights to material unsuitable for sawmilling within the licensed area for twenty-one years, after which CFP would need to prove its need for raw material rights.

We won our application and history was made with the signing of the first Pulpwood Harvesting Area agreement—PHA 1—on
November 22, 1962. The agreement covered roughly eight million acres of timber in the Prince George Forest District—an area
approximately the size of Belgium.

It reportedly took Minister Williston two and a half hours to
explain the new agreement to an audience of a hundred jammed
into the Elks Hall in West Quesnel. He stressed that CFP was going
only into the pulp business, not the lumber business, in Prince
George. His words were clear and forceful: "They will not, I repeat,
they will not interfere with any sawlog operation going on in the
area. And Canadian Forest Products must subject itself to a form
of checks and balances."

AFTER WE were granted the award, Cooper-Widman announced
that they were forced to shelve their plans for a pulp operation because of the new PHA, which blocked a timber supply for
any other pulp mill. They resented that Minister Williston had
rejected their arguments along with Noranda's, denying them an
extension to prepare proposals that would have asked for a portion of the timber we had been awarded.

Canadian Forest Products was taking a big risk. Nobody,
including us, really knew whether the economics of harvesting
smaller timber would work. A PHA gives no right to timber other
than that which falls below the sawmill standard size; and at first,
pulp companies had first refusal for chips made from any timber
going to the sawmills from the PHA. Williston had noted that the
idea of superimposing a PHA on sustained yield forest areas was
unique in North America.

Pat Carney, then a journalist and later a Cabinet minister and
more recently a Conservative senator for British Columbia, published an article in an industry magazine noting how the hearing

had failed to answer a number of questions. "The hassle over chip prices promises to be quite a poker game," she said. Carney also pointed to Williston's doubts when he said that the operator would be gambling millions "before he finds out whether he will get his wood and get it economically. It will take years before the details of his operation can be worked out."

Of course, we were well aware that the challenges would be enormous.

EACH OF THE PULP MILLS we built, Prince George Pulp and Paper (PGPP) and Intercontinental Pulp Company, cost us about $74 million at the time, which was a huge investment. Prior to the public hearing, our initial concept had been that CFP would own 60 percent of the pulp mill, with the remaining ownership split between four equal partners who would each own 10 percent and take 25 percent of the mill's production. That way the mill would be sold out when we began, with a guaranteed wood supply. Ideally, we wanted partners from the United States, continental Europe, the United Kingdom, and the Far East (Japan at the time).

The plan did not work, however. We came close to getting a Japanese partner but never concluded the deal; we were unable to find a U.S. customer willing to participate; and though we located two European companies, they did not want to be only ten-percenters.

We had proceeded to the hearing on our own and the initial PHA was awarded to Canadian Forest Products. Then we had the good fortune to meet with the Reed Paper Group, an international organization that employed close to 24,000 and was the world's largest buyer of wood pulp. Reed showed no enthusiasm for a minority interest. Instead they made us a counter proposal for a 50 percent partnership on the condition that in addition to pulp, we agree to produce specific materials they required—unbleached sack kraft (for products such as grocery bags) and linerboard (for making cardboard boxes). If we agreed, then Reed could close several of their antiquated smaller mills in the United Kingdom. They were willing to take the paper products but not the pulp, which we were happy to sell on behalf of the partnership.

We went back and forth with these ideas and we also talked with representatives of a company from Düsseldorf, Feldmühle AG, which hired a New York consultant to look into the feasibility of working with us. The resulting report advised that a joint venture would fail for two reasons: one, it was too costly to ship product from Prince George to Bremen or Hamburg, and two, it was too cold to log in the winter. (This latter point, of course, was absurd and clearly false, as winter had long proved to be the ideal time to log in the B.C. Interior.)

In response to the report, the Feldmühle executive declined the opportunity to partner with us until their purchasing man, Hans Klagges, who had been keen on the venture from early on, persuaded them to rethink their position. As a senior official and head pulp buyer with Feldmühle, Klagges had visited British Columbia with a view to a joint venture in coastal pulp with MacMillan Bloedel. But since Feldmühle was a growth company accustomed to high-quality Scandinavian pulp, they preferred the idea of accessing additional long-fibred product from the Interior. Once Klagges realized that the New York consultant they engaged had been incorrect in his evaluation of winter logging, he also questioned and proved incorrect the advice that pulp could not be hauled to the coast and shipped to Germany at competitive costs.

We had already signed on with Reed to build a 500-ton daily capacity pulp mill and a 300-ton brown-paper mill when Feldmühle came back to us. They had reconsidered and were offering to take a significant amount of pulp under contract and buy into the mill. We turned them down because we did not want to give up any part of our fifty-fifty ownership with Reed.

At the time, Reed was the biggest U.K. paper company, with Don Ryder having recently taken charge as CEO. Ryder was later knighted and subsequently became Lord Ryder. Feldmühle was the largest such company in Europe and was owned by the Flick family, who also owned 59 percent of Daimler-Benz. We knew that both companies would make excellent partners.

It was my dad who came up with the idea of building a second pulp mill, the Intercontinental Pulp Company Ltd., to accommodate another partner—though a major hitch arose. According to our agreement with Reed, everything we did in Prince George and the PHA, we would do equally with them.

In short order, a board meeting took place in Europe, which I did not attend. Our directors returned and reported the outcome: in dividing the ownership of the second mill, we would take 25 percent, Reed 50 percent, and 25 percent would belong to Feldmühle. I was most unhappy about breaking our fifty-fifty concept with Reed, and I objected to proceeding unless we found a way to remain equal. We had fought to get equal ownership with Reed, which was a much bigger company than we were. We could not opt for second position. As a director of CFP, and as a shareholder in the company, I had to object.

In no time, I was sitting in Don Ryder's London office, telling him that the plan approved at the meeting was unacceptable to us. I explained that we would rather not build this second mill if it meant taking a minority position. "We won't proceed unless our concerns are addressed," I told him. "Feldmühle has accepted 25 percent and we're not going to take less than Reed. To keep it fair, each of the three companies should take a third of the new mill. We go equal, or we don't go at all."

A long silence followed. In fact, not a word was spoken between us as we sat on either side of Ryder's desk for a good twenty minutes. When you have a deal that is about to fly or die, that is a very long time. The ball was in Ryder's court and he was busy staring me down, waiting for me to capitulate.

"I've got it," Ryder said at long last. "CFP and Reed will go 37.5 percent each. I refuse to have the Germans' share increased."

"Done," I replied.

It was a good solution. In the end, CFP and Reed shared Prince George Pulp and Paper equally and the PHA was transferred from Canadian Forest Products to PGPP (with CFP still holding the guarantee). The Intercontinental mill would proceed with CFP and Reed holding 37.5 percent each and Feldmühle taking 25 percent.

I WAS THRILLED at the prospect of building a mill in Prince George, a small community that held so much promise. The town sits at the junction of the Fraser and Nechako rivers and at that time was surrounded by immense forests.

We had many sites to choose from, but we had not wanted anyone to know where we were looking until our arrangements were finalized. At one point, John Liersch and I snuck off on our own search, which proved problematic when we got stuck in the gumbo on a steep slope and spent an entire day extracting ourselves because we did not want to be seen calling for help.

We found an ideal site to the east of the town centre, situated alongside both rivers. The location's main advantage was our access to the clear water from the Nechako River, which we could take into the mill while pumping the treated effluent back into the Fraser. Thanks to the Alcan dam system, the water in the Nechako did not discolour as much in the spring freshet, whereas the Fraser grew dirty with silt during the runoff. (The freshet used to prevent us from producing bleached pulp in the early days but, with new technology, it's hardly a consideration in our current operations.)

Before we started building and, during construction, I spent at least a week or often two weeks or a month in Prince George and up and down the Interior. I got to know the people and the sawmill industry very well and developed enduring friendships as I gradually convinced them to centralize and build a new industry. Those who were willing to centralize would have to junk their existing equipment, but they would benefit from higher recovery and lower production costs. Because the industry was brand new and would use the best technology of the time, the region was about to become probably the world's most effective and efficient lumber producer.

I enjoyed meeting with many managers and owners, including Gordon Brownridge of Eagle Lake and Mel Rustad and his nephew Jim, both of whom were leading citizens in Prince George. Sawmillers like Bob Stewart and the Andersen family were farsighted and outspoken about issues in the region. Bob always insisted on holding breakfast meetings in a small hotel restaurant on the highway where Skip Cleave still organizes the Canfor Coffee Club gatherings for Canfor retirees in Prince George. They not only meet to socialize, but also to make toys for underprivileged children.

Some sawmill operators were more cynical than others. I recall paying an early courtesy visit to Martin Cain, an amateur prospector and a lumberman at the very end of planer mill row. His office was in a little shed, with a desk and two chairs, where we sat and talked about our plans for Prince George Pulp.

"So where are you going to build this goddamn mill?" he asked me.

I told him the exact location, just across the river and downstream.

"You guys are smart cookies," he said, shaking his head. "There's a lot of gold on that site. You'll mine it and never build a mill!"

We never did locate gold, and of course we did build an impressive mill. We placed the site preparation for both of our Prince George mills in the capable hands of Ben Ginter, quite a wild guy who owned the local brewery. He and his son often joined me for breakfast at the hotel in town and we would talk about the project. After the site prep was complete, Ben was hell bent on building his own mill, which materialized in the form of Eurocan. In hindsight, it might have been better if he had stuck with what he knew best.

For a while, rumours circulated among our competitors that we were not proceeding with construction since neither of the major local engineering companies, Sandwell and Simons, had been awarded an engineering contract. Sandwell had done an early feasibility study for financing, but that was the extent of their involvement. What no one knew was that we had chosen an engineering firm that was a subsidiary of Anglo-Canadian Pulp and Paper Mills Ltd., an eastern Canadian company controlled by Reed. Bob Chambers was the chief engineer of Anglo-Canadian and the top pulp design expert in those years. We knew he could create the most modern and efficient of operations, which he did in the engineering of PGPP, followed by Intercontinental two years later.

We did not have to look far for a builder. B.C. Bridge and Dredging had constructed our mill in Port Mellon. They had since been taken over, first by Marwell, another B.C. company, and subsequently by the Dillingham Corporation of Hawaii, an international construction company that was ready to start work.

One of the most exciting moments of my career was standing at the north end of what would become PGPP and admiring the steel skeletons of the warehouse, the pulp mill, and the chemical side of the operation. I loved watching the construction all the way down that endless half-mile before it was obscured by floors and walls. Our recovery boiler and digesters would be housed in structures as high as a sixteen-storey building. Between reinforcing steel and concrete, the entire vast complex would require countless tons of underpinnings. It was quite a sight.

W.A.C. Bennett, British Columbia's premier at the time, always described our mill as his favourite project. He called it his first baby of Peace River power, even though we agreed to go ahead with the project before the Peace River project was complete. Another preoccupation of Bennett's administration was the Pacific Great Eastern Railway (PGE), the predecessor of the British Columbia Railway (B.C. Rail). Known variably as the "Prince George Eventually" railway, or as I remember it, the "Please Go Easy," it had been painfully slow to build. The rail line reached Prince George in 1952 (almost forty years after construction began) and extended north later. The line was critical to all business interests in the area. It provided a crucial north-south link that contributed greatly to the growth of Prince George and other communities to the north.

Bennett would park his private railroad car on our track lines so he could share in the excitement of watching our progress. He and one of his ministers, Waldo Skillings, along with Bill Clancy, his private public-relations man, always wanted me to join them as a fourth for a game of bridge in that railcar. We would meet there frequently, though I could never stay very long.

"I have to go," I would say.

"No! I'm the premier and I want you to play bridge," Bennett would say.

"Sorry, Premier," I insisted as I jumped from the car. "I have a job to do."

Our operation occupied a large site on the north side of the Nechako. As construction continued in 1964, we were racing to get many tons of concrete poured and the buildings closed in before the cold weather arrived.

Noranda purchased the Penny and Shelly sawmills in 1961, so it seemed natural for them to expand a few years later into the pulp business. Along with the Mead Corporation, they built the Northwood Pulp Mill, which changed the conceptual agreement under which we were working.

Until then, our PHA agreement had excluded Reed and CFP from being in the sawmill industry in the Prince George Forest District. With Noranda and Mead already in the forest business and now entering the pulp business with their own PHA, we knew that it was only fair for us to have the same permissions as they had. We went to the B.C. government and explained that the situation was no longer equal. Williston agreed and arranged a policy change that allowed us to own sawmills in the region.

Because of our agreement to do things equally with the Reed group in the Prince George Forest District, we could not have CFP buy the sawmills, so we went on to create Takla Forest Products, a subsidiary owned equally by the two pulp companies, Prince George Pulp and Paper and Intercontinental Pulp. Under this new arrangement, Feldmühle, owning 25 percent of Intercontinental, had only 12.5 percent of Takla, and Reed and CFP were equal partners in the remaining 87.5 percent. CFP agreed to manage Takla and act as its sales agent. (When CFP bought the Chetwynd mill in 1963, it was outside the PHA boundary and we cleared the purchase with the Reed Group.)

Ray Williston had been enthused by the idea of a second pulp mill and he encouraged us to build a major sawmill and veneer plant in Fort St. James since none of the timber in the Takla region had been awarded. A series of public hearings led to PHA 7 being granted to Intercontinental. Takla Forest Products went on to buy Lloyd Brothers (now our Isle Pierre mill), followed by River Bank and Parmill in Fort St. James, both of which were closed when we built a new sawmill and a veneer plant in Fort St. James.

IT WAS MORE and more thrilling for us to see the steel frames transform into a working mill. Around 1,200 people were involved in the construction and we looked forward to employing 375 once we were fully operational. At the time, John Prentice was CFP's president, my father was senior vice-president, John Liersch was vice-president, and our profile was about to expand more than we could have imagined. In my diverse roles as a director and manager of our Northern operations, I was very proud to be a part of the company.

On Saturday, August 27, 1966, Premier Bennett officially opened Prince George Pulp and Paper Ltd. The mill was producing 750 tons of kraft pulp and sack kraft paper per day—250 tons more than we had originally committed. Four hundred people attended the ceremonies, including government and industry representatives as well as investors and suppliers. A big pile of stockpiled chips worth more than $2 million sat prominently in the mill's yard that day for all to see.

We were the first company to manufacture pulp in British Columbia's northern Interior and we were exactly where we wanted to be. What followed was the dynamic expansion of the pulp and paper industry in an area where that had seemed impossible only a decade earlier. By the time we were up and running, reportedly more than one billion dollars was invested in the planning of new mills in the north.

British Columbia was about to double its pulp output and others were noticing. As Premier Bennett said at our opening, "Great industrialists around the world are taking an interest in our province. We have the resources, the climate, and the best-trained labour force anywhere, anytime."

I appreciated my father's thoughts that day. He acknowledged the hundreds of people who had helped us get to this important turning point for CFP and for the province. Then he said: "I spoke a moment ago about the partners in Prince George. However, the people of British Columbia as a whole are really a third important and sometimes-not-too-silent partner. The B.C. government is deeply involved in almost every aspect of operation, being the owner of the wood resource, the transportation system, and the power authority."

Dad ended his short speech with a cautionary acknowledgement of increasing costs and our dependence on world markets and prices. "If we're to survive and make a success of our operation," he concluded, "these facts of life must be recognized by the government and the people of British Columbia."

When PGPP was completed, we kept our construction camp intact and carried on with the building of Intercontinental next door. We all knew that a combined larger mill would have been more efficient, but as different financial institutions were the bondholders in the two mills, they could not be combined and had to be separate and freestanding.

Minister Williston would make numerous speeches in British Columbia about the opening up of the Interior. In 1967, he reflected on how he had originally just envisioned one mill, yet by the time Intercontinental opened in 1968, Prince George had three mills and more pulp production than any other city in Canada. It had become the "Pulp Capital of Canada."

It may be an understatement to say that the introduction of pulp mills in the Interior completely transformed the sawmill industry—and the entire region. Over the following decade, in addition to our two pulp mills, more mills followed, namely, Noranda and Mead's Northwood Pulp in Prince George, Weyerhaeuser in Kamloops, Weldwood and Marubeni in Quesnel, and B.C. Forest in Mackenzie.

The rapid growth of Prince George was not without its challenges. For a time, the population increased by 2,500 per year and construction activity averaged more than $40 million per year. The schools were working double shifts and the bars, hotels, and restaurants were bustling. New buildings were going up everywhere.

The first time I visited Prince George was in January 1961, when the population was 12,500—a fraction of what it is now—and only a few of the roads in the "downtown" area were paved. The tallest building was three storeys high, including two hotels that were the primary places to go. With the building of PGPP, Intercontinental, and Northwood in quick succession, not only did the population grow, but the type of people who came in dramatically changed. New Caledonia College, followed by UNBC brought new levels of education and cultural diversity. The hospital was enlarged and later, UNBC's medical school, part of UBC, was hooked up through video conferencing to the Vancouver campus, the University of Victoria, and more recently to UBC Okanagan. Shopping centres appeared along with art galleries, libraries, convention centres, hockey arenas—you name it—and changed the life in the community.

SAWMILLS WERE MODERNIZING throughout the province, but the change was less dramatic on the coast. To extract the highest value from larger timber you could not process it using the same methods employed in the Interior. You had to selectively cut on the head rig (a combined head saw and log carriage used for the initial breakdown of logs) and turn the log and make adjustments to ensure that you were recovering all the clear lumber. I always felt that head sawyers at the time had the greatest job in the industry, with their intuitive eye for making decisions about how a log should be cut, work now done by computers.

In the Interior, sawmills improved at a faster rate with the processing of smaller timber, which was usually less than thirty inches in diameter. Anything bigger than that would be sold to another mill.

Automation of the Interior sawmills had a number of effects. The mills we bought after building PGPP and Intercontinental, like the two in Fort St. James, were simple operations and it was easy to substitute for absenteeism. When we built the new centralized sawmill and veneer plant at Fort St. James the way of life changed. It was no longer possible with absenteeism to bring in any untrained people to do the jobs, as was done before the two former mills closed. The new plant demanded varying degrees of technical experience. The first year we ran the mill, the turnover rate was horrible, exceeding 400 percent at its worst. Over time, it gradually reduced. The employment situation changed dramatically with the economic times, as it was important for people to hold steady jobs, and we improved the housing conditions by building about twenty new homes to accommodate key employees we wanted to attract and retain.

CANADIAN FOREST PRODUCTS was well established in British Columbia by the 1970s. As it had done before, the industry was changing under the guidance of individuals and companies that wished to improve all aspects of our operations. Peter Pearse was a good choice to chair the last Royal Commission held in 1976 on the forest industry. I have great respect and admiration for him. Among other things, Pearse probed the industry and our company on the topic of more private ownership of the forestland. Although the concept of owning private timber made a lot of sense, the previous NDP government had undermined it by making royalties (the payment on private timber) essentially equivalent to stumpage on public timber. There used to be an economic benefit to owning private timber if it was bought at the right price because royalties were a fraction of the price of stumpage. To explain this in lay terms, it was like making a decision on buying or leasing a condominium: if your monthly cost after buying would be the same as the total lease cost, there was no incentive to buy.

Other changes were afoot for CFP in Prince George as the seventies came to a close. Both Reed and Feldmühle had been responsible in taking their agreed percentages of Intercontinental's pulp and paying promptly, and they were good partners. There came some difficult times during our partnership, however, when business was down and we needed to inject capital. Reed and CFP were forthcoming with their capital, but Feldmühle lagged behind.

In 1978, because of changes in their business, Reed came to us and indicated their readiness to sell their position in both mills. My first response was to approach the owners and management of Feldmühle to see if they wished to participate by increasing their share. They declined, explaining that their only interest in Prince George was maintaining their supply of quality pulp. Their partnership commitment was to take half of Intercontinental's production, but as the mill improved over time and the production grew, they did not want to be locked into taking half of an unknown, fluctuating quantity.

In 1985, Feldmühle announced that they also wished to exit the partnership.

"What's left on your books for your interest in Intercontinental?" I asked.

"Seven million dollars," they replied.

"If you agree to a pulp contract that we can work out with you, then we're prepared to pay the $7 million for your shares," I said.

We negotiated a contract for the tonnage that they were committed to take with the proviso that they only increase or decrease by 10 percent a year after giving us twelve months' notice. That arrangement allowed us to plan our sales and them to plan their purchases. We had a deal.

Each of the original partners in PGPP was satisfied. The settlement with Reed had been fair and equitable. CFP bought Feldmühle's 25 percent share of Intercontinental for a bargain and Feldmühle kept a good supply of pulp under contract. We ended up with 100 percent of PGPP and Intercontinental, and all of Takla Forest Products. All these operations became a part of Canfor.

I remember well the timing of the Feldmühle negotiations because I was meeting with them in Europe shortly after Brian Mulroney had become our prime minister. I arrived in the dining room for breakfast one morning at the hotel, where they knew me from several previous visits.

"I did you a favour last night," the concierge told me. "You got a phone call after midnight from a fellow who claimed to be your prime minister. I knew it was a phoney call because Mr. Trudeau is your prime minister."

"Was his name Mulroney?" I asked.

He nodded slowly.

"He is indeed our prime minister," I said.

Mulroney laughed when I finally reached him and apologized. He had been calling to ask me if I would lead a study on the

Canadian Postal Service. I declined, explaining my full schedule with Canfor. I added that because we had been hit with a slump due to poor business conditions, I thought it politically unwise for him to appoint someone who would be vulnerable to public criticism: "How can this man fix the post office when his own company isn't doing all that well?"

Mulroney appreciated my point of view.

7

Victoria
Our Landlords

CANADA'S PROVINCES CONTROL our forests and all other natural resources outside of our national parks, which fall under the jurisdiction of the federal government. This means of course that the B.C. forest industry operates under the watchful eye and at the (sometimes arbitrary) mercy of our forests' de facto landlords in Victoria. The premiers, their ministers, their deputies, and a host of less visible advisers are responsible for the final decisions that affect communities, industries, and the environment.

Thankfully, their decisions are often informed by important others: members of the legislature, who advocate on behalf of their ridings; expert representatives from industry groups, whose experience naturally exceeds that of most politicians; and the UBC Faculty of Forestry, who bring technical expertise to the discussion. I have known a good many people from all those categories, and many have left their mark on my memory. Most of them have contributed greatly to the health of our forests and our province.

We always knew we had a partnership with our landlords and, if we worked together for mutual benefit, we would be successful. Still, some of the ministers and civil servants felt we were adversaries, and that made life not only difficult and unpleasant, but also nonconstructive.

My first dealings with the B.C. government were nothing but positive, as shown by the enthusiastic welcome we received in Prince George. Premier W.A.C. Bennett and Ray Williston were both committed to the economic development of the north-central Interior, and I give them full credit for the region's transformation. Both set themselves apart as optimists who looked for ways to make things happen instead of ways to block them.

The people of British Columbia elected Bennett as their premier in 1952. A Social Credit politician with a colourful personality, "Wacky" (as he was known) surrounded himself with a limited circle of close friends that included Waldo Skillings, a member of his Cabinet, and Bill Clancy, a public relations consultant. Beyond our bridge games played in his railcar at the PGPP construction site, I shared memorable times with Wacky when he was premier. The last transpired in 1965 when I chaired the Canadian Open at the Shaughnessy Golf Course in Vancouver. Preparations were in full swing but we had not yet wrapped our heads around the major parking problem.

A solution began to take shape when we learned that the province had sponsored a float in the Rose Bowl Parade depicting "Beautiful British Columbia." The sponsorship gave them a very expensive, one-time, thirty-second, nationwide television spot. Jack Randall, club chair for the Canadian Open, and I invited the premier and Skillings to join us for a midday meal at the Union Club in Victoria.

Over lunch, we presented the idea of a different advertising plan. If the premier was willing to expand Marine Drive from two lanes to four lanes from the end of West 41st Avenue to the UBC campus, and leave the project temporarily unfinished so the two new lanes could be used as a parking lot during the Open, we would offer him two-and-a-half-minute spots both on Saturday and Sunday on national television in the United States and in Canada. For no cost at all, he would do something constructive for future transportation to the university and get much cheaper advertising for British Columbia.

Bennett supported the idea. In fact he got so enthusiastic he also offered to clear two acres opposite the Shaughnessy driveway as a "construction site" so we had more parking close by. When we played bridge after lunch, I think we took them for $100 each in addition to getting our wish.

RAY WILLISTON was a wonderful man to work with and he was very intelligent and perceptive. He had only one fault: he would sometimes make a policy to suit the circumstances of the moment without regard to how that policy fit the overall plan for the province's future. Consequently, he made a few technical mistakes. But thanks to the joint vision and assistance of Bennett and Williston, all the new mills in the Interior—Prince George, Kamloops, Northwood, Intercontinental, Cariboo Pulp, and Mackenzie—were built, and their communities prospered.

Ray had travelled on an exploratory journey to Europe to find out more about European forestry practices. He visited my father at Offensee at Emperor Franz Joseph's former hunting estate, which my father leased for a few years. While he was there, my father introduced him to Hans Klagges of Feldmühle, who subsequently became our partner in Intercontinental. Ray learned about the potential of the B.C. Interior's pulp as a quality fibre that could potentially make the finest paper in the world. Even then, he saw the breadth of opportunity in the northern Interior.

I enjoyed my travels throughout the Interior with Ray, and I saw him regularly there, right up until the year he died. I have good memories of our many enthusiastic discussions in the woods about the region's potential. Together we went to Chetwynd, Fort St. John, and Fort St. James. We had quite an entourage and travelled in two planes. We renamed the Chetwynd airport "Chetwynd International" because up to then they had never had two twin-engine aircraft there at the same time. They have since moved to a new location.

I WENT ON to work with leaders of a different political stripe. As the first NDP premier elected in British Columbia, Dave Barrett meant well and I found him likeable. We had a good rapport, yet his forests minister, Bob Williams, made it clear from the beginning that he had no interest in working with the forest industry. Instead, he worked against us, which was devastating. He was discourteous to the forest companies and alienated us at every opportunity.

During Barrett's tenure, which began in 1972, we were told that the government did not want Canadian Forest Products to get any larger. Had we been a public company at the time, we would have been fine, but we were the biggest private company in the industry and in the eyes of the NDP government we had gone far enough. We could do nothing more in the industry but maintain our operations. With good cash flow, it was time to diversify.

We were surprised by this unexpected change of direction, but it has never been my practice to speculate about what socialists think. Although I have met many bright individuals who ascribe to that philosophy, it seems to me that socialism has failed everywhere it has been attempted in the world for two reasons: first, it removes incentive and, second, it works everything down to the lowest common denominator.

When I was Canfor's executive vice-president, for a while we arranged annual dinners with the Forest Service in Victoria. The ground rules for this event involved my bringing a half-dozen of our top people, and the Service attending with ten or twelve of their top people. We would always invite the minister, who would occasionally accept and often did not. We agreed not to discuss negotiations or outstanding issues during our time together, as it was meant to be a social evening. We talked about their general concerns, and we would share our observations about the state of the market for our products. We had a lot of fun, got to know each other better, and developed mutual respect and trust.

That tradition came to a crashing end in the early 1970s, when we invited Bob Williams, Premier Barrett's minister. On receiving the invitation, he wanted no part of it. Instead, he decreed that we could not have such dinners, that he would not allow it. Whereas we wanted to work in partnership with the Forest Service and discuss issues openly, he was acting as an adversary of industry. And that was the end of a healthy and productive tradition.

We had our frustrations with Bob Williams, but Barrett's minister of labour was an excellent choice. Bill King hailed from Revelstoke and had been an employee of the CPR and a member of the rail union. He was a personable, fair-minded, and able minister and a pleasure to deal with.

Barrett's snap election in 1975 led to Bill Bennett (W.A.C.'s son) becoming our premier, and we were back on Social Credit ground. I have always liked Bill very much. He did a lot of good things for the province, as did his minister of forests, Tom Waterland.

Austin Taylor, my closest friend and best man at my wedding, was with the brokerage firm McLeod, Young, Weir Co. and Ltd. when he was Bill's top fundraiser. The three of us enjoyed a pleasant tradition of meeting once a month for breakfast to talk in depth about our favourite topic—British Columbia. We continued to get together when Bill became leader of the opposition and even after he became premier, though less frequently until we stopped altogether. With his re-elections, Bill did not appear to want any more advice and, as many politicians do, he started to slip and get stale.

Bill called me one day in 1980 to discuss an issue that Marie Taylor, the president of Vancouver General Hospital, had brought to his attention. Her father served in Bill's Cabinet, and she had spoken to him about an important matter.

"Peter, we have no hospital foundations in the province," he said. "I would like you to start one."

"Well, I'd be pleased to try and do that," I replied. "But I feel strongly about appointing my own board because it will have a fiduciary responsibility. So don't appoint Socreds who didn't get elected. It's not a paid job; none of us will take any money. It will all be volunteer."

We agreed and, in 1980, we launched the Vancouver Hospital Foundation. I appointed a couple of past hospital chairpersons with a high profile in the community and a solid understanding of the challenges, and I invited individuals from different ethnic groups to ensure that they were represented and involved. I served as chair for five years and remain committed as chair emeritus. We have raised almost $300 million since we started thirty years ago. Although the initial start was slow, in recent years the annual donations have been in the $30 million range.

BILL BENNETT'S term ended in the summer of 1986 when Bill Vander Zalm stepped up to the plate as premier. Bill was an experienced politician but somewhat naive. He is likeable and hardworking, and from the first time we met in his office to discuss the gas station at Englewood, we have had an amicable rapport. Initially, he was a good premier to work with, but he made the mistake of giving a disproportionate amount of power and control to David Poole, a close friend, as his executive assistant or "principal secretary." Poole made things very difficult for the industry by making changes to the stumpage system that had nothing to do with the value of the timber or the quality of the mills or the cost. The formula should have considered all those factors. The new system was destined to create enormous waves and it did just that.

Premier Vander Zalm's minister of forests for the last two years of his tenure was Claude Richmond, whose intentions were positive. We became personal friends and, as a sitting member for Kamloops, he hosted an annual Open Golf Tournament and invited an interesting crowd. I remember attending one year and having a lot of fun as Claude's partner, playing alternate shots. From Claude's first putts and chips, it looked like I had a four-foot putt left on almost every hole, which is a tough distance. I was under considerable pressure.

"Claude, do we lose our tree farm licence if I miss this one?" I asked from time to time.

Vander Zalm wanted a major project for the coast, and we managed to deliver what he was looking for in a deal we reached with Oji Paper. With them we decided to rebuild Howe Sound Pulp and Paper, transforming it from a modest-sized pulp mill that might well have closed down to a larger pulp mill and a newsprint machine.

Bill Vander Zalm left office under the dark cloud of his infamous brown-paper-bag-full-of-cash incident on the sale of Fantasy Gardens. Some felt that he used the premier's office to conduct his private business. I believe that, in his own mind, he had not abused his office and I am inclined to agree that he was not in a conflict of interest.

Bill became a good friend, but I was disappointed in his stance regarding the Harmonized Sales Tax (HST), where he aligned his position with that of the NDP. Bill likes publicity and, with his charisma, he succeeded in gathering enough signatures throughout British Columbia to force the government to hold a referendum. The government had made a mess of the way the HST was introduced, because frankly they had not intended to implement it. However, when the Ontario arrangement was negotiated with the federal government and British Columbia was offered a "me too" deal, they realized it was an opportunity they should not ignore.

The government lost the HST vote, which will be a big setback for years to come. In my view, Bill did the province a great disservice by staying with his position. I fault him for not changing his stance after Premier Gordon Campbell resigned and amendments were made, including the subsidy for lower-income families and a proposed reduction of the tax.

I HAVE FLOWN over British Columbia hundreds of times and always look down at the forests with a mixture of pride and concern. Canfor has taken excellent care of the timberlands under its control.

To this day, I get angry with Vander Zalm's successor, Mike Harcourt, for not authorizing the logging of Tweedsmuir Park, 350 kilometres west of Williams Lake in the Chilcotin, when we first saw the pine beetle outbreak as a real problem in about 1995. The chief forester at the time tried to convince Premier Harcourt that something had to be done with the beetle infestation in that enormous park so it would not spread through the whole province.

He called to tell some of us in industry that he considered the situation critical and that he had failed to persuade the premier.

Dave McInnes of Weyerhaeuser Canada, Tom Buell of Weldwood, and I on behalf of Canfor, being the three largest Interior operators at that time, met with Harcourt in Victoria and pleaded with him to act. It was not a question of our wanting to harvest; we told him another option was to burn the infested area down, but he could not leave it as it was.

"Forget it, guys," the premier said. "The park boundaries are sacred."

"Mr. Premier, the beetle doesn't recognize the boundaries and this is a very high risk you're taking," we insisted.

He said the meeting was over, we went home, the beetle survived, and history will tell the rest of the sad tale. The annual harvest will be reduced for many years. It's hard to put a number on it, but certainly the damage to the B.C. economy lies in many jobs lost and billions of dollars in lost revenue. There is no guarantee that the beetle would not have had a devastating effect even if Harcourt had taken action, as we did not have any cold snaps during the winters to kill off the beetle, but I think it could have been more controllable had he acted in a timely fashion. Every time I see those red skeletons turning grey as they die, my heart sinks.

I knew Harcourt and saw him as a fine person and a lawyer with good intentions; he and others like him mean to do good but, in my opinion, they don't know how. I felt that he had little leadership ability, yet he wanted to be loved by everyone—and that's difficult to achieve, particularly in politics. Of course, he wanted to do well by the province.

Harcourt gave a lot of responsibility and authority to two of his ministers, Glen Clark and Moe Sihota, both of whom were willing to run with the ball. I knew this because of a curious message passed along to me over the course of two meetings in Vancouver, one on the CNR chair's railroad car and the other at a small lunch. Clark attended one and Sihota attended the other, and each gave us the message that, if we in the business community wanted anything, we should see one of them and not waste our time with the premier. That notion struck me as very odd.

Not long after those meetings, I travelled to Halifax for a Bank of Montreal meeting. Sheila, as president of the Canadian Ladies' Golf Association, was also there at the time, so I invited her to come with me to the bank dinner. I expected to be placed beside her, but Matt Barrett of BMO had another seating arrangement in mind. Because I knew the Nova Scotia premier, John Buchanan, from my dealings with the Business Council on National Issues, Barrett asked me to sit on the other side of the premier so we could have him between us and enjoy some lively discussion.

During our meal, I turned to Buchanan and asked how Premier Harcourt was doing as president of the Premiers' Council that year. He did not want to comment and suggested that I ask Harcourt directly because he was at the hotel himself. Given my unease about Clark's and Sihota's strange instructions, I wanted to find out what was going on.

After dinner, I called our premier and asked if he and I might have a "Peter to Mike," one-on-one discussion. Over a drink in the bar, I was blunt and told him the story about those memorable meetings in Vancouver where we had been advised to consult his ministers and not him.

"Well, that's exactly how I want it," he said.

"Mike, if that's what you want, you're finished as premier. You have to go back and call those two guys in and pound the table so hard that they bounce out of their chairs. Then you tell them that, if they ever say that again, you'll park them so far away on the back bench that they won't even hear what's going on in the House."

"Peter, you don't understand," he said. "I don't want that. I want them to run the place because they're very good. I want to enjoy myself and make friends and get around and see what's going on."

I was astonished by his reaction.

"Mike, you've had it if you want it to be that way."

A year later, a call came in from the premier's office.

"Peter, do you remember our discussion in Halifax?" Mike asked.

"I will never forget it as long as I live," I said.

"Well, I want you to know you may have been right. I'm now going to take charge and I'm giving them new marching orders."

"Mike, it's way too late. The game is over."

"What do you mean?" he asked.

"Well, your ministers have been running the show. If you're doing this for optics, so be it. But in reality, you're not going to change anything."

The next thing we knew, of course, Mike was out of the leadership and Glen Clark won the runoff to replace him.

That was an unforgettable experience. I could not believe a premier wanting to let two of his ministers have so much control.

Our dealings with Victoria were generally positive, always interesting—but not without further difficult moments involving the same government. One disappointed me greatly and threatened British Columbia's business reputation.

In December 1994, Canfor attempted to acquire Slocan Forest Products Ltd., a public company, and I made sure that the provincial government had no objection to our doing so. The minister of forests, Andrew Petter, was on vacation at the time so I spoke only to Premier Harcourt. He said that our reputation in smaller towns where we operated was better than that of Slocan, and on that basis he would approve the takeover.

Gordon Armstrong, Canfor's senior vice-president, finance, accompanied me on a Sunday night to the home of Ike Barber,

Slocan's president and CEO. We had a pleasant visit with Barber and his wife, Jean, explaining that we were interested in coming together. We acknowledged that the takeover was unsolicited, but we wanted it to be friendly. We told him of our plans to make an offer with assurances that we had room for him in the company. I felt the evening had gone well. Apparently, I was mistaken.

Shortly after my return home, the phone started ringing. Our takeover was going to be fought and Barber was not going to take it lying down. A great deal of water went under that bridge and Barber subsequently employed an array of tactics to block us. One was buying back stock in the company, which weakened their balance sheet. In the end, Gordon and I went to Toronto to meet with the major institutions, who told us if we made it 25 percent cash instead of an all-Canfor stock offer, they would vote in favour. We made the change and it looked like we would succeed.

Our offer was still pending when I attended Premier Harcourt's two-day economic summit in Victoria and sat with either the premier or one of his ministers, including Andrew Petter, at each of our several meals together. Our conversations revolved around the big issues and nobody spoke to me about company matters. I returned on the Helijet to Vancouver and was handed the phone as I walked into my office. It was the deputy minister of forests calling to say that his minister had instructed him to advise me that as we spoke he was going to announce publicly that it was not in the province's interest for us to do what we planned and, accordingly, he would not approve our purchase of Slocan.

"See if you can stop him," I said to the deputy. "There are a few things the minister does not know, and he has never discussed any of this with me. The premier already encouraged me to proceed. The three of us have to meet."

It was too late. The minister made his announcement and the damage was done. I later phoned the premier, who was also in Vancouver, and he came to my office. I was furious.

"You clearly don't have control over your Cabinet," I said. "Why did you not override Minister Petter? He sat beside me at the conference and never said a word. He has no idea what's going on and he's damaging B.C.'s credit rating by intervening."

During the following weeks, I went public myself and announced that, in my opinion, the government had done an unfortunate disservice to British Columbia, that the decision had cost Canfor a lot of money, and the same held true for Slocan, which had worsened its position by using capital to buy back stock. It had cost everyone, including the Province. Their interference in a deal that the marketplace supported hurt the image of British Columbia as a place to do business. I was disgusted by the whole affair and wasn't interested in hanging around for the post mortem. I headed to Palm Springs, where I finally heard from the minister.

"I couldn't have you disrupt the Interior pulp industry by taking chips from the south to your mills in Prince George or Port Mellon," he said.

"Minister," I replied, "all you had to do was talk to the other pulp companies. I had already met with them. They supported us taking over Slocan because we had reassured them that they could keep their chip supply. They knew us, they trusted us, and I was not about to change the geography of British Columbia. In the public interest, those chips would continue to go to the closest pulp mill to save transportation costs. You had no valid reason to do what you did in interfering."

Andrew Petter was and is an intelligent man who has gone on to serve as president of Simon Fraser University. He could not be

more pleasant to me now and I wish him well. I still do not understand his intervention back then, though it echoes my impression
that Premier Harcourt did not communicate well with his Cabinet.

We did end up acquiring Slocan some years later.

GLEN CLARK WENT on to win the leadership race in 1996. It was
always my impression that, although he was a good leader, the
New Democratic Party by that time realized they were not going
to be re-elected and they proceeded to make questionable decisions that made things difficult for their successor.

Clark was the second-youngest premier to be elected in the
province, and his time in office is remembered by many for the
unsuccessful "fast ferries." So much publicity resulted from that
situation that it became the focus of Glen Clark's existence in
Victoria. Glen himself is bright, and he had a close relationship
with the unions. Like other premiers before and since, he ran into
criticism for concentrating power among a small group of advisers. I have come to know Glen better in recent years, as he is on
our board and makes a good contribution on our safety and health,
and pension committees.

After Glen left office, Dan Miller was appointed interim premier. He was a neutral party in the leadership campaign that
followed, as he chose not to run. At one time, Miller was minister
of labour, and as minister of forests under Premier Harcourt he
was businesslike and not opposed to industry like so many politicians were at that time. Miller was a personable man who earned
everyone's trust.

IT WAS AND STILL IS important for British Columbia's forests
ministers to recognize that for the province and the industry to
be successful, we have to work as partners rather than in opposition to one another.

B.C. constituents have consistently applied pressure on two main issues: one, the desire for each constituency to control the forest around it, which does not bring the best economic result. And two, the wish to have "appurtenancy," whereby forest licences dictate that certain mills located in the community have access to timber. This often makes sense when the licence is granted, but can easily become less relevant and economically damaging. What some do not understand is that there is no constant ideal. The forest industry has evolved with a move from bush mills to modern, centralized operations, and the surviving mills are now many times bigger. The size of these new operations requires extending the radius from which you draw timber and, in such cases, appurtenancy makes little sense.

A good example of why a larger scale in our capital-intensive industry is necessary relates to the one and only mill we purchased in Quebec. After Canfor bought the Daquaam mill in 2003, I went to see Premier Jean Charest, who I knew when he was in the federal Cabinet. I told him how pleased we were to be doing business in his province, and that we hoped to expand our operation.

"How will you do that?" he asked.

"We'll try to buy timber from adjacent enterprises and consolidate our operation," I explained.

"I don't want that," he said. "I want a mill in every town."

"Unfortunately, Premier, that's a formula for bankruptcy," I replied. "The little mills can't make it. You need a capital-intensive big mill and we can provide that, but we need access to more timber."

He could not see the economics of it at the time, but he must have given it some thought after seeing how so many little mills did go bankrupt, which was entirely predictable. A number of years later, we saw each other at a dinner in Ottawa, and he indicated that on further reflection, having larger centralized mills was a better solution than having a small one in every town.

Charest's initial wish was similar to how B.C. municipalities all want their own fiefdoms, and how the NDP always wanted small, specialized units, or "boutiques" as they called them.

Michael Phelps was CEO of Westcoast Transmission and a director of Canfor when he hosted a dinner party at his house one year for Klaus Schwab, the chairman of the World Economic Forum, to give him an opportunity to meet some of the B.C. business community. Harcourt was premier at the time. At our table, Sheila and I were seated with Schwab, Michael and Joyce Phelps, and Mike and Becky Harcourt. I had been having a good conversation with Becky, trying to give her some messages of what the industry was looking for, when in an unlikely moment of dead silence in the room, we all heard Sheila say to the premier, "I have never heard anything so stupid!" Later, I learned that Mike had been lecturing Sheila on why we needed not big mills, but a whole bunch of boutiques that each did their thing and how that would bring prosperity to every town. Sheila rightly told him that was nonsense.

AS I GREW into my work in the industry, I was impressed by British Columbia's Forest Service with its many forestry school graduates, both at the district level and in Victoria. Over the years, the percentage of professional foresters in the civil service seems to have declined. We are still dealing with competent people but from backgrounds other than forestry.

Mike Apsey is a great friend of the B.C. forest industry, having worked at different times with MacMillan Bloedel, as deputy minister of forests, and with the Council of Forest Industries (COFI). With his diverse experience, he is perhaps the person who best understands the many issues we have faced over the years. Mike knows how people reject the idea of the Forest Service working together with industry and asks how can it be any other way? The service has to work with the forest companies to manage the people's resource. They cannot sequester themselves in Victoria, as some have done in the past. They have to be travelling around the province, working with us on the ground and listening to our concerns. It's that kind of partnership between government and industry that gets things done responsibly.

8

An Ugly Rumour
Balco and the Road to Diversification

I WAS GETTING FRUSTRATED in 1970 by Canadian Forest Product's lack of profitability and internal communication. Moreover, it had been seventeen years since I had joined my father and uncle in the business, and I was ready for more responsibility. The largest annual profit the company had made by then was $7 million, and I knew we could do a great deal better than that. I was also disappointed by the weak communication links between our operations: my uncle ran the plywood and hardboard mills as well as the Building Materials Division; my father was in charge of the Eburne sawmill and pulp sales; Bill McMahan supervised all logging and pulp production; and Victor Whittall was "Mr. Shingles and Shakes." We did not have a complete picture. Everyone worked in his corner and had no active connection with the other divisions, and many service functions were duplicated. I wondered quietly whether I should be moving on, and was seriously considering a job offer from Weyerhaeuser.

We travelled to England that year for a board meeting of Prince George Pulp and Paper and Intercontinental. We settled into the large sitting room off the main lobby at Claridge's Hotel, and then I gave my father and uncle an ultimatum. I told them that I was very appreciative of the opportunities they had given me, but that I had received a challenging offer. If I accepted, I would owe Weyerhaeuser at least three years before I could return to CFP. I reassured them that my preference was to remain with the family company—but only if I could be assured more authority and if our key employees were granted more information and responsibility.

I told them explicitly that I never could have done what they had: starting with an investment of $260,000 and building an integrated forest company, which by then had annual sales of more than $178 million. What I could see after my many years with CFP, through my exposure to other companies and my time at business school, however, was that they were making the mistake of looking at everything in terms of the impressive returns on their *initial* capital, rather than the return on the investment they had since made. They had also developed an operational style that was not using our capable people in a meaningful way. Furthermore, I explained, the company was too private. Beyond the family and the chief accountant, none of our senior employees really knew how we were doing. I felt that had to change.

Dad and Uncle John were understanding and receptive, and we came up with a plan. I would become executive vice-president, fully responsible for all of the operations except banking, my uncle's territory, and pulp sales, which my dad would keep.

At last, I was free to form the operating group that I had long imagined would improve our progress. I wasted no time in calling on the heads of our major business units to meet with me every month to review their statements and their outlooks and to jointly assess all capital expenditures that came to us for approval. Before that, they had not been aware of the financial results beyond their own respective operations, and I was gratified to see concrete results. I would also insist that safety be on our regular agenda and that all monthly reports start out with their safety statistics.

My new position in the company afforded me some interesting challenges, and one in particular. As I took on my responsibilities as executive vice-president, I heard that a public company called Balco had built a new plywood mill near Kamloops alongside their sawmill. I could not understand why our staff had not convinced them that we should be their plywood sales agent. They told me Balco was uninterested.

I headed up to Kamloops myself to meet Balco's owners and see if I could shift their thinking. Dave and Alf Balison extended a warm welcome and treated me to an extensive tour of their impressive mills. I met with their chief forester and decided to push harder for the opportunity to become their sales agent.

"I just don't understand, with all the good decisions you've made so far, why you would want to try and sell your own plywood when the industry is quite complex," I said. "I'm telling you we are an open book and we can ensure you get the same net mill price that we do in our own two plywood mills. CFP would only get a sales commission, and that's it. Our goal is not to get an advantage, we just don't want the market to be hit by a new supplier coming in on top of MacMillan Bloedel, Weldwood, and Canfor, because between us we have sold plywood for almost every other manufacturer."

It took most of the day, back and forth, to get to the reason for their reluctance. Dave and Alf were guarded and secretive, but they finally responded with a surprising explanation: they could not enter into this kind of sales relationship because they were being taken over. They were not in a position to launch a new long-term contract, which the new "American owner"—who remained unnamed—may not want. They felt their hands were tied by a delay in completing the sale of the company. Dave was a modest shareholder in Balco, whereas his brother Alf owned 51 percent of the outstanding shares, with most of the balance held by the public. Alf was not in good health and was waiting to leave for Hawaii.

It turned out that the provincial government, namely the minister of forests, was holding up the transaction.

I returned to Vancouver and discussed the issue with Ron Longstaffe, our corporate secretary and in-house lawyer. We contacted the superintendent of brokers to ask if there was anything wrong with CFP purchasing 51 percent of a public company if we intended to keep it and run it as a public company, and not buy any more stock. He reassured us that such a purchase would be perfectly acceptable.

I called Alf and told him his cheque was ready and that he should drop by and pick it up on his way to Hawaii. We were both happy to agree that CFP would purchase 51 percent of Balco. Their management would stay in place, and we sent one of our MBAs to help tie their accounting system in with our operation. It was a damn good little company and we enjoyed the association from the outset. The situation got a great deal more interesting when I received a call from the deputy minister of forests in Victoria who I knew well.

"There's an ugly rumour going around that you people have bought Balco," he said.

"That's true," I replied. "We bought out one shareholder but it will remain a public company. Why is it ugly?"

"Well, the government doesn't want this to happen. You'll be hearing from the minister."

In no time another call came in from Bob Williams, Dave Barrett's minister of forests. It was a conversation I will never forget. I had to hold the phone at arm's length while the minister swore at me for the longest time. I could not understand why he was angry. He railed at me about our purchase of half of Balco, about how he did not want this to happen, and he swore that he was going to change the law and take our timber away from us. He went on at length about how he would punish our company in every way possible.

And he did change the law. In a matter of weeks, the Forest Act was adjusted in what would become known in the industry as the "Balco Amendment" to say that a controlling interest in any lumber company that held Crown timber rights could not be purchased without the minister's prior consent. It went on to say that, if permission were granted, the minister would take away 5 percent of the seller's Crown timber rights and put it in the "small business program," which would reallocate the timber to smaller firms. We felt it was a ridiculous policy, as the "small businesses" often did not do a good job of reforesting and frequently did not have good logging practices. It took away timber that the companies needed to be more self-sufficient and effective. It was a bad deal all around, but we knew truck loggers wanted it so they would have their own timber instead of being restricted to contracts with bigger companies. Eventually, the policy was changed when it became obvious that most companies with 5 percent taken away would have insufficient control of the log supply.

THE BALCO DEBACLE with Williams had been destabilizing to say the least, and we had to wait a few weeks before fully understanding what was behind it all and why the minister had been so upset. I was at my desk at head office when the switchboard buzzed to say that someone whose name I did not recognize was there to see me about Balco. I asked that they send him in.

My unannounced visitor turned out to be the president of the Kamloops NDP riding association. After our introduction, he explained that he had come to express the association's disappointment as a Balco shareholder that we were not buying any of the remaining 49 percent of Balco, and he offered us its shares. He had expected that the buyer of Balco would buy their stock. He said Williams had told them that when an American company bought Balco, which one apparently was about to do, it would have to buy all of the shares. I explained to him that we had undertaken not to buy any more than we already owned.

"I've publicly announced that we are not going to trade in the stock," I said. "We're going to keep Balco as a public company, and we would be restricting the float if we bought more. However, you're in luck because reaction to our takeover has been positive and the stock has gone up nicely, which means you can liquidate your position at a profit."

The man then dropped the other shoe: he explained that the minister had alleged that an American company might buy 100 percent of Balco.

The riding president thanked me for my time and went on his way. After he walked out of my office, I phoned Premier Barrett and told him I wanted to see him on an urgent basis. I was in his office that same afternoon, telling him everything I had heard. He clearly had no idea what was going on.

"What do you want?" he asked.

"I'm going to give you a choice," I said. "You can join me at a press conference I might call or you can become minister of forests for CFP and Balco. I never want to lay eyes on Bob Williams again."

"I just became your minister," he said.

ABOVE As a boy, I frequently accompanied my dad on visits to the mills such as this one, where I am standing above the booming grounds.

FACING PAGE My mother and me on a visit in the late 1940s to the Nimpkish Valley, where she was always interested in what was going on.

TOP My father, Poldi, and me.

ABOVE Poldi on one of his hunting trips in the Rocky Mountains.

ABOVE A winter view from The Crescent of our family home at
1402 McRae Avenue in Vancouver.

FACING PAGE From left: me, Russell Mills, and an unidentified man
in front of a giant fir tree in the Nimpkish Valley, around 1950.

ABOVE Sheila McGiverin and I were engaged in December 1952 and had our portrait taken soon afterwards.

FACING PAGE, TOP During the Second World War, Pacific Veneer became a leading manufacturer of the lightweight plywood used in the wings of the de Havilland Mosquito bomber, also called the "Timber Terror" and the "Wooden Wonder."

FACING PAGE, BOTTOM One of my father's passions was cars, and here I am in my own Mercedes-Benz 300SL gullwing preparing for a race.

TOP The only way to fell these giant trees was by using a manual saw.

ABOVE A typical scene from one of CFP's logging-camp cookhouses.

Despite Williams's threats to take our timber away, common sense prevailed. Otherwise, what would have happened to the Balco employees and the shareholders? Balco remained a public company and, as we grew in northern British Columbia, we did not use Balco chips. We always believed chips should go to where the freight rate is the lowest, so they were sent to Weyerhaeuser's nearby pulp mill in Kamloops.

In time, we wanted to invest more in our own backyard, and we needed the cash for acquisitions in the north to solidify Canfor's chip situation. We sold Balco to Tolko Industries, which was expanding in the area. Thanks to Al Thorlakson, Tolko has since grown into one of the biggest private forest companies in the country.

Premier Barrett kept his promise and became Canfor's and Balco's minister of forests, and I never spoke to Williams again.

THE GOVERNMENT had made it painfully clear that Canfor was not to expand further in the B.C. forest industry. No other firms were similarly affected, as we were the only private forest company of significant scale at the time. The others were smaller and of little concern to the government. Our choice was either to pay out substantial dividends to ourselves, which we did not wish to do, or find more creative means to deal with our cash flow. It was time to look elsewhere for business opportunities, a push supported by my normally cautious Uncle John. As we began to diversify outside of the industry, he was all for expansion and my father became the cautious one.

Soon after the Balco incident, Crédit Foncier, a mid-sized financial institution controlled from Paris with headquarters in Montreal, asked me to be a director on the Yorkshire Trust board. I accepted on two conditions: that I would have a free vote and I could own a few shares. I learned a great deal through that experience and admired the way Crédit Foncier operated. They owned 70 percent of Yorkshire Trust, and the Toronto Dominion Bank owned 10 percent. The remainder was held by other individuals, but primarily by Frank Trebell, the trust company's excellent CEO.

In time, Frank grew impatient with Crédit Foncier's ownership and arranged to buy them out. Because Crédit Foncier had invited me in the first place, I felt it was an appropriate time to resign from my position on the board. Both the TD Bank and Frank objected and asked me to stay on, which I was then happy to do. Frank brought in some first-class people, including Gerald McGavin and Peter Cundill. The company remained in sound shape, but Frank was charged with profiting improperly and found guilty. As a result, he had to sell his shares in Yorkshire Trust and, of course, resign. I knew Yorkshire Trust was a solid company, so Canfor stepped up and became the controlling shareholder. Later I joined the Bank of Montreal board, replacing Uncle John, and I had to give up my directorship at Yorkshire Trust.

Peter Cundill, who had left Yorkshire Trust, had recommended that we invest in Crédit Foncier, and we surprised ourselves by becoming the company's second-largest shareholder. We declined an invitation to be on their board, because we viewed it as an investment. We did well with both Yorkshire Trust and Crédit Foncier and eventually sold both.

Our next step in venturing beyond the forest industry took us to Cornat Industries, a growth company started by Peter Paul Saunders. Cornat owned diversified holdings that, among many others, included two major coastal shipyards, Burrard and Yarrows; B.C. Ice and Cold Storage; Johnson Terminals; and Quadra Steel. Because we purchased 51 percent of Cornat for the tax benefits and not to operate the company, we chose to hold only three positions on a twelve-person board. The company showed a good growth pattern, acquiring Bralorne, a gas company also specializing in manufacturing equipment for the petroleum industry; Versatile Industries in Winnipeg, which manufactured agricultural tractors; and Canadian Vickers, an industrial ship-yard in Montreal.

Borrowing the name of one of the companies it purchased, Cornat became Versatile Industries, a more descriptive title for their diversified holdings. Versatile was successful under its new management until the economic downturn, when they attempted to sell the tractor company to John Deere but were blocked by the U.S. government under their combines legislation, as they thought John Deere would have too much of a monopoly. That cost us dearly. We eventually sold the tractor company to the Ford Motor Company at a far lower price.

AS WE EXPLORED other ventures, our family was continuing to diversify in an interesting array of investments. My uncle was an avid sports fan and became immersed in the Westminster Royals soccer club and the Salmonbellies lacrosse team as an owner of both. Soccer was his first love, and he brimmed with pride when his team won three national titles. Several of his players ended up working at the Pacific Veneer mill and the Building Materials Division.

My father was a great car fan and he was quick to order a 300SL gullwing Mercedes soon after it was released. When the car arrived, he realized that no mechanic in Vancouver knew how to service the vehicle, and that it had to be serviced from underneath. He had a pit installed in his garage and located a mechanic in Los Angeles who had been with the Mercedes racing team and who would journey up to Vancouver and service the car.

Mercedes had no Canadian sales organization at the time, and my dad wanted to fix that. He, my uncle, and I, along with a number of prominent local partners, including Fred Brown, Ron Cliff, Frank Griffiths, Senator Stan McKeen, and Bob Simpson, formed Mercedes-Benz Canada, the national distributorship. We made a few wrong turns at the outset by operating our own retail outlet in Vancouver on Georgia Street instead of appointing dealers with their own locations. A distributor by definition does not deal with the public, and we naturally began to receive calls from people looking for a deal.

Mercedes were very much in demand globally, to the extent that, if you ordered a silver, a red, a white, and a black, they might well ship you four black cars and say you were lucky to get them. They wanted us to sell Unimogs, four-wheel-drive trucks, which were unsuitable for British Columbia, and they also asked us to take one DKW (a two-door car not unlike the Volkswagen Beetle) for every two Mercedes. Their demands were excessive and it seemed that we were constantly battling. In the early 1960s, we gave it up and sold the Mercedes distributorship back to the factory. All shareholders were left with an ongoing right to buy one car a year at landed costs plus a nominal service charge.

One fine day when the German Trade Commission hosted me at an international trade show at the Pacific National Exhibition, I spotted a silver BMW coupe on a black velvet wall. I had no idea how they had got it up there.

"What do you plan to do with the car after the show?" I asked the representative, knowing BMW did not have a dealership in Canada.

"Oh, we'll ship it back to Germany," he said.

"Tell you what," I said. "If you can get it off the wall without damaging it, I'll give you $5,000 for it."

He just laughed and we left it at that.

I didn't give it another thought until the following week when I received a call from the German Consulate asking me to pick up my car. When I got home that night, I told Sheila I had lost eight cylinders. Instead of my V12 Ferrari, I was now the owner of a four-cylinder BMW. My dad agreed that it was great fun to drive and before long we were visiting the BMW factory in Germany, where we negotiated the Canadian distributorship. We kept the business in western Canada, and we asked our friends Alf Powis and Adam Zimmerman of Noranda and Northwood to be our partners in the eastern Canadian distributorship. We were rivals in the industry, but we got on well with them, respected their business acumen, and recognized the importance of having local attention in the other half of the country.

The distributorship was capitalized at $1,000. My father and I each kept 35 percent, and our key employees who joined us from Mercedes put up only $300 for their 30 percent equity. My dad and I guaranteed a note at the bank, but it was never called upon. The company made money from the first day and was a very successful venture. BMW wanted to take it back in 1983 when it had become the largest independent distributor that they had (without having equity in the distribution). They offered us a chance to be fifty-fifty partners ongoing. We turned that down and said that, if they gave us three more years and then bought it on fair terms, we would sell 100 percent. We were concerned that we might have conflicting objectives: they might not care about their profit in Canada and may want to dump volume through the system, whereas we aimed to be profit-oriented and we wanted to be able to control any speculation on hedging currency, which we dealt with every day at Canfor. They kindly agreed to that and treated us very fairly. We eventually sold the entire distributorship back to them in 1986 and kept the right to buy two cars a year for immediate family use on favourable terms.

MY FATHER was also an enthusiastic amateur photographer. Somewhere along the line, he met Eddie Lee, a bright employee at a Vancouver photo business. Dad and Eddie joined three professional photographers and with them formed the ABC Photo Company. They started out in a small-scale shop and later moved to a property they bought on Fourth Avenue. ABC did a superior job of developing and printing photographs, and the partnership was a success.

After my father died, I inherited his shares in ABC Photo and met with Eddie and his partners to talk about the direction we would take. They accepted my offer to stay on, which saved them from having to manage a payout and afforded them some business advice from time to time. Of course, with the advent of digital photography, all shops like Eddie's were forced to change drastically. The company did not incur a loss, but the volume plummeted. Eddie did a superb job of downsizing, staying at the forefront of technology, and the business remained profitable. We eventually agreed to sell the property and then to sell the business to some of the employees.

My father had many interests, but none perhaps as intense as sports. I fully shared that passion. We were very disappointed in 1966 when the National Hockey League decided to expand and Vancouver was bypassed. The original Vancouver bid was made by Cy McLean of B.C. Telephone; Coleman Hall, who owned the Devonshire Hotel (and had been running the Canucks for many years even though he never owned any players); and Foster Hewitt of CBC *Hockey Night in Canada* fame. My teenagers could have done a better job of completing the NHL paperwork. All the bidders had

done was include a photo of each of them and list their directorships and affiliations, even though the form clearly requested
financial data and responsibility.

When we heard that the league intended to expand further,
from twelve to fourteen teams, we put together a group that
would make an impression on the governors. The group included
my father, Uncle John, my lifelong colleague and good friend Ron
Cliff, and me; Ron's father-in-law, Fred Brown; insurance man
and great sportsman, John Davidson; Frank McMahon, whose
horse Majestic Prince had won the Kentucky Derby that year;
entrepreneur and philanthropist, Max Bell from Calgary; and Cy
McLean and Coleman Hall, both involved with the Canucks at the
time. We gathered letters from the five major chartered banks
saying that they would stand behind any of our financial under-
takings. We then prepared a colour brochure describing hockey in
Vancouver going back to Cyclone Taylor's day, when the Vancouver
Millionaires won the Stanley Cup, and showing our plans.

I then jumped on a plane and visited the twelve existing franchises, to give them a copy of the brochure, to meet them, to tell
them how we intended to operate and to answer any questions.
We were well received by eleven cities. Only the Toronto Maple
Leafs owners, Harold Ballard and Stafford Smythe, did not support our entry, saying that they did not want to lose the western
Canadian market for the Leafs.

Rumours floated that an existing team or two might be for
sale, and we thought a quick way in might be to buy one of them.
The media were full of interest in this and very critical that we
were not bringing Oakland to Vancouver because Oakland was
not doing well. We of course had explored that. I had had meetings with their owner and management but had learned that
Atlantic Richfield had helped finance both Oakland and Jack Kent

Cooke with his Fabulous Forum in Los Angeles on condition that they remain in business for five consecutive years, during which they would have exclusive advertising rights. So the Oakland club could not move even if they wanted to. The media kept hammering us, and we explained that legal issues made it impossible to buy Oakland.

We next learned from the NHL that they would like to see Pittsburgh moved because they were not doing well. I went back to meet Pennsylvania state senator Jack McGregor, and I offered him the opportunity of a minority 49 percent interest in the franchise so our Vancouver group would be in control. I told him that we would buy the club for very little but give them a profitable location instead of a losing franchise. He said he was most embarrassed because he would have loved to make that kind of deal, but they had already sold the franchise.

I was aware that you cannot sell a franchise without the consent of the board of governors. To make a long story short, they had sold it without NHL approval. The senator agreed to phone NHL president Clarence Campbell to explain what was going on.

After we obtained the franchise, we started to buy players in addition to those we got in the draft because we wanted to produce an early respectable winner for Vancouver. We also bought the Rochester franchise from the Toronto Maple Leafs. Punch Imlach owned a portion of the Rochester franchise, and we told him we would pay him a good price if they loaded the roster with quality players, which he did. We won both the Western Hockey League and the American Hockey League in 1968 and in 1969 without losing a single game in the playoffs.

When I attended the last NHL board of governors meeting before we were to play our first game, the first item on their agenda was a reverse draft to take six players away from Vancouver because we were too strong for a first-year club. I objected strenuously and said that, because it had not been put on my agenda, they could not discuss it.

"If you do choose to discuss it," I continued, "then we don't want any part of this league."

They decided they would go ahead.

"You should find someone you can work with for Vancouver," I said as I got up to leave. "We're not in this for the money. We wanted to get Vancouver into the big league and we have achieved that. If you aren't prepared to allow us to build a winner, we want out."

Ice impresario Tom Scallen was a name put forward to replace our group, though international skating champion Peggy Fleming may have been Tom's only visible asset. He was not very credit-worthy, and we were advised not to transfer the ownership until we were able to cash his cheque. That was done properly and Tom took over. Unfortunately, when he put out a public offering I bought a few shares and, when I got my copy of the prospectus, I found mistakes. Because of that prospectus, Tom Scallen went to jail.

The franchise was then bought by the Griffiths family, who meant well and were good owners from an ethical standpoint, but not very efficient in building a team. They didn't make the most of their opportunity. It then went to a Seattle family, who joined with the Griffiths and eventually took over. The Griffiths' demise was hastened by the fact that they built the expensive new stadium (then called GM Place, now Rogers Arena) with the idea that they would have both the hockey and basketball franchises to help increase its occupancy. The basketball did not go over well in Vancouver, which resulted in their having to sell the whole thing.

From my standpoint, we accomplished our mission of getting Vancouver into the big time. However, we did not like the way the league operated and I doubt that it is much better today.

OUR CORPORATE SITUATION changed in 1983 when we took the company public. We did not want to be a conglomerate, and we made sure that we sold off the nonforest products assets that had become part of Canadian Forest Products. We came out of our diversification investments quite successfully and had no regrets. From a corporate point of view, our adventures in diversification were over.

Our decision to go public was partly a response to a conversation I had had the year before with the ministry when we were discussing a tree farm licence for Chetwynd. During our conversation, the minister, Tom Waterland, and his deputy, Mike Apsey, informed us that it was not politically prudent for the government to grant our "family fiefdom" another "huge area of land." I saw this as strictly a matter of optics, which should not have made a difference when we knew that a licence would help the industry build an effective base in the region.

"Would it make a difference if we were a public company?" I asked.

"Most certainly," was their reply.

"I'll be back," I said.

And a year later, I was back.

My father and uncle had fully understood our predicament: if we wanted to stay in our business and grow, we had to go public. They accepted our need for growth and the government's concerns about the size of the company. We had nothing to hide and we were proud of our record and our reputation. CFP was a significant participant in the forest industry and we were fully committed. We had also gained valuable experience in running Balco and through our directorships on the boards of several other public companies.

The family kept 65 percent of Canfor and we sold 35 percent, the largest initial public offering that had taken place in

Canada to that date. The issue was well received and fully sold out. From then on, Canfor Corporation would replace Canadian Forest Products as our official name, and colloquially it became Canfor instead of CFP. We appointed some top-notch external board members. At one point, I assured these directors that, if a major issue ever arose, even though we controlled the company by ownership, we would abide by their wishes so they felt comfortable serving on the board.

9

Unfinished Business
Deals Negotiated but not Completed

ONCE WE HAD understood the problem, the Balco deal became very simple. Through the years, we considered three other significant possibilities, which we negotiated but never closed. Two unfolded in British Columbia and these stories have never been told before. Had either one or both been completed, they would have significantly changed the structure of British Columbia's coastal forest industry.

Long before we had even contemplated our move to the Interior, Harold and Joe Foley of the Powell River Company contacted my father and Uncle John with the idea that their business and ours could be a good fit. It was 1959 and the prospect of such a merger was appealing. Powell River had a long and successful history in newsprint, dating to the early 1900s, when three partners from Minnesota acquired land and water rights, formed a subsidiary company, and built an impressive townsite complete with hundreds of homes, a hospital, and two schools.

Fifty years later, the Powell River Company was still big in newsprint with a shingle mill and some other products on the side. The Foleys had come to the West Coast from Florida, and they hired and developed good people, at one time employing Fred McNeil, who went on to become the president and CEO of the Bank of Montreal. Harold Foley had become chair, his brother Joe was president, and they were looking for potential partners. Their best year had been 1950, but recent competition had started to impact newsprint sales and production costs were on the rise. Although CFP then had only a modest-sized pulp mill, we had diversified plywood lumber and shingle mills in addition to significant timber holdings, which they felt might be complementary.

At the time, I was working as an understudy to Bill McMahan, a wonderful man who contributed a great deal to our business over many years. Bill's strength, however, was not communications. As talks began with the Foleys, I was asked to take charge on our end, and John Liersch led the Powell River side as executive vice-president. I liked John immediately and knew it would be a privilege and a pleasure to work with him. Together we visited both companies' operations and developed a valuation formula, which included appraised values, historical and potential earning power, and replacement value for insurance. After weeks of intensive research, we balanced it all out with our auditors and managed to shape a promising deal.

It turned out that we were a larger company than Powell River had envisioned, but the arrangement John and I had designed still made sense; our thorough research proved that integrating the two companies would give us both more clout. We agreed to manage everything related to forestry and wood production, sales and distribution, whereas they would take care of pulp and paper. The Powell River group, comprising the Foleys, the Brooks, and the Scanlons, held a little more than a one-third ownership of the Powell River Company. By joining forces and forming a voting trust, their group and our family would own more than 50 percent of the new company, which would jointly give us absolute control over the public company—a beneficial arrangement for all concerned.

We gathered at my father's home on McRae Avenue on a Sunday evening to sign the documents. My dad, my uncle, and I welcomed Harold and Joe Foley and John Liersch. The Foleys had brought along Al Williamson, the head of Wood Gundy in Vancouver, as their consultant. The meeting got off to a good start until Williamson spoke up. To our surprise, he said that because of CFP's size, we as the Bentley-Prentice family would own more than the Foley-Brooks-Scanlon group. Consequently, he added, they should issue us only the same number of shares as they would have in our voting trust. This made no sense to us, but he was locked in. We felt that the advantage of having joint full control of the company was more important than equality within the voting trust. Furthermore, they would pay us cash for the balance of our agreed-upon value.

"No," we insisted. "We're in the voting trust together. It's in your interest that we don't take cash, and we don't want to take cash."

Our concerns were heard, but we were surprised that Harold was immediately convinced by Williamson's rationale. Joe was apologetic and John and I just looked at each other in frustration. This had never come up as an issue during our long evaluation period.

The deal fell apart that night. That was the end of it.

Two ironies emerged from this episode with Powell River. The first of these was our good fortune in meeting John Liersch, and our delight a year later when he accepted an offer to join us as our executive vice-president. The second was the deal the Foleys forged with MacMillan Bloedel within a year of our failed efforts. That merger resulted in the creation of MacMillan, Bloedel, and Powell River Ltd., the largest forest products company in Canada. Even though MacMillan Bloedel was much larger than Canfor, there was no question with them as there had been with us about voting protection. Harold Foley reasoned that his friendship with Prentice Bloedel would protect him. Well, Prentice was a good man, but business was not his strong suit. By 1962, the partnership turned sour. The Foleys were kicked out and ended up on the outside looking in. With us, they would have had protection through the voting trust and by the predetermined management controls over different sections of the business. With MacMillan Bloedel they had nothing.

This failed merger with Powell River is a little-known chapter of our corporate history. If we had succeeded, that joint venture might have changed the pattern of the industry on the coast. Our combined companies would have been only slightly smaller than MacMillan Bloedel, but significantly larger than any other B.C. forest companies. It's difficult to know what might have transpired for us, however, as that arrangement would have conflicted with our subsequent move from the coast and into the Interior.

ANOTHER OPPORTUNITY occurred when Ian Sinclair expressed interest in exploring the possibility of merging CFP and his company, Canadian Pacific Logging. If completed, this deal would have assured us a superior supply of timber on the coast, and it would have led to us expanding our coastal operations.

Canadian Pacific Logging was a B.C. company that owned private timber on Vancouver Island. It was run by Bill Sloan, a brother of Chief Justice Gordon Sloan. The business was a wholly owned subsidiary of Canadian Pacific Rail (CP) in Montreal, headed by

Ian Sinclair, whose maxim was, "At Canadian Pacific, you don't come to work. You report for duty."

When Sinclair expressed interest in joining us, we saw that the merger would make us stronger and help CP integrate. By then we had already established ourselves in the Interior, with Prince George Pulp and Paper up and running and Intercontinental under construction. But Sinclair showed no enthusiasm about that side of our business. We were disappointed that he was only interested in our coastal operations and did not want to recognize our Interior values. Based on these differences, we stopped negotiations.

Sinclair would later make a bid to purchase MacMillan Bloedel, which he discussed with my father and me on several occasions. In response to his interest in MacMillan Bloedel, Premier Bill Bennett coined his famous statement, "B.C. is not for sale."

ANOTHER DEAL WENT AWRY in the early 1980s with a company in Saskatchewan. The Landegger family of New York owned a company called Black Clawson (a machine manufacturer) and several pulp mills, including Prince Albert Pulp (PAP), which they owned with the provincial government.

The Landeggers were looking to sell their two-thirds interest in PAP. We were eager to expand in pulp and more than ready to talk to them, but I needed clarification before proceeding. I made my way to Regina to speak with NDP Premier Allan Blakeney about two important questions: was CFP an acceptable buyer, and would they like to increase their ownership share from one-third to 50 percent? The answer to the first question was positive: we were acceptable, the premier said, and particularly so as a Canadian company with an excellent reputation. I suspect it helped that Blakeney had known Harry Macdonald, our vice-president, pulp, when they were both attending Oxford University as Rhodes

Scholars. Addressing the second matter, Blakeney stated clearly that the government wished to stay with their 33.3 percent share of PAP.

Based on that successful meeting and with those assurances, we carried on. In the course of our investigations, I discovered the need for some minor amendments to the Saskatchewan Forest Act, which predated the province's entry into the pulp industry. After the authorities agreed, we moved into active negotiations with the Landeggers and the provincial government regarding our potential two-thirds–one-third ownership. Before long, we agreed on a price with the Landeggers and had a deal. Or so we thought.

It looked like a go until twenty-four hours before the final documents were mailed to us for signatures. That day we received a call from Saskatchewan's minister of economic development saying that in the province's view, the company would be profitable, and since the government was not interested in paying federal taxes, the minister was proposing significant and unexpected changes to our arrangement: PAP would become a fifty-fifty partnership between us and the provincial Crown corporation. To make the deal more palatable for us and to minimize our taxes, the minister conceded that all depreciable assets could be on our books. If we formed an equal partnership with each owning 50 percent, as opposed to a company with them holding shares, the Crown could avoid paying income tax on their half. The price we had negotiated was for two-thirds, but with the deal they were proposing, we would have wound up with only half. The deal also meant that Canfor and the Saskatchewan government would have the same number of seats on the pulp company board instead of Canfor controlling the board, reflecting its two-thirds ownership as intended. Above all, the fact that they changed the deal without consultation or discussion is what turned us off.

I asked the minister why he was being silent on the price and was startled by his answer: it would be the same as the figure we had negotiated with the Landeggers. In fact, he continued, the Saskatchewan government had already gone ahead and purchased the Landeggers' two-thirds.

I tried to keep calm while explaining that Premier Blakeney had told me specifically that he did not want to increase the government interest from 30 to 50 percent, and that our negotiated price was for two-thirds of the company, and not half of it. The minister stood his ground. Thanks to corporate aviation, I was in the premier's office that afternoon.

"Mr. Premier, congratulations," I said. "You and your ministers are now the proud owners of a pulp mill. In light of the way the government has acted, we do not wish to proceed."

Premier Blakeney was a decent, straightforward man who clearly had been unaware of the radical changes his minister made to our original agreement. All he knew was that the government had gone ahead and bought the Landeggers' shares in Prince Albert Pulp in order to form a partnership with us.

As we talked in his office, Blakeney agreed that the new deal was unacceptable for us and asked me to please ignore what his people had done. The government wanted Canadian Forest Products as a partner. He was prepared to go back to the original deal and eager to change everything to our satisfaction.

Despite the premier's good intentions, we were anything but satisfied. I told him that we appreciated his prompt reaction, and although he had complete credibility with us, his government did not.

"You may well not be here forever, Premier," I said. "We cannot be comfortable in a partnership with a government we do not trust."

We lost faith in the Saskatchewan government to the extent that our original plan became unworkable. After the deal collapsed, the government announced that we were jointly buying PAP. We felt compelled to correct them publicly.

Another deal had eluded us.

IN THE END, the Saskatchewan mill was not successful. Harry Macdonald eventually left Canfor and became the president of PAP to help his friend Allan Blakeney deal with the mess they found themselves in. What followed was a market decline when few private enterprises wanted to buy pulp from the government company and instead purchased it from their regular suppliers. It was a tough business, but we had escaped.

The impact of our lost opportunities with Powell River and Canadian Pacific are hard to measure. If the CP merger had been completed, we probably would have spent more capital on the coast and delayed or lost the opportunity to move to the Interior in a big way. Since we went on to make such strides in the B.C. Interior, it seems best that the deal fell through.

With the decline in newsprint, Powell River as an entity did not fare well. In hindsight, we may have been lucky that neither of these deals was finalized. However, I came away from those experiences having learned something. The fact that we negotiated each of the deals but didn't complete them showed me that when opportunities arise, they are worth pursuing, but not necessarily worth finalizing on any terms. We were right to stick to our guns.

Staying on course was an important theme throughout my career and one that informed the many roles I would play in Canfor and beyond.

10

Linking with Ottawa
A Voice from the West

ONE OF THE unanticipated results of the time I spent in our family's business was my role that evolved as an industry voice from western Canada. Thanks to my position, I had the opportunity to meet several of the prime ministers in charge of our country.

I learned from my father at a young age that we had been very lucky to immigrate to Canada. At first, he believed that the Liberal Party was one the average worker could support, and coming from Europe, where leaders could be autocratic, that appealed to him. He was a strong Liberal until Pierre Trudeau took office, when he began to have doubts. He took a liking to Brian Mulroney when he was running for leadership, and he supported him all the way. I had my own issues with Trudeau.

Prime Minister Trudeau and I first met one day in the early 1980s. Jim Coutts, Trudeau's right-hand man, had called to invite me to have dinner with the prime minister at his residence on short notice. I was on a few prominent boards at the time, including that of Shell Canada and the Bank of Montreal, so I was known by some in the eastern corporate world. I was outspoken and had voted Liberal more often than not—until Trudeau came along. I saw him as an intelligent man with a great personality. He was brilliant on the theoretical side, standing his ground on issues such as Quebec sovereignty and matters concerning First Nations. But during my fourteen years on the Executive Committee of the Business Council on National Issues, I saw that once Trudeau had discussed a topic and dealt with it intellectually, he thought it was done and he would lose interest. He did not behave like an executive, who would follow up and see that solutions were implemented.

I had no idea what to expect at the dinner, but Coutts told me that I should be prepared to talk about the B.C. economy. It was an exciting proposition and a welcome opportunity. Four of us were to enjoy an open and candid discussion at 24 Sussex Drive.

The mood was initially light as I sat opposite the prime minister and we talked briefly about our favourite cars and his new convertible. The subject then turned naturally to the reason we were all there. Knowing that the only useful information I could offer was the truth, I did not hesitate to say that the prime minister's government was not thought well of in British Columbia at the time. I explained that we felt as if the world ended at Ontario's western boundary, where all the government's interests lay. The National Energy Program had already been a disaster; in our view, it had split Alberta. Nothing in the most recent budget encouraged exports from the West, and nothing was being done for the port system on our coast.

My views came as a disappointment, as Trudeau had wanted a more balanced report than the one he got. I contributed a fair and honest view of the perspective shared by many people in British Columbia, and I tried to do so in a nonpolitical way. My efforts failed, however, and my message was badly received. Those sitting at the table fell silent in the wake of my presentation, and the hour that followed was unpleasant and argumentative. They questioned the bad news I was giving them and insisted that I recognize some of the "good" the government was doing. When I challenged them to describe what that might be in the eyes of a western Canadian, they did not come up with anything. I was never invited back to share my views.

Trudeau was still in office when I received an invitation to sit on the selection committee for the Outstanding Achievement Award for Public Service, a group of five, each of whom served a maximum three-year term to avoid patronage and ensure a healthy turnover. Our job was to honour the outstanding employee every year.

In 1975, the United Nations designated International Women's Year. Although the government was not supposed to have a say in the Outstanding Achievement Award, the prime minister came to us with the suggestion that we choose a certain person. We agreed that his choice was a deserving one but, after our usual careful deliberations, and to the prime minister's disappointment, we chose a man to receive the award—Jake Warren, the former ambassador to Washington, who was outstanding.

Before I started my third and final year on the committee, an official in the Prime Minister's Office told me Prime Minister Trudeau wanted me to chair the committee. I replied that I would be pleased to consider the opportunity, but requested a one-on-one meeting with the prime minister before I accepted. We arranged the meeting for a much later date, which gave me the chance to further investigate a matter that I wanted to discuss with him.

In the meantime, my old university colleague, John Turner, who was then minister of finance, kindly helped me arrange meetings with people at the Public Service Union and the Public Service Alliance (PSA). The problem I discussed with them and that I wished to present to Trudeau involved a subject that I had found increasingly worrisome: Ottawa was severely over-staffed.

I had enormous respect for the Canadian civil service and I felt we had one of the best in the world. For years, they had been hiring some of the brightest graduates and developing them well. Most deputy ministers were exceptional and our trade commissioners in foreign countries were top notch; it was always a pleasure to deal with them and they were helpful to Canadian business. I thought, on the average, they were much better than the majority of the elected members. But the negative aspects of the service were twofold: one, too many employees did too little work; and two, if the elected party wanted to change direction, it was difficult to do so. Unlike the U.S. system, where they can kick everybody out at the senior level and make their own appointments, our civil servants were kept in place through all changes of government.

The joke being tossed around at the time went something like: "Why do civil servants never look out the window in the morning? So they have something to do in the afternoon." Senior civil servants were well aware of the problem, and the union agreed that morale was low in some departments.

I had given a great deal of thought to a scheme for reorganizing and downsizing the civil service. My plan was simple: we would take some of the best civil servants in every function of government, whether it be secretarial, legal, accounting, or whatever, and put these very capable people into a spare department. All other departments would be staffed with just enough people to look after their everyday needs and, when the workload peaked, the spare department would offer them expert staff on a temporary basis. Those staff would become more and more experienced, and eventually would become the most promotable civil servants to jobs such as assistant deputy minister.

The plan did not involve dismissing anyone; rather, we wouldn't replace the first one thousand civil servants who left their positions (unless they had skills that were not available internally). I presented this idea to representatives from the union and the PSA, and it met with their approval. Turner was optimistic, since gradually eliminating a thousand people at an average cost of $50,000 or $60,000 a year would have been a worthwhile saving. I thought we would be making an enormous contribution by improving efficiencies in Ottawa—if we could do it.

When I finally met with Trudeau, the timing was good. He had just given a televised speech on the need for us all to cinch our belts and mind our expenditures. I unfolded my proposal, and he appeared to listen carefully. I explained that I was too young to have been in the Second World War, and I guessed that I would be too old for a third world war, which I hoped would never happen. Because Canada had been so good to my family, I was prepared to act like the former wartime "dollar-a-year men." I offered to take a year off from my job to implement a restructuring of the civil service—at my own expense.

When I was finished explaining my plan, the prime minister got up from his chair, came around to my side of the desk, and put his hand on my shoulder.

"Peter, do you really think I would be party to you laying off a thousand Liberals?" he asked.

"Mr. Prime Minister, you haven't heard me," I said. "We wouldn't be laying off anyone. These employees would be leaving of their own free will or retiring; we wouldn't replace them."

"I won't hear of it. I don't want you to do that," he said.

I had nothing to lose in pressing my point.

"Mr. Prime Minister, in authorizing this plan, you could lead by example on the cutbacks you talked about in your public address after returning from Cuba. Let me help you reduce the civil service by one thousand people, which would offer enormous annual savings when you consider their salaries, benefits, and additional costs. If you won't let me implement this plan, I can no longer serve on your committee."

I reported the conversation back to the committee, and the other members resigned as well, with the exception of one of the McCain brothers of McCain Foods. He was a staunch Liberal supporter and happy to take the chair and form a new committee.

I FELT THAT civil service incident was well behind us when I booked a table for the company, as I often did, at a Vancouver fundraiser for the Liberal Party. The mood was upbeat and Trudeau was shaking hands enthusiastically as he made his way around the room. When he came to our table, he shook everyone else's hand, but he did not shake mine. The person escorting him introduced me as the host of the Canfor table.

"Peter and I know each other," Trudeau said and walked away.

The last time I saw him was in China in September 1997. The Bank of Montreal had taken its board there to open their third Chinese branch in Beijing. Prior to the opening, the chair of the board, Matt Barrett, and I attended an international banking conference in Hong Kong. I knew Matt had the company plane with him and asked if Sheila and I could hitch a ride to Beijing. He welcomed me graciously, saying that he had Mrs. Barrett and Trudeau with him, but there was ample room.

We flew together to Beijing and Trudeau could not have been more charming. He had forgotten our earlier experiences and kept telling me that he was grateful for all the good things I was doing for Canada.

I must give Trudeau credit also for being effective in China. The people had great admiration for him because he had agreed to recognize the regime long before the United States was willing to have anything to do with them. His popularity was evident when we were invited to President Jiang Zemin's residence for a meeting one morning at seven-thirty. We had thought it would be a quick photo op, but it turned out that the president wanted to have some fairly serious dialogue with us. After a half hour or so, he surprised us all by saying in perfect English words along the lines of, "I like you all so much and my interpreter has made two mistakes, so I'm going to excuse him."

He then suggested we take a tour of his residence, where we continued our fascinating and blunt discussion. We talked about the world scene and I mentioned the reluctance to invest capital when no reliable legal system of appeal existed in China. To which he responded, "But in the United States and Canada, you have too many lawyers and lawsuits. I could put in all the laws you want, but we don't have the infrastructure to deal with them. We don't want to get ahead of ourselves."

"I notice also that on your cable television you have CNN and BBC," I said. "I didn't expect that you would allow your people to watch those networks."

"We are happy to let our people see that, if they work hard, they can expect better things," he said.

We continued to be surprised at the royal treatment we were afforded on that visit. Each of us had a separate car and driver with a police escort wherever we went. It struck me as a little ridiculous when we held a board meeting in the Great Hall of the People, as we had to make it a dummy meeting because of our certainty that all proceedings were being photographed and recorded.

Like so many wealthy, left-leaning people who never had to meet a payroll, Trudeau was in my view an idealist who could not deliver because his objectives did not add up. Left-wing social policy exists to help the poor, and although I am all for that, it has to be affordable. We cannot bankrupt the country in our efforts to address social problems. I have always believed the enterprise system to be the best system yet devised, under which you work toward the highest common denominator.

I GOT TO KNOW Brian Mulroney better than I did Trudeau. The first time I met him he was running for leadership of the Conservative Party. Bruce Howe of MacMillan Bloedel (who, like Mulroney, was from Baie-Comeau, Quebec) brought him to our office to meet with my father and me. We had a longer conversation than any of us had planned because we were getting along so well. My father and I found him engaging and bright. We were immediately impressed, to the extent that we both donated to his leadership campaign at that first meeting. Mulroney lost that leadership bid, but we stayed in touch and went on to become friends.

During his term in office, from 1984 to 1993, Mulroney appointed Peter Lougheed as chair of the Canada–Japan Forum 2000, and I had the privilege of chairing the Forum's trade and investment section. My two other committee members were Raymond Royer of Bombardier, who went on to become CEO of Domtar, and Jack Munro, who was appointed because of his union leadership. We were working toward getting some kind of free trade going with Japan, or at least an expedited method of dealing with investment and trade disputes.

Working with Lougheed was a real pleasure, principally because he ran his meetings efficiently, with everyone reporting back on assignments he had given us. We were asked to write reports with our Japanese counterparts. Mine was Koichiro Ejiri, then chair and CEO of Mitsui and Company and a wise and fine gentleman. We reported regularly to the minister of external affairs and the minister of finance. We all knew that we were working for something worthwhile. When it appeared that the committee might be appointed for a second term, however, I asked to be excused in order to attend to a heavy workload.

Prime Minister Brian Mulroney made two very courageous decisions that were good for Canada: he brought in the North American Free Trade Agreement (NAFTA) and the Goods and Services Tax (GST). Free trade was essential for Canada to become competitive once again and for job creation. Yes, it was unpopular, but it was a key issue that went hand in hand with the equally unpopular tax. Many dissenters did not understand that we could not have free trade and maintain the manufacturers' sales tax, as that would have put Canadian-made goods at a disadvantage. They had to change it to a GST, so products were taxed equally regardless of where they were made.

Both of those decisions involved big fights, but I am confident that history will show Mulroney to be one of our country's best prime ministers. He restored our international image and developed a solid relationship with the United States. Some were convinced that the link was too close, but in my opinion, there is no such thing as being on "too good terms" with your best customer, your best supplier, and your neighbour.

The Conservatives came under fire and eventually Brian Mulroney stepped down as leader. Both Brian and his wife, Mila, were considered extravagant in their personal expenses, from the number of pairs of shoes purchased to the redecorating of 24 Sussex and the summer home, Harrington Lake. It was time for them to move on.

Before I met Kim Campbell, I knew her first husband, a skilled bridge and chess player, who would often challenge Uncle John to a game of chess. I then got to know Kim on the local scene and remember her being quickly appointed to Cabinet after she was elected.

Former minister of finance and Campbell supporter Michael Wilson called to ask if I might be in Toronto for a dinner he was hosting for Kim when she was prime minister and running for re-election. I knew Michael well. In honour of this dinner he had assembled a who's who of the corporate world—the banks, the auto industry, the oil industry—everyone. Sadly, Campbell gave an unfortunate talk that evening that had little to do with business and might better have been delivered to a school board in a small community.

Michael and I stayed behind after everyone had left to talk frankly with Campbell about her need to reach the audience. We explained that she would need a completely different theme for her campaign than the one we had endured earlier that night. I offered to meet with her the next day in Ottawa if she was interested in learning more about what the business world would wish of her as the nation's leader.

I received a call the next morning from Campbell's chief of staff, Jodi White, who said that they were sending a car to pick me up at my motel and take me to Harrington Lake, where I would dine with Campbell and discuss her campaign. There, I explained how I had been disappointed at Wilson's dinner to find her in a defensive mode about the Tories. I insisted that she would fare better if she went on the offensive, reminding people of what the Liberals had done before, and challenging Jean Chrétien's decisions. Instead of trying to defend the Conservative policies in a television debate, for example, she could say, "Mr. Chrétien, I'm surprised, after your record as minister of finance when interest rates reached an all-time high, that you would attempt to seek a leadership that would take us back to that level of disastrous fiscal management. And you are telling Canadians that you want to run the country?"

Campbell is a bright, multilingual person I admired very much, even if she got killed in the debates and the Conservatives were wiped out in the election. She called me a few times during the campaign because we had become friends and I believe she trusted me. I advised her on those occasions to change directions. She never did.

WHEN JEAN CHRÉTIEN became prime minister, he wanted to continue the Canada–Japan Forum. The original committee was disbanded and Chrétien chose Ed Lumley, a former minister of trade to replace Peter Lougheed. Ed called one day to invite me to return to the committee, which I declined as I was very busy at the time.

Within minutes, the phone rang again.

"This is Jean," someone said in a rough voice.

"Jean who?" I asked, not registering.

"The prime minister," he replied. "You've turned down Ed, but I would like to ask you for a personal favour and have you serve again on the committee."

"Well, Mr. Prime Minister, I thank you for the invitation, but please excuse me—"

"Furthermore," he said before I had finished, "Mr. Ejiri, the CEO of Mitsui, has been reappointed and, as your counterpart, he has requested to work with you."

I couldn't refuse. I went back to the work we had started, and Ed Lumley and I grew to be close friends over the four years we served together. Although nothing concrete came from that work, I believe we helped some of the student exchanges. It was great to get to know our friends in Japan and to learn more about their country. Not much was achieved, but then to be successful, you need a willing government.

The degree to which the government at the time had lost interest in Japan became obvious at our final meeting in Ottawa. Lloyd Axworthy, minister of external affairs, had arranged a dinner hosted by Don Campbell, the deputy minister and former ambassador to Japan, who was acquainted with the five high-calibre Japanese counterparts with whom we had worked for so long. Axworthy excused himself from the dinner, as he had not seen much of his family, and I was embarrassed by the fact that so little attention was being given to this group of distinguished guests. I decided to make a phone call.

"Mr. Prime Minister," I said, "I understand you're home. We're at a dinner at external affairs and it would be wonderful if you would allow us to come by so our Japanese colleagues, after four years of service, can have their photograph taken with you. You don't need to entertain us; just a hello would be fine."

"Peter, don't you know the Chinese are where it's at?" he replied. "The Japanese connection doesn't mean anything."

"Mr. Prime Minister, you asked me to work for four years for something that does not 'mean anything' and you cannot be bothered to say hello to the president of the University of Tokyo, the chair of Mitsui, and the chair of Nikkei?" I asked.

"You come over, Peter," he said. "We'll have a drink together."

I hung up on him.

I was not a fan of Jean Chrétien's style, but he was an astute politician. He had what I consider to be a good political gut feeling, more so than any of our other recent prime ministers.

That I have to respect. On one occasion he came to talk to the Business Council on National Issues, and as the chair was absent it was my role to host the luncheon in Toronto. Chrétien got up to speak, and gracious as always, assured us he would be brief in order to allow ample time for questions. Then he went on to say, "I make you just one promise—the GST will be gone when I'm elected."

After he got through his brief speech, I had to clear something up.

"Mr. Chrétien," I said, "before I invite questions, I have to tell you that this group, I think to a person, favours the GST because keeping the old manufacturers' sales tax was not an option, and the GST is bringing in several billion dollars a year. If you eliminate it, can you tell us how you're going to replace it and with what? I'm sure the group would be interested."

His response was an underwhelming: "I'll think of something."

Fortunately, as we all know, the GST was not eliminated, and Chrétien did not think of something. His political understanding was not matched by his economic understanding.

Chrétien's statesmanship never failed him, however. After he was prime minister he spoke at the Carlyle Group's annual conference in Washington, D.C. He was charming and gave an excellent speech that made me proud to be a Canadian.

I HAVE KNOWN Paul Martin for many years, having met him way back when he was still a shipping company executive. He and I worked together as members of the Business Council on National Issues and I always liked him. We were lucky to have him as our minister of finance and he did a first-rate job. I once had the pleasure of chairing a fundraising dinner for Martin in Vancouver. I was a much bigger fan of him than I was of Jean Chrétien, and I was pleased when we reached our goal of raising more money for Paul than the prime minister's dinner raised for him.

I remain a big fan of Paul on a personal level, but unfortunately found him a disappointment as prime minister. One incident that occurred before he got the top job remains in my mind as the moment I recognized where his priorities lay. He was minister of finance when the Royal Bank and the Bank of Montreal announced their intention to merge. Owing to a misunderstanding, it turned out that Paul was not in his office when the banks' two vice-chairs arrived to brief him about the plan. When he learned of it instead through the media, he stated that the merger was definitely not going to happen.

Paul was coming to Vancouver two days after that incident. In anticipation of his arrival, John Cleghorn, the chair of the Royal Bank, Matt Barrett, the chair of the Bank of Montreal, and I had a discussion because they knew that Paul and I were good friends. They agreed that I should try to approach him, but that it was important to ensure we were alone and unaccompanied by any of his executive staff or aides. So we arranged to have breakfast in his hotel suite to discuss the issue.

Before that meeting, I had checked with David Dodge, the former deputy minister of finance, who was on sabbatical at UBC. He assured me that his department had seen the need for possible mergers so our banks would remain meaningful on a global basis. He explained that the changes enabling mergers to happen had already been made. I realized then that it was just Paul and not the department who was objecting to this merger.

When I met with Paul, I told him how sorry we were that he had been blindsided by the merger announcement and that the media had reached him before the banks had. I also pleaded with him to reconsider his initial reaction that there wouldn't be enough competition.

"Whether there is or not doesn't matter," he told me. "The fact is, if I recommend this, I'll never be leader of the party and I'll never be prime minister."

It seemed to me that Paul's desire to become prime minister outweighed all other factors. I got nowhere with him that day. We had a polite exchange and then agreed to disagree. My impression of him then was later confirmed when he did become prime minister, as I saw that he was always trying to do the right thing according to what the polls indicated. It appeared that he never wanted to make the final tough decisions. I'm sorry about that because he is a highly competent person.

At an anniversary dinner in Ottawa for the Business Council on National Issues, Sheila and I happened to be sitting at a table with David Dodge and Hartley Richardson and their wives. Paul was sitting at the next table. During a break in the proceedings, with the women away from the table, Paul came over to sit with David, Hartley, and me.

"It must be difficult for you sitting in the House after having been prime minister," I said to him.

"No," he replied. "I'm enjoying myself. I don't have to make the big decisions."

"Paul, if you had made the big decisions, you would still be prime minister," I said.

AS THE POPULATION and economic importance of Canada's two western provinces continues to grow, they have a stronger political voice today than in the past. The premiers play a bigger role at the First Ministers' Conferences and in the federal government. On a business level, however, the eastern business community continues to dominate the national economic environment.

I have had no business contact to speak of with Stephen Harper, but I see him as an extremely intelligent and impressive leader. I had thought he might not be electable, but my admiration grows for him because he is doing the right things and not necessarily the popular things. To me leadership is not about popularity. Having known a number of prime ministers, I would stress the importance of accountability in that role. The most important quality, however, is the ability to make hard decisions.

The fact that Harper remained in control of a minority government for several years and is now leading a majority government speaks to his leadership ability. I think Canada is very fortunate to have him in charge.

I HAVE GREAT RESPECT for all those who allow their names to stand for public office because in most every case, it involves great personal sacrifice. Being in the resource business, we must get to know the politicians whose decisions have such a profound influence on our ability to operate. Despite the importance of what Ottawa does, most decisions that affect our industry are made at the provincial level.

11

Howe Sound Pulp and Paper
From the Worst to the Best

RETURNING TO THE Canfor story, in 1951 we had purchased a controlling interest in an old shuttered mill at Port Mellon from Sorg Paper of Middleton, Ohio. The original mill was established in 1908 and had numerous ups and downs, producing unbleached kraft pulp and running intermittently. The operation had always been an integral part of the Sunshine Coast community, but in 1949, mill workers were unemployed once again and the operation was closed and put up for sale.

Pulp and paper had been thriving in Canada for two hundred years, primarily in the East and initially as a domestic industry. With the discovery that paper could be manufactured from wood rather than cotton and linen, the industry took off, aided in time by the prohibition of pulpwood export from Crown lands and the removal of the U.S. tariff on newsprint in 1913. By the end of the First World War, Canada was the world's largest exporter of pulp and paper. Like most other sectors, the industry slowed to a crawl during the Depression but recovered with the economic boom after the Second World War.

It was Bill McMahan who had urged my father and uncle to acquire a controlling interest in Howe Sound Pulp and Paper Ltd. Always interested in further integration, they knew a good opportunity when they saw one, but their eyes were open to the challenges.

"We were not financially strong enough to build a pulp mill from scratch, and we liked the location," my father once told me. "The mill was a very poor mill. We knew we would have to spend a lot of money to convert Port Mellon into an efficient operation."

Howe Sound had been hopelessly out of date when CFP took over. A large sawmill on the site was useless to us, so we moved all usable equipment to the Eburne operation and then tore it down. We had a double incentive to get the Port Mellon mill up and running again. The first we had negotiated with federal finance minister Donald Gordon: we would achieve tax-free status if we agreed to reinvest 100 percent of our net cash flow into the plant's refurbishing and conversion into a larger bleached pulp operation that would resurrect much-needed jobs lost when Sorg had shut the mill down. The other motivating factor was a pulp shortage created by the Korean War, when more demand existed for all sorts of products. So began our long history of effort, hope, and cash poured into Port Mellon.

We realized we had much to accomplish as we looked over the two hopelessly outdated antique machines that managed to pump out 100 tons of unbleached pulp every day. Our first step was to take the mill's capacity up to 350 tons of semi-bleached pulp and gradually build up the operation to 650 tons of fully bleached pulp.

Rudy Paradis was the initial mill manager, and Harry Macdonald, who was involved in the hiring process, subsequently moved on to oversee our pulp sales. Phil Strike worked as one of Harry's right-hand people. His dad, Bill Strike, had been a sales manager at Eburne and one of the original CFP directors. During Phil and Harry's long association with Howe Sound, they each had five daughters. Between them, they produced ten girls and no sons. They began to place blame squarely and good-humouredly on the Port Mellon environment.

Our next challenge was covering the expenditures necessary to meet modern environmental standards. As we slowly breathed life into the mill, production costs were astronomical. "In 1952, or so, we sold unbleached pulp for $400 a ton, which was unbelievably high," my father recalled years later. "Our costs, though, were close to $200 a ton, whereas our competitors' costs in modern mills were much lower."

Fortunately, our profits were relatively substantial. Two years later, we were able to buy the balance of Howe Sound shares and assume full ownership of the mill, and it became a division of Canadian Forest Products. We continued to improve the mill in every way possible.

With the increased need for chips, we wanted flexibility so we could whole-log chip should we need the extra volume. We bought Westcoast Cellufibre, a small sawmill at the foot of Manitoba Street in Vancouver, and processed pulp logs there to recover some lumber but primarily to make chips. We added a second line to whole-log chip the really poor logs.

IN THE MID-1980S, we recognized that the mill would not continue to meet ever more stringent environmental requirements, nor was it big enough for us to afford the type of capital it would take to correct the environmental issue.

That was when the Oji Paper Company from Japan came along. We had come to respect and trust the company as a reliable friend in the industry, and one that was well equipped to assess Japanese markets. Oji asked us to consider building a freestanding newsprint mill with them on the B.C. coast. The idea did not appeal to me or to the company, and despite the excellent friendship we had developed, we turned them down. We were interested in a joint venture, we explained, but only if the addition of newsprint included the expansion of pulp at Port Mellon.

In one early meeting with Oji, they wanted everything to be secretive, for two reasons. First, they did not want word circulating about a mill that might not be built. Second, they did not want news of any discussions getting out before things were finalized since they were aiming to get our product from Howe Sound to Japan at the time of or before a new joint venture between Weyerhaeuser and one of their competitors was established. We met with them at the Red Lion Inn at SeaTac airport in Seattle. The meeting lasted less than an hour because we refused to budge on the matter of building a freestanding newsprint mill and they refused to budge on entering the pulp business. We parted friends, but with no deal.

It became obvious to us later that Oji had then proceeded to talk to MacMillan Bloedel, to B.C. Forest Products, and, possibly, to Crown Zellerbach, all of whom produced some newsprint in British Columbia. Oji had already entered into a joint venture with Canadian Pacific Forest Products (CPFP) in the Maritimes, and like these other B.C. companies, CPFP had been in the newsprint business for some time. As a result, Oji found that it could not exert enough influence to get the newsprint up to the standard they needed for Japan. Although CPFP and Oji produced a good product in the Maritimes, it still did not live up to the quality they wanted. After talking to the other B.C. companies and reflecting on their partnership with Canadian Pacific, Oji saw the advantage in joining us expressly because we were not in the newsprint business. With Canfor, they could have full control over paper quality at Howe Sound.

Oji came back to us in 1987, and we eventually agreed to expand the pulp mill and install one new, first-rate newsprint machine—but only after some gruelling and rigorous discussions in Japan. As before, Oji insisted that our talks be kept completely secret. On our travels to Tokyo, they did not want my colleagues or me mixing with the normal industry group, so we stayed at their "guest house," a magnificent facility behind the royal palace. It was not much bigger than a normal two-storey residence, and it was an ideal, isolated place for them to put us up. We had no access to the industry or even to our own office in Tokyo. (At various times, CFP ran sales offices overseas along with pulp offices in Montreal, London, Milan, Brussels, and Tokyo.)

The first day of negotiations went badly. Studies we had conducted recommended that Oji pay us for 50 percent of Howe Sound, and we would agree to reinvest that money right back into construction of the new Howe Sound Pulp. The study assumed Oji would pay $300 million.

After they pummelled us in that first session, Mark Gunther, Gordon Armstrong and I gathered at the guest house to talk strategy. Mark and Gordon suggested that we would lose the deal unless we came down to $285 million. They were convinced that Oji would not go for anything higher.

"No," I said to Mark and Gordon, intent on convincing them. "We're not going to come down after they hammered us yesterday. If we don't like the number they come up with, and we're high, we can ask for an adjournment and review it to see whether we want the deal at a lower number."

The following day Oji suggested we each write down a number and then disclose the figures, one after the other, by turning over our pieces of paper. If we were close or in "the same ballpark," we would make a deal; if we were not close, we would not make a deal. It was a high-stakes game—and one I was good at from my mis-spent youth at UBC.

We all sat in the guest house meeting room with our num-bers on our respective pieces of paper lying face down on the table. A tossed coin decided that we go first. I turned over my sheet—$315 million. They all clapped. Then they revealed their number—$300 million.

"We're in the same ball park," they said with obvious relief.

I responded cautiously and asked for a caucus, explaining that this was a difficult decision for us. We went upstairs and I ordered some sandwiches—we made them wait for a while. Of course, we were delighted with the result, but we had a further decision to make. After we had our lunch and talked it over, we came back.

"We recommend we split the difference at $307.5 million," I said.

"It's a deal," they said, clapping once again.

When we had gone out for dinner at the end of that difficult first day of negotiations, the chair of Oji had picked me up at the guest house. He spoke very little English and I of course did not speak Japanese.

"How was it?" he asked me.

"It was a bad day," I said.

"Tomorrow will be better," he promised.

In hindsight, I knew this subtle reassurance was responsible for my having put a higher number on our piece of paper than what the study had showed.

THE VENTURE WE AGREED TO build with Oji and the refurbish-ing of Port Mellon was to cost $850 million, of which $268 million were for environmental improvements. With state-of-the-art emission controls, it would be the largest of its kind in North

America. Even Greenpeace showed interest in what we were doing because we voluntarily went beyond the regulatory requirements of the day.

To get the project on its feet, I enrolled Bill Hughes, a highly technical man and a former manager at Port Mellon who had moved north to head up Prince George and Intercontinental Pulp. He was happy to return to Port Mellon to oversee such an exciting new development.

Looking back, I see now that both Bill and Oji's project manager were technocrats who became engrossed in creating a gold-plated mill. They seemed to lose sight of the budget. Instead of $850 million, the actual cost was $1.3 billion. Examples of gold-plating at Port Mellon were everywhere. Bill Hughes and his counterpart ordered the best of everything and overbuilt the facility for its intended production. The most wasteful single expense was made without ever seeking board authority, when a foundation was built on the site for a *second* top-notch newsprint machine. The reason they gave for this astonishing cost was that they felt we could not afford to have blasting in the proximity of the first machine if we should ever decide to put in a second machine. That alone was a multi-million-dollar expenditure for a machine that would never be built. We did not have anywhere near the amount of fibre to consider it. The board did not have a handle on the level of expenditures that members of our senior staff were making. With Oji's desire to deliver newsprint from Howe Sound a priority, the emphasis was a "hurry up" process. Looking back, that was a very, very costly mistake.

In addition to those expenses, we paid a price for producing Japanese-quality newsprint. Oji required us to blend a percentage of kraft pulp with the CTMP (chemi-thermomechanical pulp) fibre to produce superior paper for their market—but the process was much more expensive and it also deprived us of pulp to sell.

In the end, the result was an artistic and technical success, but one that would cause us to suffer on the financial side from an unreasonably heavy debt load.

IN 2010, TWO investments for $6 million and $36.7 million in Howe Sound funded by the federal government's Pulp and Paper Green Transformation Program allowed for further environmental upgrades at the mill, placing it at the forefront of clean energy production from wood biomass in British Columbia. We also hoped that such changes would improve the mill's sustainability and maintain the operation's 450 jobs.

Positive news in the industry reported that mill effluent losses had been significantly reduced. Despite our efforts, however, the plant at Port Mellon was still struggling financially and talks were already under way about selling. Further bad news followed: Howe Sound was lacking residual fibre because of the closure of our other coastal operations. In addition, markets were shifting and world newsprint technology was changing. Recycled papers were in demand and Japan no longer required the same high-quality newsprint from British Columbia.

We could not have asked for better partners than Oji, whose people were honourable and helpful throughout our relationship, but the simple fact was that Oji had no further need for the Port Mellon newsprint. We had to turn to other Asian and North American markets, which were also diminishing in the face of new digital technology.

With these dramatic changes, both Oji and Canfor wanted to sell the mill. Neither of our major shareholders, Stephen Jarislowsky nor Jimmy Pattison, was keen on pulp; both preferred the wood product side of the business.

The sale of Howe Sound Pulp and Paper—our last operating concern on the B.C. coast—was completed in 2010. Canfor and

Oji sold it along with Westcoast Cellufibre to Paper Excellence BV, a Netherlands-based unit of Indonesia's Sinar Mas, the same company that bought a mothballed mill in Mackenzie, British Columbia, only three months earlier.

I respected our board's decision to sell Port Mellon, but I regretted letting go of the best pulp and paper facility on the B.C. coast. With all its outstanding improvements, I believe Howe Sound will be the last surviving pulp mill on the coast. Personally, I am sorry that Canfor will not be involved in its future.

Even though we are no longer participating in Howe Sound, we remain very much involved in Canfor Pulp Products Inc., comprising our three mills located in Prince George. If we had abandoned pulp altogether, we would be sitting on a one-legged stool, and that is a difficult way to survive in an integrated business.

12

The Leaders
Industry Icons

THE B.C. FOREST sector has always been a close-knit community, albeit an odd mix of individuals, companies, and organizations, where most of the players, large and small, have enjoyed respectful relationships. I am privileged to have known many of the "greats" in the industry, my father and uncle among them. Several leaders stand out in my memory as remarkable characters who variously challenged me, annoyed me, mystified me, and impressed me—depending on the circumstances and the vagaries of our fluctuating industry. We may have been strong competitors in the marketplace, but we were also a group of friends, who formed what I experienced as a rewarding fellowship.

Early on, many of the people at the top were either foresters or individuals who had been more or less raised in the industry. They understood all levels of integration, frequently visiting mills and staying close to operations on the ground. They also understood the markets and the financial side of things because they were always out talking to customers. Their thinking addressed what was best for the company and its shareholders in the long term—and they worried about the forests, the mills, and the markets as a whole package.

Reflecting on the giants I met as a younger man, I remember a series of eccentric individuals who were passionate about their work and the enterprises they built. Those memories offer a few stories that deserve telling.

HARVEY REGINALD MACMILLAN, familiarly and fondly known as "H.R.," was British Columbia's first chief forester. Before his appointment in 1912, he worked for the Dominion Forest Service. As the province's industrial boom became apparent, he resigned from his government role to enter the private sector. The rest, as they say, is history, as he went about building a modest operation that would become the biggest forest company in the province—MacMillan Bloedel.

H.R. had a profound impact on the creation of B.C. forest policy; his influence continued throughout his long and impressive career and even after he retired. I recall how he favoured forest management licences as the best way to go, yet after his company got what they wanted at the 1955 Sloan Commission, he was decidedly less committed. When my father privately challenged him on that apparent change of heart, H.R. answered in his typically direct way: "I already have what my company wanted and I don't want others to get the same."

My father and H.R. respected each other and they went back a long way. When H.R. first saw the timber in the Nimpkish Valley, he put two survey crews in the woods at Englewood while negotiating with Puget Sound Pulp and Timber, which had decided to sell it. In the meantime, our close family friend, Fred Brown, convinced us that the best timber stand in British Columbia was growing at Englewood. We should buy it, he insisted, even if it was a larger operation than we wanted at the time. After flying over it and liking what we saw, my family jumped at the opportunity. H.R. had assumed MacMillan Bloedel was the only potential buyer at the time. When the deal was done, he complimented my dad, saying that it was a brilliant move that he had not expected.

I had two memorable personal encounters with H.R. The first was in England, just after Sheila and I were married in 1953, when I was learning both the pulp and paper business and the lumber business through the Seaboard office in London. Several companies were exporting hemlock to the United Kingdom at the time—MacMillan Bloedel, Seaboard, and East Asiatic as a distant third. Prices were ostensibly set according to what MacMillan Bloedel and Seaboard did, and for the first time since the Second World War ended, the price of B.C. hemlock was dropping. One problem was the confusion between dormant wormholes in our hemlock and the worms actively burrowing into the Paraná pine imported from South America. I kept myself busy reassuring our customers that the residual wormholes had no effect on the structural strength of our B.C. wood.

The drop in hemlock sales also had to do with timing. When someone in the United Kingdom bought lumber, they had to wait six weeks before it arrived because of the lengthy shipping time. Our customers were taking inventory losses before the product even landed on their shores. All this, along with the wormhole misunderstanding, was scaring them off. They stopped buying, which induced the B.C. companies to keep lowering their price to attract the U.K. buyers. But the low prices were having the opposite effect on the market.

I saw all this as an unnecessary, stupid, and vicious cycle, and I was wrestling with it when officials at Canada House invited

me to attend a function welcoming a Canadian fishing delegation. H.R. MacMillan was a member of the delegation as a board
member of B.C. Packers. I had met H.R. at my family's home in the
past but did not know him at all personally. It seemed an opportune time to speak with him about the hemlock issue, and there
appeared to be no conflict in doing so. Under Canadian law, you
cannot discuss domestic pricing with any competitor, but it is
legal to work together on export prices.

I saw H.R. at the reception, a tall man with bushy eyebrows
and a perpetually determined look on his face. I approached him
and meekly introduced myself.

"Mr. MacMillan, my name is Peter Bentley," I began. "You know
my father, Poldi. Even though you're here with the fish delegation,
I wonder if it would be appropriate to talk to you about lumber?"

"To hell with the fish, I want to talk lumber!" H.R. barked in his
characteristically strong voice. "What's on your mind, Peter?"

I went into some detail explaining how we might improve the
market for hemlock and that, if the MacMillan Export Company
was agreeable to the strategy I had in mind, I was sure we could
manage it.

"That makes sense," H.R. said. "Come and have breakfast with
me tomorrow at the Savoy."

The next day I arrived early to find H.R. sitting in the dining
room with his U.K. manager.

"Peter has explained all this to me and I want to know what you
think," H.R. said to the man.

"I don't think we can make it work," he said.

"Well, you're stupid and we're going to do it," H.R. snapped.
"Peter is quite right. Why should a customer buy into a falling market? If we do a price increase, they'll buy immediately. And once
the volume starts going, we can gradually increase the price from
there. That's exactly what we're going to do."

We did implement what I had suggested and we were completely successful in restoring the U.K. price of hemlock. I was glad my first interaction with H.R. led to a happy conclusion.

MY SECOND ENCOUNTER with H.R., however, many years later, was one of the most uncomfortable moments of my career.

It was the early 1960s, and what we called a big "road show" was in progress in the Interior, involving a series of public hearings for the award of several potential Pulpwood Harvesting Areas (PHAs), which would allow for the construction of pulp mills. The hearings included applications from Columbia Cellulose, MacMillan Bloedel, Harry Hagerman at Smithers, and Canfor on behalf of Intercontinental Pulp.

Jack V. Clyne, a man of high integrity, had resigned as a B.C. Supreme Court Judge in 1958 to head up MacMillan Bloedel. The company had prepared a brief for their application at the hearing in Smithers. Its chief forester and Bert Gayle, another member of their forestry staff, had already explained what they were planning and they seemed to have won support from the local community. In addition to the pulp mill, they were also going to build a sawmill to make chips and use the better part of the log for lumber. MacMillan Bloedel had an excellent brief to present and two executives giving evidence: Clyne, who was very adept on his feet but new to the forest business, and Ernie Shorter, MacMillan Bloedel's vice-president, wood products. Following the usual protocol, Minister Ray Williston questioned them, as did the adversaries to the application.

"Will it be a market pulp mill?" a young lawyer asked Clyne, meaning would they sell the pulp it produced in the market.

"No," Clyne replied, not yet having a good grasp of the industry and responding to the lawyer as if he were still on the bench. "When we build something it's not for sale."

That of course, was the wrong answer, and on top of his gaffe, he was implicitly scolding the young lawyer for asking such a question.

More queries followed about the proposed sawmill, which was to be about five times larger than any other sawmill in the area.

"Are you just going to use the better portion of the logs coming in?" another lawyer asked.

"I don't want to talk about it," Clyne said. "The sawmill is just a sideline."

Well, that was a devastating answer; for the local people, this "sideline" to the pulp mill they were going to build represented employment and their livelihood.

Ernie took the stand next and his answers were equally weak. He was an expert at what he did and very knowledgeable, but he was strictly a coastal lumberman who did not know the Interior. He and Clyne blew it on the witness stand to the extent that Larry Harris, MacMillan Bloedel's vice-president, pulp, asked after the hearing if he could fly back with John Liersch and me on our Grumman Goose. He was afraid that he might say something to his own people on their plane that would get him fired.

John Liersch walked into my office the next day and asked if I was a MacMillan Bloedel shareholder. I acknowledged that I was a small one.

"Then get the largest brief case you own and come with me. We're going to the MacMillan Bloedel annual general meeting," he said.

"What will I put in the case?" I asked.

"Nothing. I just want us to sit there and scare them."

So off we went, carrying our large empty brief cases, which made it look like we had a lot of questions. On the way in, I saw that the scrutineers were rejecting Jean Southam, H.R.'s daughter, because she did not have her proper identification. I vouched for her so she could attend. As we walked into the meeting room, she thanked me and extended an invitation.

"Peter, I'm hosting a reception for the directors later at the house and I'd like you to come," she said. "Daddy always talks well of you, and although he won't be here at the meeting, he'll be at the reception. Why don't you come a little early and have a visit with him?"

I was happy to accept. When I arrived at the house, I was shown into the library. There, sitting tall in a large armchair, was H.R. by himself.

"Close the door, Peter, and have a seat," he said. He clearly had something in mind to discuss with me.

"I guess you were up north at the hearings?" he said.

"Yes, I was, Mr. MacMillan," I replied.

"Are we going to get our licence?" he asked.

"In all honesty, sir, I don't think you have a chance," I said.

"I don't understand. We're the logical choice," he said.

"Yes, you are," I agreed. "But instead of putting the people who did all the preparatory work and who know the local situation on the stand, your chair and Ernie did all the talking and didn't answer the questions well. In fact, the way it all unfolded, it would be difficult for the minister to award you the licence."

The door opened and J.V. Clyne joined us, taking the chair beside me. There I was, sitting between two great men, and things were about to get very uncomfortable. H.R. turned to Clyne and let loose.

"Peter tells me you fucked up," he said as I sunk lower into my chair.

"What did I do wrong?" Clyne asked me.

"Obviously, you didn't mean to do anything wrong, Mr. Clyne, but your answers to the minister and the lawyer fell far from the mark," I explained. "It wasn't what they were looking for. Then you gave the lawyer hell for a question you had misunderstood and, on top of that, Ernie answered incorrectly on the subject of the log use."

It came as no surprise that MacMillan Bloedel did not get that licence.

I HAD FIRST MET J.V. CLYNE through St. George's School, where I also knew his son Stewart, who was a year or two behind me. David Wallace, Chunky Woodward, Ron Cliff, and I were all friends and alumni who had risen to a level of business stature in the local community. We loved our old school, but we felt it was time to share our collective opinion on the teaching staff's lack of competence and professionalism. We drew straws to see who would invite the board and the headmaster to a meeting. I lost the draw and the obligation fell to me to host a Sunday afternoon gathering at my home on West 32nd Avenue.

That day the four of us announced that we were ready to head up a campaign to build a new and larger school, which was sorely needed. We would only do so, however, on the assurance that they would hire the best teachers available and that they would pay the public school wage or higher. We demanded quality.

After a short discussion and the sharing of a few concerns, the board members agreed and were unanimously committed. The headmaster was less enthusiastic, as were all his old cronies on staff, many of whom were wonderful people but not quality teachers. Then and there, the board decided to appoint two of us, David and me, as directors. That marked a significant breakthrough. Until then the board's membership consisted of men who were much older and no longer had boys at the school. David and I were also the first two old boys ever to be elected to the board.

At first, Clyne had jumped all over our new plan for the school, saying that it was too small. We argued that we did not yet have the money and we could not risk putting the school in debt. After the meeting, he seemed to change his mind.

"Peter, I was wrong," he said, putting his hand on my shoulder. "You're doing exactly the right thing and I respect and appreciate what you're doing." We were off to a good start.

LATER, WHEN CLYNE first joined MacMillan Bloedel, he used to call me in advance of certain meetings.

"Good," he would reply when I confirmed I was attending. "I want to talk to you. We can walk over together."

On our way, he would ask me for background as he learned the business. Sheila and I were invited to his home a couple of times a year, and we got along very well notwithstanding our age difference. MacMillan Bloedel was a great company in its time, but I could see a lot of mistakes being made; I felt it was not my job to tell him.

Another side of Clyne was more colourful. He drew attention at a cocktail party to celebrate MacMillan Bloedel's purchase of Powell River; Harold Foley said something that prompted Clyne to throw whiskey at him. I was not there for that incident, but I remember hearing from those who were that Clyne was right and Foley was wrong.

SOMEHOW, DESPITE THE INCIDENT in Jean Southam's library, I managed to maintain a good rapport with Clyne. Another encounter with him I remember well occurred in the late 1960s when Canfor was growing rapidly in the Interior, but there was a serious shortage of managerial types in the industry. We had a lot of new sawmills starting up and they desperately needed experienced supervision. My friend and fraternity brother, Mike Robson, whose father had been a key player with Bloedel before it joined MacMillan, had grown up in the business, and he was the number two man in MacMillan Bloedel's sales organization for wood products. I went to Mike and asked for his help in finding management.

"This may sound strange," I said, "but as our production is growing at these mills, I don't have people to man them. You must know some bright people at MacMillan Bloedel. If I sign a letter of agreement promising not to steal them, I could appoint them for one or two years as mill managers. If it doesn't work they would come back sooner and, even if it does work, you have the right to recall them whenever you want. I just need some good people!"

Mike said he would get back to me the next day. The following morning he was sitting in our waiting room when I arrived at the office.

"I want to come and work for Canfor," he said before we sat down. "Not as a temporary manager, but as head of your sales organization."

I was pleasantly surprised. Our sales team at the time was not great and Mike knew he was way ahead of them. But I was also worried.

"Mike, I can't just hire you like that. MacMillan Bloedel will never forgive us," I explained. "You're right that we have a weak team, but let's do this properly. I will run an ad and you can respond to it. If you're the best candidate, then we'll talk again."

We posted the job and, not surprisingly, Mike was the best candidate by far.

"But I'm not hiring you yet," I told him.

Before that I had to call Clyne and request a meeting. Always gracious, he invited me to his office.

"This is a small industry, and one of your people has applied for a job with us," I explained. "I intend to give Mike Robson the job because he is the best applicant, but I wanted to talk with you first so it wouldn't be a surprise."

"Wait a minute," Clyne interrupted. He picked up the phone and called Denis Timmis, a senior MacMillan Bloedel executive, later to become CEO.

"Denis, get in here!" Clyne commanded.

Timmis swiftly obeyed and strode into the office.

"Explain to Peter why he can't take Mike Robson," Clyne said.

"I don't see how we can do that, Jack," Timmis said. "Mike applied for a job and Peter wants to give it to him."

"We're not letting Mike go," Clyne insisted, offering up another senior person who was equal to Mike in the sales department.

"He hasn't applied," I said quietly. "But he's a good man, so you're left with a quality senior sales executive, even without Mike."

I left, having made peace with Clyne once again, and Mike joined us at Canfor.

I respected Clyne enormously but, as time passed, I felt that he was a poor choice for MacMillan Bloedel. No doubt he had integrity, but it was amazing to me that they did not have an internal person to follow H.R. who knew the business well. They went on to make more errors in judgment, including hiring Bob Bonner, a politician, a good lawyer, and an honourable person but again someone who did not know the industry.

AN OUTSTANDING LEADER among the "old guard" of MacMillan Bloedel was Bert Hoffmeister, a natural leader and close friend to my father. He and I were two of the original eight partners led by Frank Wilhelmsen of Garibaldi Lifts, a company we created in the early 1960s, which was the start of skiing at Whistler Mountain. I remember Bert as a very military and businesslike man with strong views and a pleasant personality. He was highly decorated in the war and one of the first presidents of the Council of Forest Industries (COFI). MacMillan Bloedel's president throughout H.R.'s tenure as chair from 1951 to 1955, Bert then carried on as chair himself for two years.

The first of the more recent heads of MacMillan Bloedel that made the grade in my estimation was Ray Smith. Ray was a pleasure to work with, and ironically, he had once slipped through Canfor's fingers. He had been looking for a job after leaving the armed forces and somehow this news (and presumably Ray's reputation) reached Bill McMahan. Bill contacted our human resources person, Arnold Smith, and suggested that he interview Ray. Arnold complied and, during their short meeting, he apparently led with his favourite human resources job interview question:

"What do you do?" he asked.

"I play the trumpet," Ray answered in good humour.

"Then go join a band," Arnold said, and sent him on his way.

CAL KNUDSEN was a senior player at Weyerhaeuser before taking the head job at MacMillan Bloedel. I remember well the day Cal arrived for his first day on the job in 1976, as it was the same day that the federal government combines people launched an investigation into plywood price fixing in Canada. Under scrutiny were MacMillan Bloedel, Canfor, and Weldwood—Canada's three major plywood suppliers.

When I came to the office that morning, I found two federal people sitting in my office. One was tasked with getting hold of files that might apply, and the other sat uncomfortably close to me at my desk, making sure that I did not do anything wrong. I surmised that Cal would be getting the same kind of treatment on his first day at MacMillan Bloedel, so I gave him a call and welcomed him to Canada.

I then turned to these government characters and insisted that the whole thing was ridiculous because our returns on plywood were so low.

"I don't understand this investigation," I said. "If we'd been fixing prices, we would have done a much better job than a 1.5 percent return (at its highest) on plywood in such a competitive business!"

As that tiresome day wore on, I telephoned Ron Basford, the Liberal member of parliament for Vancouver Centre and the minister responsible for the Competition Bureau. I wanted to give him a piece of my mind.

"Have you ever bought a light bulb?" I asked him.

"Yes, I have," he replied.

"When you went to the store to get the light bulb did you go to get a 60-watt bulb, or did you go with a view to buying a GE or Westinghouse or Sylvania brand?" I asked.

"I just wanted a certain power of bulb," he said.

"Well, when you buy sheathing plywood, people want so many four-by-eight sheets and they don't specify the manufacturer," I explained. "It's inevitable that after a day or two, as the market changes, the prices will be the same because the retailer could not exist if we were all at different price levels. At Canfor, we are selling a *commodity* and you're wasting a lot of the taxpayers' money chasing this issue. Anything you ever want to know, you can get from us, but I don't like being under this cloud. It's an insult that you're doing this when our returns are so pathetic."

The minister hemmed and hawed. What had prompted that investigation remained a mystery. The only information they were permitted to share with us was that it was not internally initiated, which led me to believe that a complaint had come from someone trying to make trouble. After a few months, they got out of our way, but we did not get a clean bill of health from them for two or three years.

MANY OF the other individuals who headed up MacMillan Bloedel through the years I can count among my friends, including Ray Smith, his successor Bob Findlay, and Tom Stephens, the last CEO of MacMillan Bloedel when Weyerhaeuser moved in.

After starting as adversaries, Adam Zimmerman and I developed a solid friendship. I admire what he did in the industry. After starting Northwood, then buying into BCFP and finally buying into MacMillan Bloedel, Adam became a major personality in the industry. He is an extremely bright man who became somewhat of a political force, which was not always in the industry's best interest because he was very outspoken. But being very vocal myself, I could not fault him for that.

I remember Zimmerman describing Pat Carney's involvement with the softwood lumber file when she was minister of international trade. He said it was like hiring a plumber to do open-heart surgery.

In the end, and despite a succession of intelligent heads, MacMillan Bloedel had a tough time and made a number of bad decisions, which radically changed their position from the strong industry leader they once were.

THE NEXT major player was B.C. Forest Products (BCFP), partially owned at the time by the Scott Paper Company, which appointed Charlie Dickie, an outstanding executive, to head up the company. After a brief stint in Vancouver, he moved on to Scott's headquarters and became the chief executive of their global company.

Ian Barclay succeeded Charlie and was also a first-rate leader who headed up BCFP during the industry's rapid expansion between the 1960s and the 1980s. He assembled a strong team and created a good culture and morale in their company. They became one of the country's largest lumber producers.

I always admired the way BCFP developed their people. Ian brought along Ken Benson and Don Saunders, both of whom looked like potential successors. Ken ended up taking over at BCFP, and Don went on to be hired by the Pulp Bureau (which bargains with the two pulp and paper unions, Pulp, Paper, and Woodworkers of Canada, and Canadian Paperworkers Union) and Forest Industrial Relations (FIR, which bargains with the IWA, the original forest union on the coast for woodworkers) when Don Lanskail moved to COFI. I always felt that the reverse would have better suited those men and their respective areas of expertise: Lanskail would have been more valuable staying where he had been with his legal and labour background, and Saunders could have been a better fit for COFI.

The three Koerner brothers arrived in British Columbia from Czechoslovakia about the same time we arrived from Austria. Unlike our family, they had been in the timber industry in Europe, and they formed a company known as Alaska Pine. They expanded quite significantly and were very successful. The two older brothers died relatively early and Walter Koerner, who survived them by several years, became the best known of the three. They were very generous in their philanthropy and Walter's son Michael, who lives in Toronto, is well known for his generosity to both the arts and education.

NUMEROUS OTHER FOREST industry players stand out as close colleagues with whom I developed a bond, both at the corporate and the personal level.

Canfor enjoyed a particular friendship with Weldwood of Canada, established in 1964. When I first took the reins at Canfor, Gary Bowell, yet another Rhodes Scholar in the industry, was in charge of Weldwood after working at MacMillan Bloedel for many years. Tom Buell, a professional forester who knew the industry inside out and got along with everyone, succeeded Gary. My father admired Tom and claimed he was the best in the industry. Should anything happen to me, he saw him as a good fit for my job. My own opinion of Tom was equally high.

Canfor always had a strong affinity with Weldwood, principally because we shared a similar culture. Tom and I made several unsuccessful attempts to get approval from Champion, then Weldwood's parent company in the United States, to merge our operations. The answer was always the same: "We are not for sale." They saw Weldwood, quite appropriately, as the crown jewel in their holdings.

Though we could never manage to join our two companies, Tom and I worked closely together and schemed to make our respective wholesale distribution operations more efficient. We decided that the building materials situation was way over-serviced by MacMillan Bloedel, Weldwood, and Canfor, with each company selling the same kind of products—paints, doors, floor coverings, and the like. To correct that, Tom and I created a fifty-fifty partnership in a company we named CanWell. We alternated each year as chair and, to avoid the risk of one of our top people taking over, we hired an independent CEO. Not once did Tom and I disagree about anything. We wanted to eliminate duplication at numerous locations. We also decided that both companies would sell the real estate at all our locations and lease back only the ones we wanted to operate. We kept the best locations, the best product lines and developed an all-star team. As plywood became less relevant, we no longer needed the company, and when we finally sold CanWell, it was like selling the hole in the donut as we had already realized the cash from the real estate sale.

Another of the larger coastal companies was Crown Zeller-bach. Frank Youngman was an early CEO at Crown Zellerbach and worked with my dad. Then there was Bob Filberg, who once headed up the Comox Logging Company and had been our witness at the never-ending Cudahy trial. Bob Rogers led Crown Zellerbach for several years prior to becoming Lieutenant Governor of British Columbia. Bob had attracted Tom Rust from B.C. Forest Products to join him and Tom proved to be a competent leader.

Crown Zellerbach had some quality people, full of integrity, and the company was a strong member of Seaboard, but it had its problems. There were no local ownerships here, so Crown Zeller-bach Canada was a wholly owned subsidiary. They ran somewhat independently yet they were saddled with some of the head office employee benefits that differed from those in Canada. This meant that in addition to their own corporate policies, they chose to do certain things in Canada according to U.S. law that they did not have to do here. They had some screwball ideas at the top of that company. I remember when all their senior people were sent to touchy-feely management training sessions, the results of which turned out to be very disappointing. Instead of relationships being enhanced, they were strained or even damaged.

Then there was Herb Doman who built his company signifi-cantly and went into joint venture with Western Forest Products, which included Squamish Pulp. Although this integrated him and his empire was growing—so was his debt. Herb was a likeable person and a real character, but he got into rough waters. In 1988, the fact that he was negotiating the sale of Doman Industries to a large U.S. company was publicly disclosed. At nine o'clock one morning, that company called Herb and advised him that they would not buy the company and no further discussion was neces-sary. Instead of immediately calling the stock exchange to advise them that the deal was off, Herb called some of his shareholders, including Premier Bill Bennett's family. Bill's brother, Russell, who ran the family affairs from which the premier had to divorce himself, promptly sold their shares. It was only later that day that Herb notified the exchange. The delay resulted in an accusation of insider trading and quite a scandal. Although everyone was ultimately acquitted, both the B.C. and the Ontario security commissions dragged the matter on for a long time.

Herb always liked to make bets. He used to call me to make a bet on all sorts of sports events. I always let him pick the team he wanted, which he frequently did unsuccessfully.

Sam Ketchum launched West Fraser Timber and was well on his way to transforming it into a major industry player when he was killed tragically in a helicopter accident. Hank Ketchum, Sam's nephew, took over the controls and has done a superb job in making the company the world's largest lumber producer. In addition to growing in British Columbia and Alberta, they have also moved into the southern pine region of the United States in a major way. They are considered an efficient, low-cost producer and have been highly successful. Hank is extremely capable and widely admired, but West Fraser's corporate culture is very different from our own. This is true on manufacturing, but particularly on the marketing side.

Allan Thorlakson built up Tolko, the company his father, Harold, founded in 1956, and now the largest private timber company operating in British Columbia. We have a joint paper sales company with Tolko, based in Kelowna, where we sell paper from both our mills.

Among Tolko's purchases was our interest in Balco, which we sold to them because it was a better fit for them than for us. Allan subsequently purchased Riverside after they had taken over Lignum, a company started by the Kerr family and built into a significant lumber wholesaler and a medium-sized independent sawmiller under the leadership of Kerr's son, Jake.

Brad Thorlakson continues to give this company good leadership under Allan's watchful eye.

CANFOR WAS FORTUNATE through the years to have many wise and capable forest industry executives leave their jobs to join us. Three of these came from Powell River: my mentor, John Liersch, Dr. Ralph Patterson, who attended the Banff business school when I did, and Bert Gayle.

I recall the day when I announced at a Canfor meeting that I had hired Bert as a senior member of our team. John Liersch started to laugh like hell, making me fear I had just made a big mistake. After John recovered and I asked him what was so funny, he commented that the news was fantastic but ironic. John himself had once made great efforts to draw Bert away from his government job to Powell River. Bert replaced me as coordinator of raw materials, becoming my right hand and then winding up a vice-president of the company.

Leadership in our industry can be remarkably transient. Many people, only some of whom I am able to mention here, promoted the growth of our industry in British Columbia and they built hugely successful enterprises. With markets constantly shifting, however, they had all learned to be flexible and alert to change.

13

The Environmental Debate
A Key Factor in Leaving the Coast

THE DEAN OF the forestry school at UBC retired in 2010. On my way to his farewell reception, I ran into a young man in the lobby of the forestry building. As we walked past the MacMillan Bloedel Room, the Canfor Room, and the Weldwood Room on the main floor he said, "I know Canfor, but who are MacMillan Bloedel and Weldwood?"

How times had changed.

The young man's question brought to mind the radical shifts I had witnessed in the forest industry since arriving in Canada as a boy—and how businesses with household names can quickly vanish. Thinking back, I could still see the numerous lumber operations such as Canadian Western and Alaska Pine lining the Fraser River's shores, with just as many mills—Robertson and Hackett, Alberta Pacific, Bay Lumber, and others—on Vancouver's False Creek, then an important hub of our industry. From a dense forest known only to local First Nations communities, the area surrounding False Creek had grown into a small lumbering village and then burst to life as an industrial community.

Lumber had been at the geographic heart of Vancouver's development, but in time it burned itself out. The Depression and the Second World War had dealt many industries a serious blow. Mills and other operations on False Creek gradually deteriorated into fire traps. Businesses began to leave the area in the 1950s and '60s in the first exodus of the smaller forest industry players, making way for housing and parks. Our industry was on the move, as it would be for years to follow, when increasing numbers of companies on the lower coast changed hands and disappeared.

By the 1980s, the situation on the coast was vastly different than it had been when our family first came to British Columbia. Many smaller companies had disappeared or merged with larger ones, and five major players—MacMillan Bloedel, Crown Zellerbach, B.C. Forest Products, Canfor, and Weldwood—although large on the local scene, had not yet reached the top echelons of the global industry. Canfor's focus had turned to the Interior, and we were not alone. We left for overlapping reasons having to do with the market, environmentalism, politics, and technology. Of those original big five, not one remains on the coast, and Canfor is the only one that still exists.

The first to disappear was Crown Zellerbach in 1981, and then B.C. Forest Products six years later. Fletcher Challenge acquired both. The next to go was British Columbia's flagship; this time no one stood up to say that the province was "not for sale" when Weyerhaeuser, one of the largest American forest products firms, acquired MacMillan Bloedel in 1999. The news startled us all; nobody knew that MacMillan Bloedel was on the block, as its profits were recovering impressively under the new leadership of Tom Stephens. After the company's long, illustrious, and controversial history, and its more recent struggle to survive, MacMillan

Bloedel as an entity disappeared completely. British Columbia had lost the indisputable icon of our industry.

The last big coastal entity to be taken over was Weldwood, the company we had always wanted to merge with, but which Champion refused to give up for sale. We were saddened to see the departure of our corporate "twin" when it was acquired by West Fraser, but we were fortunate to inherit a few of Weldwood's key players, who helped us greatly. Eventually Canfor was the last of the original five on the coast.

COMPLEX INFLUENCES had led to the exodus. One was the shifting demands of our customer base. The global market for certain wood species and products was changing. Cedar was (and remains) a specialty product that weathers extremely well. Because that market differs somewhat from the commodity business, we still have surviving cedar mills on the coast. Hemlock, however, was a different story. Because of its high moisture content, it was slow-drying, which made it expensive to treat before shipping. A better solution was spruce, pine, and fir from the Interior, which was quickly becoming a preferred building material, especially in North America.

All the changes that resulted in companies leaving our coast similarly affected Canfor and our employees. Closing mills is always difficult. In smaller communities dependent on a particular mill, closures can be devastating. We considered it fortunate that the coastal mills we closed were all in populated areas where other job opportunities were available to our employees.

The shutting down of the Panel and Fibre Division probably affected our personnel more than any other closures because that was where Canfor began and where, at one time (when it was Pacific Veneer), we had a work force of one thousand. Of course, we did not terminate that many people, as the business had been shrinking. When we finally shut that operation's doors, it had become a hardboard mill only that employed relatively few.

The demise of pulp mills has probably delivered the biggest blows to communities on the coast, such as Gold River, Ocean Falls, Prince Rupert, and Squamish. We sold Howe Sound Pulp and Paper, but Canfor has never closed a pulp mill.

BY FAR the biggest factor in Canfor's departure from the coast was environmentalism—a topic that fills volumes both inside and outside our industry. A well-known chapter in British Columbia's recent history tells how our coastal industry came under attack by environmentalists. The image of old-growth logging was a major trigger.

I have commented often that, like people, trees die, even though their life span is much longer. I believe strongly in pre-serving parcels of beautiful trees for people to see and enjoy. To keep them all, however, makes no sense to those in our industry when the land the trees are on is not productive. The older trees do not grow, nor do they convert air to good oxygen. In fact, they become users rather than givers of desirable gases. Some of the tree is still alive, but barely so. A young thrifty forest has a much higher incremental growth per hectare than an old one.

Selective logging is often suggested as a viable option, which in my opinion it is not. People who advocate for this technique do not understand that young timber will not grow well under a can-opy of old growth, and that the selective logging of an old tree will crush a lot of young trees on its way down. Replacing old timber with young timber is the way to go, but I agree that this should be done with much less wide-open clear-cutting. Logging on a patch basis—cutting smaller areas and separating the patches with liv-ing forests—is one of the best ways to disperse seeds and prevent the fire hazard imposed by a huge area of slash.

We have been criticized in British Columbia for clear-cutting, yet that is exactly what is done in Europe. The only logging they do there other than clear-cutting is the thinning of young forests, which accelerates growth. The difference is that they create far smaller clear-cuts, as we do now, but in Europe they are already on their third, fourth, or fifth rotation, so the trees are more uniform and the terrain is easier for operations. On the coast, we have had a different situation because of the enormous variance in the size and diameter of the old-growth trees. To try and selectively fall older timber would be inefficient. In addition, if we selectively logged, the newly planted trees would not do well because the remaining standing timber would shelter them from sunlight, resulting in much slower growth than the alternative.

To face a battle every time a tree was cut made business difficult. The debate about clear-cutting versus selective cutting was long-standing and the argument around the size of the clear-cuts was legitimate. The logging of old-growth timber may have been in our opinion a wrong issue to argue from an ecological standpoint, but it had enormous public support. Protests impacted not only our biggest customers, such as Lowe's and Home Depot, but also their customers, who objected to the practice. Though Canfor was not directly involved in many of those battles, we saw that operations in the Interior were not confronted by the environmental movement owing to the absence there of old-growth timber.

In the Interior, we faced environmental issues, too, but less momentous ones, such as the sulphur smell from the pulp mills, which is now negligible compared with what it once was. Sulphur levels have been reduced by 98 percent since the 1970s, when you were greeted in Prince George by the stench of gases in the air. Some referred to it then as "the smell of money," and we used to joke about how the smell cleared our nostrils. It's difficult to get the sulphur compounds down to an entirely undetectable level, but the odour is now a minor nuisance rather than a problem.

We recently spent $8 million of Green Transformation Program money in Prince George to eliminate the last of the odours. The program is the Canadian government's response to the United States spending $6 billion to help pulp mills that burned "black liquor." (The burning of black liquor restores it to white liquor in a closed cycle, and in the process creates both steam and energy for use in the pulp mills.) Our federal government put up only $1 billion, and restricted the funds to environmental and energy upgrades for our industry. The awards were based pro rata on the amount of black liquor burned. In total, Canfor received 12 percent of the funds, or $122 million.

Canada's billion dollars was small in comparison to the U.S. subsidy, but by spending our billion dollars wisely, we probably have a more enduring benefit.

IN THE 1980S AND '90S, we were also under siege from European customers, who wanted pulp to be chlorine-free. Bleaching was a big issue that we had to overcome. The industry as a whole responded well to the problem of dioxins and furans (common names for the toxic chemicals found in small amounts in the environment and linked with a wide range of health effects). The main source of these toxins was the burning of municipal and medical waste, but many industrial sources were also culpable. In the pulp business, we were using chlorine to bleach our product, and until technology could measure the levels, we were unaware of its danger. Once toxins were identified in the environment, we sought to change the technology. Prior to this change and during the time it took to make the necessary improvements, we did face some difficult challenges. At Canfor, our new methods do not create the dioxin hazard that was previously caused by using elemental chlorine in our pulp mills.

Two memorable events arose on the coast around the Howe Sound shellfish closure in the 1980s because of pollution. One involved a crab fisherman who sued both Howe Sound Pulp and Paper and Western Pulp for his lost income during the fishery closure. During the proceedings he reported the revenue he had been making before the closure, and when our lawyers checked that his income tax was based on a lower number, his credibility disappeared. Although the fisherman may well have suffered financially, in court it came out that either he was not declaring his income or he was exaggerating his loss. Either way, he lost credibility and the lawsuit quickly disappeared.

The other memorable event related to constant criticism from Terry Jacks, a local pop singer and self-described environmentalist. I invited Jacks several times to visit Howe Sound or my office to talk, but he refused to come. On one occasion, he did travel to the mill by boat with the federal environment minister, Lucien Bouchard, but they did not look at the mill or talk to management. Instead, Jacks dumped garbage on our dock, addressed to me.

Jacks finally requested a meeting with me. He still refused to come to the mill or to my office, but suggested we get together at the home of my son's parents-in-law, Dr. Clem and Heather Williams, in Lions Bay. When Jacks arrived, he insisted that our hostess leave because he wanted no witnesses present. After that curious awkwardness, the two of us sat down and Jacks showed me photos of the Port Mellon mill taken when Sorg Paper had owned it before it was shut down. The images showed raw effluent flowing into the Pacific.

"Isn't that terrible?" he said.

"Yes, that's awful," I agreed.

"Aren't you going to argue with me?" he asked.

"Why would I?" I said. "What we're looking at has nothing to do with Canfor. I'm inviting you to come to the mill and see what we have done since that time. And if there's something we haven't done, I'd like a recommendation from you instead of all the lies and criticism."

"I have two possible solutions for you to stop my criticism," Jacks said. "One, you can hire me as your vice-president of the environment, or, two, you can buy my house for a million dollars." He wanted to sell his house on Howe Sound and move away.

"Get out of here," I said.

That was Terry Jacks and his reluctance to have witnesses to our discussion about Howe Sound.

A RELATED FRUSTRATION cropped up for me when David Suzuki hosted an entire television show on Howe Sound. He spent a lot of time at the mill interviewing Bill Hughes and others and he also asked to have a session with me, which I agreed to on one condition.

"I want integrity to this," I said. "I'll give you straight answers and you can ask me anything you want. But I don't want my words edited. I want you to show the entire answer and not just bits and pieces of it attached to other questions."

Suzuki seemed willing to accommodate my request, and we had a twenty-minute interview. He thanked me for our time together and I thought it went very well. When the show was aired, not one mention of our interview was made. It seemed that he didn't like any of my answers.

Most administrative players in our industry have had considerable experience with the media. In my estimation, our team at Canfor has always been direct and straightforward with the media, and for a time I nurtured those relationships myself. I enjoyed my interviews with Gary Bannerman and Bill Good on radio and with Jack Webster on television.

The only difficulty I ran into was with Rafe Mair. I was one of his early guests during the first week of his CKNW radio show. He gave me a beautiful, complimentary introduction—and then he launched into a lengthy diatribe about the forest industry. After he had finished, many minutes later, he turned to me.

"Would you agree with that?" he asked.

"Well, you covered a lot of ground, Rafe," I said. "Some of it was right and some of it wasn't—"

I was about to continue when he said thank you and dove into yet another one-sided speech.

"Rafe," I said when he was done. "I thought this was a talk show, not a Rafe Mair monologue."

Only then did he get flustered. I suppose he had just emerged from the world of politics and wanted to get his opinions about the forest industry out to his listeners. Of course he didn't need me as a guest to do that. I was never invited back.

AMIDST THE ENVIRONMENTAL pressures of the 1980s and '90s, one of our foresters travelled extensively in Europe, talking to people in the industry, to our customers and to the public. The industry opened a European office, and we had an office in Brussels devoted entirely to environmental issues. Back home, we hired Patrick Moore, one of the founders of Greenpeace, and one-time IWA president Jack Munro, to form the B.C. Forest Alliance, sponsored by the industry to address complaints about its environmental impact. There was no shortage of objections.

On both sides of the debate around clear-cuts and old-growth logging, everyone had been through the ringer, but by the turn of the last century things were looking up. The industry was paying close attention and positive changes were afoot. Of course, this did not mean that those concerns were behind us. Our sensitive relationship with the environment would remain.

I like to think that Canfor has played a leadership role in our industry and a significant one. Even in our early days at Englewood, we took a long-range view, marking every area we logged and posting signage along the roads so people driving through the valley would see exactly what we were doing. The signs indicated when the area was logged and also the date that it was replanted. We did not limit our logging to the valley bottoms as some companies did; rather than taking most of the prime timber found at lower elevations, we kept a balance of quality and size in the timber stands that remained. Consequently, when interest arose in preserving the big timber on the valley bottoms, a substantial amount was left.

In 1987, the rules dramatically changed in British Columbia: the Crown moved responsibility for reforestation to the companies logging Crown land. But since we began logging in the 1940s, we had always replanted. Much later, when Canfor operated at capacity, we planted seventy-seven million seedlings per year, which represented roughly three trees for every one that we logged. Our efforts extended far beyond replanting, and I am proud of what our foresters and logging managers accomplished in differentiating ourselves.

As the forest sector began to wake up to certain environmental issues, Canfor was already at the leading edge of the industry. Unlike other public companies, we have never had to employ security guards at our annual meetings to deal with demonstrations. Aside from minor complaints, we have had few challenges to our practices. I give management and our staff throughout the province full credit for the way they conduct their operations and activities at all levels.

KIRK MCMILLAN was vice-president, environment, and played an important role, which led to the hiring in 1989 of Michael Jordan, our director of environment, energy, and climate change policy. It was time to bring in someone of Mike's calibre to create and implement our environmental plan at the mill level, and to set up an environmental audit program that would guarantee we were living up to our word.

That same year we announced our environmental policy, put together by Canfor's environment and energy group and our environmental experts, including Mike. That policy was our commitment to exceed compliance and to communicate about our environmental performance with our shareholders and the public. Our audit program covers the mills as well as the woodlands, and I believe we were one of the first forest products companies to make that kind of commitment.

In the early 1990s, Canfor began the voluntary climate registry, which reported the industry's tracking of greenhouse gas emissions. At the same time we issued our first stand-alone environmental report, one of the first such submissions from a Western forest products company.

Our first stab at an environmental audit of our facilities involved simply looking at whether we complied with regulatory requirements. In the mid-1990s, we moved from there to examining what we needed to do to ensure we were meeting our policy commitments and compliance. In short order, by the end of the decade, we were setting up environmental management systems at our pulp mills in Prince George. We followed a process to become certified through ISO (International Organization for

Standardization), first at our pulp mills and then in our woodlands, and we established ISO-standard-based environmental management systems at all our solid-wood operations.

THE DIOXIN FURAN issue in the pulp industry had gained momentum because of the development of analytical equipment that could measure toxins in parts per billion (and it was not long before they could detect parts per quadrillion). In 1983, the U.S. Environmental Protection Agency (EPA) inadvertently detected dioxins in fish downstream of pulp and paper mills. Then, in 1988, a multi-mill study in the United States confirmed the link between dioxins and furans, and the chlorine used in the bleaching process. The information from that study was a call to action for all of us in the industry.

For the decade to follow, the B.C. ministry of environment, lands, and parks reported significant improvements in effluent, including an 83 percent decrease in AOX (adsorbable organic halide), the surrogate measure used to detect chlorine compounds in the effluent emerging from pulp mills, and efforts to make further reductions were ongoing. With our membership in the Pulp and Paper Research Institute of Canada, we would be at the forefront of implementing 100 percent chlorine dioxide substitutions at our mills to eliminate the dioxins and furans.

Historically, AOX presented an interesting challenge, which had not been without its political implications. On a Thursday evening in 1989, John Reynolds, Premier Bill Vander Zalm's minister of environment, summoned pulp company CEOs to the government office on Vancouver's waterfront. There, he shared a piece of confidential news: he would be announcing the following week that all mills had to be at "zero AOX" within two years.

Because our mills were considerably better than the industry average at the time, I became a bit of an unofficial spokesman at the meeting. I told Reynolds that we were prepared to meet the toughest known achievable standard (which he reminded us was in Scandinavia), but we could not live with the zero-AOX target for one reason: it was not technically possible.

"How can we ask people to sit on our board, knowing that we cannot possibly comply with the regulation?" I asked.

Reynolds assured us they would not enforce something that was not doable. I returned to my office and called Vander Zalm. I told him that his Cabinet had not understood the consequences of their action in approving the zero-AOX standard recommended by the minister. I asked him to please consider taking back to Cabinet some facts on the best standard in the world anywhere, which we would make available to him before their Wednesday Cabinet meeting. I did not know at the time that his deputy, David Emerson, was on the line with us and later encouraged the premier to follow my recommendation.

On the following Monday, Vander Zalm called me at home at seven o'clock in the morning. He told me that Reynolds had resigned, accusing the premier of being in the pocket of the pulp industry. The premier wanted me to know that the story was out and there would probably be a media scrum outside our office. He was right.

"Why don't you come inside and I'll get you some coffee?" I said to the media group gathered in the elevator lobby of the thirtieth floor of the Bentall Four building downtown. "We can talk about this in civil terms so you can understand the whole story."

The group accompanied me inside, where I gave them the facts.

"I don't know what the government will do, but I know what we in industry cannot do," I explained. "Mr. Reynolds is way off base. The premier was simply willing to look at realistic numbers after being misled by the minister about this new, impossible regulation."

The news covered the story for three days or so. The zero-AOX target was indeed legislated but it was soon rescinded after the intervention.

Much later, in 2001, an expert independent panel headed by John Carey of the federal National Water Research Institute reviewed the levels, the technology, and the environmental implications and reported that a zero-AOX requirement would not have any "demonstrable environmental benefit."

ANOTHER ENVIRONMENTAL IMPROVEMENT the forest sector needed to accomplish was a move away from fossil fuels to using wood residue, much of which we previously wasted. Some of these changes began in the late 1970s, when we started using planer shavings as fuel. In the process of replacing the old steam plant at the Eburne mill at the time, we installed two platforms for energy systems when in fact only one was required. Modernization had so improved operations that we seriously miscalculated the heat demand. (It was not one of our better moments.)

A priority for us and for the provincial government has been to eliminate the old conical wood-residue burners, commonly known as "beehive burners." These conspicuous structures once burned our "waste," which is now a valuable resource. No matter how well the burners operated, they always smoked on start-up and in shutting down, and concern about air quality was increasing.

In the mid-1990s, the provincial government committed to a mandatory phase-out of the burners. Of the 125 or so in the province, about 84 were "tier one" burners, located in the more populated areas and designated by the ministry of the environment as the first to go. Canfor had six or seven that we would have been happy to eliminate, but at the time we could not afford any alternatives. As a show of good will, we closed down our

Chetwynd beehive burner in 1996 and separated the bark from the white wood. We sent the wood to Mackenzie Pulp as feedstock for their sawdust digester, and the bark went to a nearby "tier two" burner owned by West Fraser. Ironically, in shutting our burner down, we were paying a competitor to handle our waste.

It seemed that we would have just rid ourselves of the last of Canfor's burners when we would make an acquisition of operations such as Northwood Pulp and Timber in 1999 that had their own sawmill burners. New permanent solutions had to be found to replace them. One was to install systems at the sawmills to generate biomass energy rather than buying fossil fuels, and likewise to increase the use of hog fuel at pulp mill cogeneration (cogen) facilities. By the end of 2012, all our sawmills will have biomass-fired heat energy systems. In July 2011, Canfor achieved the milestone of shutting down its last operating beehive burner at our Plateau mill near Vanderhoof.

THE FOREST INDUSTRY has come a long way in being far more sustainable and more cost-effective than it once was. Further opportunities have arisen in the form of carbon offsets. In 2003, Alberta passed greenhouse gas legislation that' required large emitters to reduce their emissions. A company could grow, but it had to reduce its greenhouse gas intensity. Companies such as Canfor that had made reductions could sell carbon offsets into the Alberta carbon offset market.

In 2001, Canfor had negotiated an agreement with Canadian Gas and Electric, a renewable energy company. In return for supplying biomass, we had an agreement to purchase renewable electricity for our Alberta sawmill and to purchase steam for heat to dry our lumber at the Grande Prairie mill. That way, we moved from buying coal-generated electricity to buying renewable electricity made from wood residues that we once treated as waste. The agreement allowed us to sell about 30,000 tons a year of greenhouse-offset credits. We shut down the silo burner at our Grande Prairie operation and became the supplier of biomass for a 25-megawatt cogen facility, which we have since acquired. We now operate it as Canfor Green Energy, Grande Prairie, and we took over their staff of twenty-four.

We have a similar situation in British Columbia, where the Crown corporation Pacific Carbon Trust buys and sells carbon offsets according to stringent requirements.

ONE OF OUR CONSTANT CONCERNS and a topical issue in recent years is the basis on which governments make new regulations. Instead of setting targets to be achieved at a particular point in the future, they are set from an arbitrary point in time. The problem is straightforward: when the government picks an arbitrary starting date, it penalizes companies that have acted ahead of the legislation and it offers benefits to companies that have done nothing.

Governments should set standards that they want met by certain dates in the future, leaving the companies to decide how to meet those targets responsibly. That way, if a company cannot meet the standards, it cannot operate.

A concrete example of this problem is the Kyoto Protocol. When Canada originally signed on, it was an undertaking to reduce greenhouse emissions by a percentage from a given date to another given date. It was not an objective to achieve a standard, but rather a percentage reduction. Consequently, a company that had not spent any money on reducing emissions had a big menu left from which they could choose to invest or reduce by the quantified objective. In contrast, a company like ours that had already spent a great deal of money prior to Kyoto may have already achieved a standard that was more than the reduction required under Kyoto. For those already at the higher standard, it would have been enormously expensive and not that productive to reduce it further. If we are concerned about the environment, this is an inefficient and unfair way to go about it. It may be acceptable globally to take that position, but individual situations should be evaluated on a case-by-case basis.

A PET PEEVE OF MINE is the way national and provincial parks are created and maintained in Canada. Whether in Victoria or in Ottawa, they designate the park area, draw a boundary on the map, and that's the end of it; everything within the boundary is "preserved" as is.

That approach represents poor management and waste. In most European parks, even in highly populated areas, they constantly rotate the locations of their picnic areas, benches, and walking trails. Over time, they log and reforest all the timber in the park, which keeps the forests beautiful and thrifty. Germany's Black Forest is a good example.

In contrast, here we lock up the parks and throw away the key—a nonstrategy that is economically and environmentally unsound. An exception to the standard Canadian practice is Wood Buffalo National Park, situated in northern Alberta, where the federal government encourages logging and does not allow replanting. Their thinking is entirely faulty; sitting in Ottawa, they assume that by logging we create more rangeland for the buffalo. The reality is that buffalo don't populate the wooded areas, nor would they likely migrate to the steeper terrain in the valleys where the logging takes place.

At one point, we operated a mill at High Level, making lumber out of timber that came to us from the Alberta forestlands—and also from Wood Buffalo National Park. Although we had always reforested, Ottawa's "room to roam" argument prohibited us from doing so. I found their reasoning so ridiculous that I flew back to try and convince them of another point of view.

"Gentlemen," I said. "You realize we are talking about a very large park where buffalo have never roamed within twenty-five kilometres of our operations. The buffalo are out on the plains and we are down in the valleys. We always replant and we will be criticized if you do not allow us to do so."

In the end, there was no changing their minds, and it came as no surprise when the *Edmonton Journal* made a story out of the fact that we were not replacing the trees cut in the park. I might have predicted that the journalists would not give me equal time to inform them that we replant every hectare we cut (everywhere of course except in Wood Buffalo National Park, where we were ordered not to by the federal government).

The Liberals, the Opposition in Alberta at the time, kept attacking Canfor in the Legislative Assembly, and the media were loath to interrupt such a good story with the truth. We were badly treated on that issue and ultimately had no other choice but to stop logging in the park. That meant we could no longer run the High Level operation at capacity, so eventually we sold the mill.

The pine beetle infestation is another example of government's control over parks. The catastrophe will affect our forests and all the communities in and around the area for most of the next century. In early 2010, it was estimated that about a billion pine trees were dead and decaying in British Columbia because of the infestation. To this day I am sure that environmentalists would have sided with us in our wish to log Tweedsmuir Park to prevent further damage. But now the whole Interior has been impacted, which is tragic. Beyond the natural disaster that it is, the damage amounts to billions of dollars of current and future lost revenue to the province, to employment opportunity, and to the industry.

We are still harvesting the wood that the beetle has attacked, but much of it has been downgraded, and of course jobs have been lost. Fortunately, we can still use the fibre for pulp. Because the wood has dried out, we had to install special air treatment systems in the sawmills to deal with the dust. The pellet business, including our joint-venture operation in Houston, British Columbia, is growing in another effort to use the dead and dying pine (in addition to other sawmill residuals), and that will go on for some time.

Until we solve the pine beetle issue through logging and reforestation there will have to be a significant decrease in the annual allowable cut. Eventually, we will overcome the problem, but it will take a very long time.

IN THE 1990S, Canfor spent a lot of time and energy on improving our practices, our environmental performance, and our sustainability in utilizing the whole resource.

Development of the Interior forest industry started later than it did on the coast, and the Forest Service data there was based on an assumption for the whole Interior. In 2001, Canfor formed a company called Genus Resource Management Technologies Inc., to study what happens on that land in every respect. Genus allowed us to determine the mean annual increment of every area (in cubic metres per hectare per year), and it was well above the Forest Service number of 2.6, which the Forest Service applied for all the Interior. We knew that even our worst sites were higher, and the better ones by a significant factor. The result of all this is that the Interior, unlike the coast, was being undercut.

In the twenty-first century we have been forced to concentrate on survival in troubled economic times—and on the need to get ourselves fiscally sound—but we still continue to make environmental improvements. Our woodlands are Sustainable Forest

Management certified by the Canadian Standards Association, and we meet some of the world's toughest standards.

Some of our customers would like to see us certified by specific for-profit companies, but environmental certification works only if regulations are addressed to local conditions, which sometimes they were not. Years ago, Home Depot, a major customer in the United States, sent Weyerhaeuser and us—two out of three of their major suppliers—a letter saying that we had to be certified by a certain company. Their concern was about the sourcing of our wood, as customers wanted to know where the products originated. In response to their request, our chief forester checked out that certification outfit and found that it had approved a company that we knew to have marginal logging practices. We concluded that their printed standards were different from ours, their methods were not applicable to B.C. terrain, and a number of other reputable certifiers better suited our business. Canfor and Weyerhaeuser told Home Depot that, if we had to be certified by that company, we would stop being their supplier. We also suggested that they send their people up to see our operations. We are still supplying them and we are now fully certified, by a different, reputable company.

Canfor's responsibility to the environment is something we have come to better understand. We also take very seriously our responsibility to our employees. Safety was always a priority for my father, and it was and remains so for me. Our employees have always been proud and appreciative of our position as industry leader in safety and I am thankful that we have had very few fatalities. Between the 1950s and the 1970s, if someone worked for Canfor, they had five times as good a chance to get home to their loved ones without injury compared with the industry average. Since then, we have continued to improve, and the industry fortunately has smartened up, rendering us only twice as good as the industry average. Much of the reduction in injuries is because of the significantly curtailed coastal logging industry, which was the most hazardous work. In the Interior, new mechanized logging techniques led to fewer logging accidents. Similarly, accidents have diminished in the modernized mills, where hand and back injuries are now the most frequent occurrences.

Wherever you go throughout our company, as you enter a mill, you will see a safety board showing the number of days since the last time-lost accident. I remember a time at the Eburne mill when we were within a few shifts of reaching a million man-hours without a lost-time accident. All our employees and management were keenly aware of that pending record. But then a small cleanup man put a wheelbarrow in front of him as he walked down an incline, fearing it might run him over otherwise. The poor man injured his back just hours before achieving the record. Everyone in the mill was furious with him even though his intentions were good.

We have made progress, but because of the nature of the work, our industry is still riskier than some other sectors. But when we say safety comes first, we mean it. Our management and board committees regularly monitor and oversee the safety of our business. Part of the board committee's mandate is working through human resources to meet with our safety leaders and organize training sessions on safety. Another of the committee's tasks involves reviewing every aspect of our operations as they relate to the work environment—every detail about what has gone right or wrong. We track every major and minor noncompliant incident at all our facilities and we track what is done to address problems. We also discuss trend information and what is happening on the regulatory front, and we keep detailed statistics to ensure that we are always improving.

Every monthly divisional financial report covers the previous month's safety statistics before going on to report financial results. We also recognize excellence through annual awards, and we make a specific point of not giving awards based on improvement over the previous year. If a business unit had a bad year, we don't want to reward that unit for coming back to where it should have been in the first place.

AFTER DECADES OF GROWTH, a degree of prosperity and one hell of a lot of change, in 2004, suddenly Canfor was alone on the coast. In 2010, we also left the coast after selling Howe Sound. It's difficult to describe the industry's mood after all was said and done. One immediate effect I noted was the loss of many head offices, which had collectively offered employment, participated actively in the Vancouver community and made significant donations to local charities. All of these advantages, which I see as very important to any large community, disappeared in a big way. Of course, since then other head offices from mining and information technology have sprung up and are slowly filling the gap.

As I write, the coast is probably at its lowest point in the evolution of the forest industry. I expect, with the enormous growth of the Chinese and Pacific Rim markets, the region will make a recovery and harvest second-growth timber, which has replaced much of the old growth from previous logging.

14

Don't Do it, Jack
Union Negotiations

LABOUR ISSUES HAVE always been a great interest of mine. Living in the bunkhouses at the camps and working at the mills as a young man taught me a great deal. The fact that I worked shoulder to shoulder alongside hourly workers in different parts of the industry gave me a feel for issues that were important to them. These issues were seldom consistent with what may have been the priorities of the union leadership. I also learned early on that nothing resolves labour matters faster than open communication.

Years ago, a work stoppage paralyzed our operation at Stave Lake Cedar and nobody appeared to understand what was going on. I jumped into my car and drove up to Dewdney to find out.

"My name is Peter Bentley," I said, introducing myself to our employees on the picket line. "I'm not here to give you a bad time, but we have a strange situation here. You guys are on strike and we don't know why you're striking. Can someone please explain it to me?"

The discussion turned into a long dialogue, and then we parted amicably with full agreement that the situation could easily be resolved. The picket line dismantled, they all went home and came back to work the next day.

I was never more involved with our crews at a local mill level than I was at Eburne, Local 1-217 of the IWA. My father and I always had a good relationship with Lloyd Whalen, who was the president of the local for a long time. But Lloyd was succeeded by Syd Thompson, who was a different kind of person altogether—a real character, whose position appeared to lie somewhere to the left of the IWA. His style was belligerent, and his arguments were always delivered in a thundering, gravelly voice.

Not long after Syd took over, reports began turning up about the union's plant chair at Eburne. Apparently he had developed the habit of slipping across the back fence, downing a few drinks at the Fraser Arms pub, and returning to work on the sleepy side. This worker was what we called a "tallyman," whose job it was to count the lumber as it moved along the chain. But in his inebriated state, he couldn't count anything. This pattern had been documented a number of times, so it was an open-and-shut case: the foreman fired him for sleeping on the job.

I first encountered Syd Thompson when this matter reached the final stage of grievance between the union and the company. I remember the meeting well. Syd walked in with his people, and he pounded the table as he delivered a loud, lengthy speech for a full forty minutes on what an outstanding individual the tallyman was, and how we could not fire him because he was so valuable to both the union and the company. How stupid could we be, he asked, in letting someone like that go? He went on and on, furthering his argument with supposed medical information about this fellow's long-standing eye problems. He was not really sleeping on the job, Syd insisted, he was simply resting his eyes.

I had told my guys to stay silent until Syd finished. When he finally paused, it was my turn.

"I owe you an apology, Syd," I said.

"Thank you," he replied. "So he is reinstated?"

"No," I said. "We're changing our reason for dismissal. Instead of sleeping on the job, it's now resting his eyes."

I got up, said the meeting was over, and walked out.

Interactions with Local 1-217 grew strained with Syd's combative approach. The plant committee began to work against rather than with the company, which regrettably was noticeable even on the safety committee.

John Auersperg, the Eburne manager, called me one day at head office. "We have a sit-in," he announced.

"What do you mean a sit-in?" I asked.

"Everyone has walked off the job," he said. "They're all in the lunchroom and they're refusing to go back to work. What should I do?"

"Don't do anything," I said. "I'm on my way."

On arriving at the site, I asked John to call the engineer and tell him to blow the whistle in exactly six minutes' time.

I then went to the lunchroom.

"Okay, guys, can I have your attention?" I said, standing on a table. "I want you to know this isn't acceptable. The whistle is going to sound in about three minutes, and I want you to know that anyone not on their job when the whistle blows is fired."

I walked out and slammed the door so hard that the glass panel shattered in its frame. Then I just about got run over by men running back to their jobs.

WE FORGED a working relationship over the years with the Canadian branch of the IWA, but our dealings with the pulp side of things were different. Two unions represented pulp and paper workers: the PPWC (Pulp, Paper, and Woodworkers of Canada) and the CPU (Canadian Paperworkers Union), and they varied markedly in their respective leadership style and philosophy. As vice-president of the CPU for many years, Art Gruntman was primarily interested in retirement benefits. Stan Shewaga of the PPWC, on the other hand, was a more radical leader who showed little respect for companies or government. At times we had our hands full.

After one of many settlements was reached in British Columbia, the IWA, which represented our employees in Grande Prairie, asked for the same settlement. At the time, the Alberta industry wage scale was below that of British Columbia, and we were offering them the same improvements negotiated in British Columbia, but on the lower base. The IWA was quick to reject our offer.

I visited then president of the IWA, Jack Moore, and showed him the monthly statement of our Alberta operations, indicating a very marginal return, to explain why we were not prepared to undermine the rest of the Alberta industry by granting his request for a higher wage rate.

"Don't do it, Jack," I said. "If you insist on your position, this will mean a strike and we will not give in."

The union struck. Ten months later, the men wanted to get back to work and the IWA was decertified in Grande Prairie. We then made the deal directly with our employees that we had offered Jack in the first place. With that chapter behind us, I believe we gained credibility with the union.

B.C. PREMIER Dave Barrett's government was suffering in the latter months of 1975 due in part to a pulp strike—one of four significant strikes in that era—that would not settle. The strike had not only shut down the pulp industry, but the sawmills had nowhere to send their waste and they were halting operations due to chip stockpiles in their yards. As chair of the Pulp Bureau, which handled labour negotiations for the pulp industry, I was involved in the tempestuous negotiations.

Barrett summoned Don Lanskail, then head of our labour negotiation agencies (FIR and the Pulp Bureau) and me to a meeting in Victoria with his minister of forests, the minister of labour and the two pulp unions, which had been on strike for a long while. I'll never forget how PPWC head Stan Shewaga spoke in uncensored terms about Barrett's government being every bit as bad as the Socreds.

"I'm not putting up with this," he barked, and stormed out. After a few moments, I turned to the premier and explained my perspective: "We've been up against this type of bargaining style since day one. We're as anxious as the government is to settle the strike, but it's impossible to negotiate with a guy like that. We can't even formulate an agenda because the conversation never moves beyond aggressive demands."

Barrett had seen enough. He moved forward with a back to work order, which made him very unpopular. To make matters worse for him, he came under attack for his government's zealous approach and declining revenues. He had been in office for three years when he called a snap election.

Around this time, Bill Daniel, in his first year as president of Shell Canada, invited me to join his board. I felt honoured and quickly accepted the invitation. As Bill did not know the B.C. business community, I arranged a dinner party at the Hotel Vancouver to introduce him to the province's business leaders.

As it turned out, we had booked the event for the same night as the B.C. election. Bill Daniel was unable to reschedule and most everyone else was committed to come, so it would have been difficult to change the timing. To stay with our plan, however, meant addressing two challenges. One, on election nights, the media always called heads of companies to get their opinion and reaction after the polls closed; we knew that it would not be wise for us to be seen in one place as if we were celebrating or otherwise. After getting consent from each person on our guest list, I called the media. The function we were holding had nothing to do with the election, I explained, but the key industry people attending had agreed to be interviewed as long as no reference was made to the dinner.

The second matter had to do with a law that prohibited the sale of liquor on election days. We were lucky that Victor Bert, the hotel's manager, came up with a solution. The royal suite was not booked the day before, so he offered to rent it to us for a dollar and stock it early with the drinks we planned to serve.

The plan worked well and we held the reception and dinner without event. We were able to serve drinks and the media respected my request not to mention the large corporate gathering. The election results poured in, we said good-bye to Dave Barrett and welcomed Bill Bennett as our new Social Credit premier.

MY FATHER was chair of FIR long before I was. Like me, he had to sit at the bargaining table before we handed that responsibility to our industrial-relations experts.

In earlier days, my father and I both found negotiations usually wound up as a forty-eight- or seventy-two-hour marathon. One always felt exhilarated when the deal was done, even if it was a lousy deal. It was not from Dad that I learned the art of negotiations, because I never saw him at the bargaining table—just as my people did not see me there. But like my father, my ability to talk the matters through came somewhat naturally. We were both analytical in getting to the meat of the situation. We saw the picture for what it was and not how it was camouflaged.

Through my years spent negotiating, I learned several things: I had to know our objectives going in; it was best to be straightforward and open; and it was important to stay firm on matters I was not willing to negotiate.

Another example of staying firm involved strikes at two shingle mills in the mid-seventies—Canfor's Huntting-Merritt Division and MacMillan Bloedel's Red Band Mill. The strike carried on for a long time and we tried our best to prevent closing our operation. Management kept in close touch with our employees who wanted to return to work. We also kept minister of labour Bill King informed, though his hands were tied. He made it clear that because the IWA had called the strike, it would be difficult for him to go against the union's wish even if our employees were getting impatient. No solution seemed to be in sight, though a lot was at stake. Between Canfor's Stave Lake and Huntting-Merritt operations, we were the world's largest producer of red-cedar shingles and shakes. The strike should never have been called and it was never resolved. As a result, the Red Band Mill and Huntting-Merritt were both closed, and many people were without jobs.

Canadian Forest Products once operated its own graphic design and print shop at the Plywood and Hardboard Division. A handful of salaried employees worked in this shop, which was located in a building at the centre of the plant. They created all manner of materials, including brochures about the different products we made, company stationery, business cards, and the like.

The fellow who ran the shop had an employee who did not work very well. But instead of terminating him under normal procedures, the manager kept him on for a few years without offering him a salary increase. The employee grew impatient and persuaded his colleagues to join him in signing up with the union that represented their trade.

When I got wind of this, I went to speak to the group about how their decision would affect the rest of the operation.

"We're not anti-union, and if you wish to be in a union rather than salaried, that's fine," I said. "But because you enter the plant premises along with everyone else and work in the centre of our operation, I have to ask you to join the IWA. We cannot put the whole division at risk in the event that you join another union and decide to legally strike and picket the whole plant. If you choose not to join the IWA, then you leave me no choice but to close the operation."

Well, they ignored my request and they joined the other union. In turn, I closed the department and laid them all off the next day. We never ran the department again, opting instead to contract out that kind of work.

WHEN I WAS chair of Seaboard and director of Prince George Pulp and Paper, we were shipping a lot of pulp to the Reed Group, along with nearly all of our paper, replacing the paper they had once manufactured in the United Kingdom. To receive the shipments, we had leased a wharf at Tilbury (one of Britain's three major ports) as a joint venture between PGPP for pulp and Seaboard for lumber.

The union decided to strike at our pier. All the other wharves at the port were fully operational, but no work was happening on ours, though office employees were allowed to cross the picket line. At the time I happened to be in England reporting to the Reed Group about operations in Prince George. I suggested to Ed Annon, the manager of Seaboard U.K., that we head out to Tilbury to see what the hell was happening.

We made the short journey to the pier and, as we approached, I could see the picket line. Ed seemed anxious and asked me to lock my door. I knew he had no labour experience, having grown up on the sales side of the organization.

TOP From left: my Uncle John and Aunt Evi with my mother and father, enjoying a twenty-five-year service banquet in the 1960s.

ABOVE John Liersch, one of my mentors, and I sharing an amusing moment at one of the twenty-five-year service banquets.

ABOVE From left: John Prentice, me, Ray Williston, an unidentified man, "Wacky" Bennett, and Philip Walker, president of the Reed Corporation, at the official opening of Prince George Pulp and Paper, 1966.

FACING PAGE Tom Wright, CFP's chief forester, chatting with a high rigger.

TOP Shingle mills were relatively hazardous work environments. Achieving one thousand accident-free days at one of them was quite remarkable.

ABOVE CFP replaced all steam locomotives, like this one, with diesel electric locomotives. CFP was the first B.C. company to use diesel electrics for its railway-logging operation.

FACING PAGE, TOP My father with Pierre Trudeau, early in his tenure as prime minister, on an unannounced visit to the Eburne sawmill on his way to the airport.

FACING PAGE, BOTTOM My father was inducted, along with Ed Bovey (left), into the Canadian Business Hall of Fame in 1982.

FACING PAGE A spar tree, used to yard logs into a central point and then load them onto logging trucks.

ABOVE Aerial view of Howe Sound Pulp and Paper before its expansion when Oji Paper joined us.

TOP Three university chancellors were on the Canfor board at the same time. From left: Eric Newell of the University of Alberta, Brandt Louie of Simon Fraser University, and me, from the University of Northern British Columbia.

ABOVE Sheila's and my joint eightieth birthday, attended by all our five children, their spouses, and fourteen of our fifteen grandchildren (with the fifteenth inserted), in Palm Springs, April 2010.

"No," I replied. "I'm going out to talk to them."

"You can't do that," he said, looking even more nervous.

I got out of the car, walked up to the line, and introduced myself.

"I'm a Canadian who's involved in both Seaboard and Prince George Pulp and Paper, the sources of all the products you handle here," I explained. "I don't know if you realize this, but a Swedish company owns an identical terminal right next door. I see that their staff are all working and I can guarantee that's where our customers will go to get the goods if we don't provide them. Now tell me, what's your problem?"

At that point, some of the men began to argue among themselves as to the nature of their complaint.

"Look, guys," I said. "I don't want you to fight over this. I'm just trying to understand what's going on. But I think there's a high risk that we'll have to close permanently if we can't use this facility constructively. The Port of London isn't on strike; it's just this pier, and that makes it impossible for us to justify doing business. I'm going in to talk to the office workers now, so when you open the gates for me, I am inviting you to come in, too. I'm sure we can give you some work, because there's work to be done."

They opened the gates and the strike at the terminal was over. Again, I was reminded that, if you can have open dialogue and good communication, most of these situations can be solved.

"MASTER CONTRACT NEGOTIATIONS" were standard practice between industry and woodworkers through FIR, and between industry and pulp unions through the Pulp Bureau. FIR bargained for all coastal employers in the logging and wood-product sectors with a capable staff of negotiators and researchers. The organization comprised an executive committee made up of CEOs of both large and small companies, and a caucus of industrial relations experts from the industry. A parallel structure existed at the Pulp Bureau, a provincial body for all the pulp mills in the province. Similar regional organizations provided support in the B.C. Interior. I was industry chair more than once on both the lumber and the pulp side.

I worked closely with Keith Bennett, former president of FIR, and the spokesperson for the wood-products side of the organization. It was there that I also got acquainted with Don Lanskail, who oversaw both FIR and the Pulp Bureau until he went to the Council of Forest Industries (COFI). I held the professionals at FIR in high regard and greatly respected the industrial relations team. Keith Bennett's equivalent on the pulp side was Eric Mittendorfer, who excelled at strategizing and negotiations.

Through FIR I got to know Jack Moore's successor, Jack Munro, as head of IWA-Canada. He was an excellent negotiator, a likeable guy, and a decent person. In my first year as chair with FIR, Keith Bennett and I met with Jack Munro and Syd Thompson to talk about how we might improve the negotiating process. We shared a variety of ideas. One way I felt we could make progress was to listen to each other without interrupting. We all agreed.

The next day we were back at the negotiating table—a rather narrow one, as I remember. Our team sat on one side and the IWA group on the other, with Jack opposite Keith and Syd facing me. Jack spoke first and talked for quite a while, covering a lot of ground. Then it was Keith's turn. He had barely started when Syd interrupted.

"Hold it," I said, putting my hand on Keith's shoulder. "We had a deal, Jack, and we honoured it. You talked for almost half an hour without one interruption. I don't think Keith will be very long, but I would like to see you give us the same respect."

Jack agreed and Keith continued. But once again, he had managed about four sentences when Syd spoke up. I have to admit,

I lost it. I reached across, grabbed Syd, and pulled him across the table.

"One more peep out of you and I'll hammer you through the goddamn table," I said.

It was a little surprising when all the union guys clapped. The incident marked a turning point in the negotiations. I guess I cleared the air.

That same year, our executive committee sat at the FIR bargaining table across from the union negotiating committee—just as we had done with Jack and Syd. Sitting behind us but not at the table was our caucus, and sitting behind the union negotiating committee were numerous union observers. The meetings were time-consuming and frustrating. With all the posturing, the speeches, and the showboating, it took forever to get to the issues, let alone begin to solve them. Often, the delays just drove us further apart. It was an agonizingly slow process and in my mind a huge waste of time.

Before the next set of negotiations in my second year as FIR chair I changed the format so members of the caucus would sit at the table, and the executive would be briefed by them separately. From there we decided which recommendations and positions the industry should take.

Pulp workers struck again in the 1990s during the NDP regime headed by Premier Michael Harcourt. Little progress was being made when Don Lanskail, then the head of the Pulp Bureau and FIR, and I as chair of the Pulp Bureau, were asked to come and meet with the premier, his minister of labour, Moe Sihota, and his minister of finance and corporate relations, Glen Clark.

The premier began the meeting by expressing his displeasure at the strike and what it was doing to the B.C. economy. Of course, we were in total agreement and told him that we had no desire to be on strike.

The premier asked Sihota to outline a deal for us that he thought the unions would accept. They wanted to know whether we could live with it. I listened carefully and needed little time to reflect before responding to Moe's surprisingly one-sided plan.

"The deal you describe is so unacceptable, that I would not even convene a meeting of our executive to discuss it," I said. "It has no chance of success."

Clark spoke up at that point. "May I give him the bottom line?" he asked the premier, who nodded.

Clark then outlined a far more realistic deal that I agreed had considerable merit, but I was unwilling to plateau the industry up to that level until they could get the union to agree. Once I was assured that they were on side, I would not only call a meeting with the executive, I would also recommend acceptance of the deal.

Before long, Premier Harcourt and his ministers were able to deliver their commitment. The industry in turn accepted the deal and the strike was over.

WHEN WE MOVED into the Prince George area, Canfor was a member of the Council on Northern Interior Forest Employment Relations (CONIFER), a northern Interior equivalent of FIR. As a member of the CONIFER executive, I once attended an emergency meeting to discuss a possible settlement to a contract negotiation. The executive discussed the deal, agreed to a package, and I returned to Vancouver that afternoon.

Driving back to the office from the airport, I heard on the news that a settlement had been reached, but to my surprise, it was at six cents an hour more than what the executive had agreed to earlier that day. What's more, the deal failed to get the operating flexibility (for shift schedules and other matters) on which we had also agreed.

I phoned the president of CONIFER and told him that Canfor was resigning from his organization. Soon after, Northwood also withdrew. Ironically, when we had been invited to join the organization they thought that the "Big Companies" (Northwood and ourselves) would give away the store, when in fact the opposite was true.

I called Jack Munro to advise him that we were now negotiating on our own together with Northwood, and that we were not prepared to sign the CONIFER deal. I cautioned him that, if he did sign it, he would find himself in a difficult situation because Northwood and Canfor had more employees than all the independent companies represented by CONIFER, and we were not prepared to give him that deal. This time we did not incur a strike, and we settled with the union on terms that were slightly better than the CONIFER package.

On another occasion, we had concluded one of our bargaining sessions when Jack Munro asked if Keith Bennett and I could meet with him and Syd Thompson. In a private room, Jack told us that he was having an internal problem with one of the locals but that a deal on the basic terms we discussed was acceptable. He wanted our okay for him to call the minister of labour, Bill King, and ask the minister to call us to Victoria. That way it would appear that the government had requested the meeting and the minister could take credit for making a deal. We were sympathetic to the request and agreed that, if the minister called us, we would immediately go to Victoria.

Something must have gone wrong in the communication. We were called to Victoria, but it seemed that the minister had not been informed that we already had approved an agreement with the IWA. When we arrived at the Legislative Building, the union was put in one room and, as we were a small group, we were put in the minister's office. While we were waiting for him to arrive, Tom Rust from Crown Zellerbach and a member of the FIR executive put on the minister's railroad hat and sat with his feet up on the minister's desk. The minister walked in and got a kick out of that, but he went on to give us quite a lecture on getting on with the process. I gathered he must have done the same with the union executive, so it took a little time to sort everything out and get us back on the same wavelength. We eventually succeeded, enabling the government to announce that a settlement had been reached.

Shortly after that, recent problems in the forest sector gave us cause to revisit a model we had developed decades earlier when we were faced with closing the Harrison Mills Logging Division. We had been managing our own logging there, and the operation proved costly. The situation was getting worse when we met with the crew to give them bad news.

"With the modest volumes we're logging here each year," we explained, "we're planning to put the logging out to bid by con-tractors—who will do a more efficient job."

The crew thought about this for a while, then came back to us with the assurance that they could do better than they had been and better than a contractor would. In short order, the Harrison loggers reduced their rates and significantly increased their pro-ductivity. In return, we agreed to a profit-sharing agreement that would not only allow them to get back what they had given up, but to do even better. The plan worked beautifully. We realized that together we had found a new way to make our employees happier and stop us from losing money.

This model was put to the test in 2010 when both the market and the pine beetle had led to the closure of several Interior mills on what we had to call an "indefinite basis." The closures under-standably upset many people.

Our first move was to go to the union, then to the employees and to the civic groups in each community, and finally to the provincial government. With each of these parties, we laid out a list of what needed to happen for us to consider reopening the mills. The feedback we received was quick: the communities wanted their people back at work and would help by offering tax incentives. The employees themselves were eager to be back at work and managed to overcome initial resistance from the unions. They forged a deal comparable to what we had achieved at Harrison Mills. In this case, they gave up 18 percent to 26 percent of their cost in benefits and direct wages and, in return, they would share in profits. The government agreed to the arrangement and helped by allowing us to acquire timber sales that made it viable for the mill to operate. We made a similar arrangement at Chetwynd with the government, the community, and the union.

The arrangement worked, and morale continues to be high among employees who are now more supportive of the company. The two local union presidents who helped us put together the deals took an active and ongoing interest and asked if they could join our board on a tour to inspect the mills. Our relations with them are excellent.

A small but telling example of renewed enthusiasm and cooperation came up at the Mackenzie operation, where our foreman hands out pay cheques twice a month. Instead of mailing the cheques, he distributes them directly to the employees, which gives him an opportunity to thank them and ask after their families. After the profit-sharing agreement was signed, the employees came to us and suggested that the cheques be given out without the envelopes they were always in. They felt that would save money. We have all benefited from this new kind of relationship, and I believe it's the way of the future.

In the case of Quesnel, we were able to resurrect operations through a package deal to sell the whole of the mill's output to one customer in China. At the other mills, however, we needed to be more creative.

In contrast, we regrettably had no choice but to close our Clear Lake operation, a nonunion mill, in 2010. The decision resulted from a combination of the diminished annual allowable cut because of the pine beetle and a weak market for studs, which was all the mill produced. They were a wonderful group of employees, and we hope that all those who want to continue working have found or will be able to get jobs at the other Canfor operations in and around Prince George.

THE WHOLE INDUSTRIAL relations scene has shifted dramatically with two major adjustments. One, we now bargain alone as a company rather than on an industry-wide basis. And two, we have moved away from annual negotiations and now tend to make multi-year contracts. Those major changes are constructive both for the employees and for the industry.

It was always my objective to improve our labour relations. In my view, nobody has ever won a strike. In fact, when a strike occurs, everybody loses. The men and women lose wages and, although after some time they might get pennies more, it's likely that the increase never makes up for what they lost. In the eyes of the customer, the company loses credibility with regular labour disruptions, and strikes always interfere with selling a product. And finally, the public is inconvenienced during a strike by the loss of revenue and the displacement of people.

The difficult times our industry has endured in the past may explain why it has been so long since the last serious strike. I hope not. I prefer to think that both sides have matured with the new realization that negotiating settlements is the best way to go.

15

Good Governance
Leadership, New Acquisitions, and Crisis

ANFOR WAS BOUND to succeed, thanks to the early influence of my father and uncle, the many individuals who headed up our divisions, their capable managers, and hundreds of outstanding employees.

From a personal perspective, I consider myself blessed to have had four significant mentors who influenced my career. The earliest of these was one of my first employers, John Hecht, of Bridge Lumber. John was a tough taskmaster who ran an efficient mill and was meticulous in details. His operation was unusual because instead of cutting its own supply of logs, customers paid to convert their logs into lumber and chips. Hecht had to be astutely competitive to get that business. I sat in on all the foremen's meetings and his negotiations with some of his customers. By working alongside him in his two-room office, I learned a great deal at an opportune time in my career.

After Bridge Lumber was sold to Crown Zellerbach, Hecht became the Austrian consul general in Vancouver and developed close ties with both the Austrian government and the provincial Social Credit government. I shall always be grateful for what I learned from John and his wife, Lotte.

John Liersch was a later mentor who had a powerful influence on my career. Above all, John taught me to never lose sight of the big picture and he showed me how to be thorough. As we began to work together in 1961, I saw how he gave detailed directions when asking people to take on a task and how he never failed to follow up to ensure the job was done. It was not that he taught me in the conventional way. Rather, I observed him in action and absorbed the high standards he demanded of the work that flowed back to him. He did not tolerate fools lightly.

My father and my uncle were my principal business mentors and they taught me well. Their genuine appreciation for our employees and their complete integrity in all our dealings were enduring lessons that have guided me throughout my working life. Over many years, I watched both men seeking good solutions for our company and for others. Whether they were dealing with a supplier, a customer, or a takeover, they aimed for a win-win result. Long after their retirement, my dad and my uncle kept offices at Canfor where they were always most welcome. I loved it when they came for mill visits, often stopping to talk to people about their work and asking after their families.

My dad was my central role model, and for as long as I can remember, I tried to earn his respect by working hard. It was not enough for me as a teenager at the Eburne mill to load lumber into a railcar with another worker and take all day doing it. I always tried to have it finished before other crews completed loading their cars.

One of my father's biggest business challenges was encouraging more cooperation within the industry. He headed up Forest Industrial Relations (FIR), as I did for a time, and he played an important role in the international pulp field by getting to know the major European papermakers. By law, Americans cannot participate in price discussions, but it was and remains legal in Canada to collaborate on the export pricing of commodities. With everyone's economic interests in mind, my dad initiated an effort to get the Canadians and Scandinavians to curtail their production proportionately to try to stabilize prices. This pleased everyone because if the price of paper dropped significantly when pulp was cheap, it was very difficult to bring it back up.

The best compliment I ever received from my father after I took over the company had to do with my continuing the work he started in Scandinavia. At one point, I had to take action on behalf of the Canadian industry when we found that two Swedish companies were cheating. I notified the Scandinavians of the problem. I told them that unless they could police that situation, the game was over. When our efforts to be diplomatic failed, I met with the group, along with the cheaters, at the table. I told them how proud I was of what my father had started, and I hated to be the one to finish it—but if we did not have concrete evidence that these two companies were in line, then our cooperation would cease. My father was pleased with the lead I had taken.

Dad was active to his last day. He played a few holes of golf at Marine Drive on a Saturday morning in 1986, played bridge with his buddies in the afternoon, and watched *Hockey Night in Canada* after dinner at home. He didn't feel well during the night and was taken by ambulance to the hospital, where they determined he had a severe heart attack and placed him in intensive care. When I went to see him on Sunday morning, he was not feeling too swift, but he remained of very sound mind. I told him the doctor was optimistic about him making a full recovery—if he behaved himself. I forget his exact words, but he told me that he really didn't care to live any longer and he had only one request of me: to make sure that my mother would remain in her house as long as she lived. I assured him I would see to that and, after a few minutes, he said, "Beat it." He died that evening. Regrettably, John Prentice died in February of the following year.

WE WERE SADDENED by the passing of our founders, but their legacy was on a firm footing. Canfor had gone public in 1983 after we had become a concern to our bankers and when we were unable to get significant additional timber rights in British Columbia because we were a private company. The combination of those two factors led us to the decision to do an initial public offering, which resolved both problems. In 1985, I became chair and CEO.

A difficult situation arose for me later in the 1980s with Ron Longstaffe, a bright lawyer, Canfor director, and our executive vice-president. Ron had been previously married to my cousin Marietta. He and I were close friends for many years, and my hope had always been that we might eventually match the strong partnership between my father and my uncle. Ron was not an operations person, so I delegated other activities to him such as representing Canfor on COFI and I asked him to take director-ships with Balco and Yorkshire Trust, where he became chair. He was also instrumental in the formation of our joint ventures, and even went to work for the Reed Group in England for a period of time.

Ron was a good board member and very capable at structuring deals, but he had an abrasive personality. He was a very political man and managed to offend a lot of people. Uncle John had been ready to fire him on the spot when Ron divorced Marietta and married one of our office employees. Everyone in the family had been naturally upset by this disturbing turn of events. I agreed with my uncle that what Ron did was unforgivable, but in an attempt to separate the business angle from the personal, I insisted that as long as he was performing well in the company, we should keep him on.

My rift with Ron followed a company conference we organized at the Hotel Vancouver. We had decided that we needed more input from all our managers to find solutions that would help us improve our performance. It was important to solicit our employees' help, and we brought in everyone in the company down to the mill manager level. We wanted to know what they could change in operations, both with capital and without. Instead of imposing our ideas, the feedback had to come from the bottom up. They were naturally interested in making changes that would help our bottom line, and they came up with constructive ideas about what we might do differently.

I tend to be self-critical, but that day I gave a good talk. Our senior management team and I had agreed in advance that I would not offer any solutions. Instead, we wanted everyone else's input, so they would take ownership of any actions we implemented. When I had concluded my remarks, Ron said, "With leadership like that, no wonder we're in trouble." His comment was completely off base.

"I'll see you back at the office after the meeting," I said.

Ron had made more than a few public statements that we did not like, and he continued to do so even when I asked him to cease. He appeared to enjoy reading his name in the media and rarely thought of how his words might impact other people. When he showed his lack of confidence in me at the Hotel Vancouver meeting that day, I had had enough. We talked later in my office.

"I'm triggering our agreement," I said.

Years before, we had drawn up an agreement that provided certain benefits for Ron, his wife, Jacqueline, and their child should he leave the company because of his decision or ours. During our difficult conversation in my office, he recognized the company's right to dismiss him but said he wanted to think about the details. When we met the next day, he said he had decided he would rather have an upfront payment instead of following the agreement. I readily agreed to that. It was a poor decision on his part—but he was gone.

We were more than fortunate when Gordon Armstrong assumed all of Ron's administrative responsibilities as head of our legal department and as corporate secretary. He later became senior vice-president, finance. I have never met anyone in or out of the financial community who did not speak highly of Gordon. He has a wonderful way with people and was closely involved with many of our acquisitions.

IN THE EARLY 1990S, I began to plan my departure as CEO from Canfor. I had become chair and CEO in the fall of 1985, at the same time that we asked Roy Bickell to move from vice-president, wood products, to fill the position of president and chief operating officer. Roy was a natural leader and we intended for him to be my successor. Unfortunately, he left Canfor so he and his wife, Noreen, could return to Grande Prairie. Roy was an excellent leader but we could not have our president living so far away.

In 1995, when I retired, we appointed Arild Nielssen, our vice-president, Northern operations, as president and CEO. I remained chair of the board. As planned, after the annual general meeting my title changed and I moved out of the Canfor office to join Ron Cliff in his office. Having stepped down as CEO, I maintained responsibility for government relations.

The Canfor board repeatedly pushed Arild to come up with a strategic plan and he would come back with two- or five-year budgets. Two years after he took over, the board held an in-camera meeting where they decided he had to be replaced. When Arild left in 1997, we had no one in-house ready to take his place, so I agreed to step in as interim CEO without compensation. Our company-wide policy required mandatory retirement at age sixty-five, and I did not want to violate our rules by accepting remuneration, which might have led others to think they could do the same.

We conducted a search and were lucky to get three strong applicants. The candidate we chose was David Emerson, who had no experience in the forest industry but came with excellent credentials. He spent two months with me so he could get off to a running start as CEO on January 1, 1998.

The company continued to grow under David's leadership. He was a good CEO and a great strategist. Over his six years with Canfor (the longest he had ever spent in the same job), he moved us forward and strongly supported the lead position we took in information technology systems as well as the development of Genus Resource Management Technologies as an offshoot IT company. David helped secure the purchase of Northwood, pushing us into our position as a major player in both pulp and lumber. We were not insignificant before, but this move put us on the map.

On another front, David developed a friendship with Paul Martin and took over from me in chairing the Vancouver fundraisers for Paul. David had been in the government world before as a deputy minister in Victoria, and Paul was trying to convince him to run for the Liberals with the promise of a Cabinet seat. He would go on to take that seat in 2004.

EVEN WHEN the family had control of the company, we always held the highest regard for the outside directors on the board. Our board has always been careful to bring in competent individuals as directors, with a focus on finding people with business acumen, integrity, and an ability to speak up. Also essential to the board's efficiency is our directors' willingness to do their homework; we need them to be well prepared for our meetings. Some boards choose to have particular directors for different roles according to their specialty. My preference is to create a blend of individuals with experience in heading up companies, or in politics or education, who bring a wide range of perspectives and skills. Business scandals in recent years have resulted in more onerous requirements for audit committees on boards, and we now bring in directors who are familiar with the complexity of that process.

I cannot say enough to adequately recognize the dedication and effort that Canfor's directors have invested through the years. We have prospered with their help and wisdom, and I am grateful for their contribution.

OUR BOARD WAS INSTRUMENTAL in encouraging three of our major acquisitions that propelled Canfor into first position as British Columbia's top lumber producer. It was a transformative leap. Early on, our acquisitions had been single entities like a mill or a logging camp. But with the industry consolidating, we were looking to buy companies with multiple operations. Such purchases made the integration process more difficult, particularly as some of these enterprises had different priorities and cultures.

The first acquisition in 1989 was Balfour Guthrie Forest Products Inc., an operation for which we paid a premium because it held significant strategic value. The original operation had been a far-flung enterprise, established in 1869 by three Scotsmen in San Francisco, who exported all manner of products such as wheat, flour, and lumber while importing industrial goods from Britain. The company was a wholly owned subsidiary of an international investment, importing, and insurance company based in London.

When Balfour Guthrie first came to Vancouver, it was in the business of importing and exporting foodstuffs, but since our region's most marketable product was lumber, they took that on, too. When we bought all the B.C. assets of Balfour Guthrie it was not just a production company but also a sales and marketing firm, working out of a building they owned on Alberni Street in Vancouver. Gordon Armstrong worked directly with their CFO, Tom Fleming, to arrange the purchase.

The strategic merit of Balfour Guthrie lay in their geography and chip supply for our pulp mills. As the largest independent chip supplier in the Prince George region, they were aware that these features meant a lot to us, and they were confident that we would pay a good price. At the same time, a large Japanese firm, Daishowa, had just entered the Canadian scene and was eager to expand into the forest products industry. It also had its sights on Balfour Guthrie and did its best to outbid us. Later, Canfor sold our High Level operation to Daishowa to service their new pulp mill in northern Alberta. We found a satisfying irony in the high price they paid us for that operation since we recovered much of the premium we had paid for Balfour Guthrie.

In the process of those transactions, we learned more about Daishowa (now Daishowa-Marubeni International and Nippon Paper in Japan), a big Japanese paper manufacturing company established in the late 1930s. The founder's son and flamboyant president, Ryoei Saito, caused a stir by insisting that two invaluable paintings he had bought at auction—a Van Gogh and a Renoir—be cremated with him upon his death. Fortunately for the art world, public protests led him to reconsider his extraordinary request, and a decline of his company's fortunes forced him to sell the paintings.

Balfour Guthrie's culture was fiercely independent, a corporate trait that continued long after we took over. The incoming team clearly believed that they should continue to operate as a separate entity with their own corporate organization. They were pleased to supply us with chips, but they were proud of what they had created and they wanted to run their own show. We had a challenge merging our operations. In our business, cooperation in filling priority orders is essential. Everyone up and down the line has to be ready to arrange timely delivery schedules that work for the whole system. The simple fact was that Balfour Guthrie could not continue doing its own thing when we had important obligations to our customers.

In the end, the one independent task we allowed them to carry on, and only for a while, was their role as sales agent for outside suppliers. We kept their personnel on to handle that side of their erstwhile business, but slowly integrated the sales group into our larger team. Despite these early challenges, the purchase of Balfour Guthrie has worked out very well.

CANFOR'S SECOND MAJOR acquisition was Northwood, a company that we had known for many years in Prince George because it had evolved around the same time as our two pulp mills. Noranda Mines had already diversified in the early 1960s by purchasing sawmills near Prince George, and when we presented our application to establish PGPP at the public hearing in Prince George, Adam Zimmerman's objection revealed that Noranda had a similar goal. It had not taken long before Noranda presented their own application and proceeded with the United States–based Mead Group to build Northwood Pulp in 1964–65, which was later expanded to twice its original size.

In 1999, a decade after purchasing Balfour Guthrie, we successfully negotiated with Noranda to acquire Northwood. Along with it, we inherited the pulp mill and sawmill in Prince George, along with North Central Plywood, the Rustad, the Houston and Upper Fraser operations, Kyahwood Forest Products, and J.D. Little Forest Centre. Given that our PGPP and Intercontinental pulp mills were running smoothly in Prince George, this purchase made perfect sense. It also made Canfor the largest producer of softwood lumber and kraft market pulp in Canada at that time. Negotiations had been tricky, however.

We had been on the verge of closing the initial deal when Noranda's 50 percent partner, the Mead Corporation, decided that it did not want to sell its interest. Mead was a large and successful U.S. pulp and paper company that purchased a large quantity of pulp from Northwood. The motivating factor behind their half ownership was their assured access to that top-quality pulp at a discount.

We had been ready to sign the deal when our agent, Salomon Brothers, and our CEO, David Emerson, announced at a board meeting that the Northwood deal would not be going through. The news came as a big disappointment. The synergies between Canfor and Northwood were apparent to anyone in the business. It was wiser and far more efficient to merge instead of continuing as rival companies that competed for fibre. The Northwood operation was located a short distance away from our two mills in Prince George, and we were in the exact same business with many redundancies: two fibre supply departments, two logging departments, distinct hauling costs and separate management teams, to name only a few. It made perfect sense for us to acquire the company.

I was convinced we could figure something out, and paid a visit to my friend Senator Trevor Eyton, who was a senior executive at Edper, the Bronfman company that had bought control of Noranda. When I explained to Trevor that we wanted to take one more stab at negotiations, he confirmed that Noranda was eager to sell. Their involvement with B.C. Forest Products and subsequently the acquisition of 49.9 percent of MacMillan Bloedel in 1981 gave them no further need for Northwood, which once offered them a foothold in the B.C. forest industry. I told Trevor that we were willing to consider buying out Noranda's half, but we were not prepared to offer Mead access to Northwood's pulp on the favourable terms they were used to.

It seemed to me as if Northwood was not even on Mead's radar, with their sole concern being the regular delivery of their product supply. They were a disinterested seller because the status quo was working just fine. If we were going to try again, Mead had to be convinced. I let Trevor talk to them, and when he explained that if Canfor bought out Noranda's half of Northwood, we would not agree to the same arrangements regarding pulp, Mead decided to sell. We went back to the table to negotiate Canfor's purchase of the whole company, and closed the deal in 1999.

We soon saw that the synergies realized with Northwood surpassed those we had anticipated. I invited Adam Zimmerman to travel with me to visit all his old operations, and he introduced us in a favourable light as the new owners.

It was gratifying on my first visit to the Northwood Pulp Mill after the acquisition to hear from employees in one of the control rooms that they knew of our high safety standards and they were pleased with the purchase.

"We're glad we can look forward to having the same safety practices and safety record that you have at Canfor," they said.

"Let's ensure that continues," I replied. "And you're the only ones who can make that happen!"

David Emerson and his management team did a superb job of putting everything together and we had full cooperation from Northwood's president, C.T. Hazelwood, who joined us as a vice-president of Canfor for the Prince George area. My daughter Barbara Hislop was our vice-president, wood products, and she oversaw the successful integration of our woodlands and saw-mills with those belonging to Northwood. I remember Hazelwood remarking that Barbara's results had exceeded what he had been able to do in integrating his own mills prior to the purchase.

Northwood and Canfor had established a fifty-fifty joint venture in B.C. Chemicals, which supplied both our operations with chlorate used in the pulp bleaching process. Once a shared entity, B.C. Chemicals became entirely a Canfor subsidiary. With North-wood on board, we melded it under the same management as PGPP and Intercon. Unfortunately, we sold B.C. Chemicals in 2003.

Our three pulp mills, all located in Prince George, have given us a highly competitive position in the Northern fibre-pulp industry.

CANFOR'S THIRD MAJOR acquisition in 2004 was Slocan Forest Products, the same company we had tried to buy a decade earlier when the minister blocked us in spite of my having precleared the purchase with Premier Harcourt. This purchase would increase Canfor's production to more than five billion FBM per year, and in capacity terms, we would become the largest lumber producer in Canada.

Sawmills were of particular interest to Canfor. We had become one of the major lumber suppliers to Lowe's and Home Depot, and to grow with them, we needed to increase our capacity. After purchasing Northwood, my preference would have been to make a deal with Weldwood, but that proved impossible. Consequently, we began to look elsewhere, finding that most options showing economic promise presented insurmountable challenges around personalities and corporate culture. Because of these challenges, Canfor had looked again at Slocan, recognizing its good assets along with a few we could have done without. Personally, I was less than enthusiastic about the new deal we had made. After Andrew Petter blocked our first effort, we had said that we would not be coming back unless Slocan wanted us to.

I was not involved with negotiations between Canfor's David Emerson and Slocan's Jim Shepherd, who had recently replaced Ike Barber as CEO, but this takeover was very difficult and the transition was anything but smooth.

Gordon Armstrong still jokes that an African spear on Ike's office wall was there in case I came to visit, and remembers Ike referring to me as "the Pope" when we had first tried to take over his company. It's true that Ike and I had had our moments, but I admired him. He had done a tremendous job building something from nothing with Slocan. I give him full credit for what he accomplished. Starting with one sawmill, he had bought relatively inexpensive assets, improved them—and then kept expanding. His operation consisted of the mill in Slocan, the Vavenby mill, the Radium mill, the Plateau mill in Vanderhoof, the Takama plywood plant and the OSB mill in Fort Nelson, and a CTMP pulp mill in Taylor.

Jimmy Pattison was a significant shareholder in Canfor, as he was in Slocan. I would like to set the record straight on Jimmy, who has been criticized by people who don't know him and who may be envious of his success, but I know him to be a fine man whose ambition for Canfor has paralleled my own. Both of us want a world-scale, British Columbia–based, preferably British Columbia–controlled, integrated forest company. Our first invitation for Jimmy to join our board had led to a courteous "No, thank you," as doing so would mean giving up his seat on the Slocan board. When we approached him again in 2003, Jimmy said yes, he would be interested, but only if he could bring a second director with him. Our board charged Michael Phelps and me with the task of interviewing Michael Korenberg, Pattison's right-hand man, to see if he would be an acceptable candidate. Immediately we found him to be a capable individual with strong credentials, including a position teaching governance at the UBC Faculty of Law. Before we bought Slocan, we were pleased to welcome both Jimmy and Michael to our board.

Stephen Jarislowsky, an even larger shareholder in Slocan than the Pattison Group and the founder of one of Canada's most respected pension fund management companies, added a condition to the Slocan acquisition: he insisted that Jim Shepherd, Slocan's top man, transfer over as Canfor's CEO. Some of us on the Canfor side were not initially aware of this, but two circumstances supported Jarislowsky's plan: David Emerson wanted to exit Canfor to join Paul Martin in the political world, and I had told our board that I thought Jim Shepherd was a good man who knew the industry.

The Slocan deal went through and I was encouraged by Shepherd's initial introduction in April 2004. But I became concerned when after a few weeks he came to review his personnel plans with me. At a meeting at my home, he told me he needed his "own team" to run the company and he was going to let go of my daughter Barbara. He explained that she would be replaced by an external hire from the United States, someone who turned out to have little knowledge of the industry. This was a tremendous personal hurt for me because in my view, Barbara had been an outstanding employee in all her Canfor assignments. Shepherd told me that he had to let her go because a number of key people would not work with her. At that point, I became suspicious of Shepherd's judgment, as Barbara was extremely popular with the people who reported to her in every job she had done.

Shepherd went on to tell me that he wanted to bring Slocan's CFO with him to Canfor. I responded that although I would not fight his decision regarding Barbara because of the appearance of nepotism, I would resist the CFO appointment. I did not believe the man was right for the job, and Ron Cliff, chair of our board's audit committee, echoed my concern. Although respecting Ron's and my position, the board felt it had to go along with the CEO's choice of a CFO. Unfortunately, the appointment did not work out, and by November of the same year, Shepherd had let him go and hired a new CFO from the oil patch. In the meantime, we had lost the leading edge we had gained in information technology under David Emerson's leadership. We had also lost a number of very capable people.

It turned out that our new CEO had no understanding of our culture and our sophisticated information systems. Furthermore, he was doing significant damage by trying to impose the Slocan culture. Shepherd generally tended to hire external people rather than trying to promote from within. I have to credit him, however, with the successful outside appointment of Paul Richards, an outstanding performer as vice-president, pulp, who subsequently became the first president of the Canfor Pulp Income Fund. Paul brought with him Mac Palmiere, who also did a good job for Canfor in wood products and then in heading up Howe Sound Pulp, where he remains. Shepherd's two other accomplishments included Canfor's acquisition of New South, and his work with the government of China to start a school there where carpenters learn how to construct frame housing.

OUR COMING TOGETHER with Slocan brought dramatic changes to our board. Ron Cliff, Jimmy Pattison, Michael Korenberg, Eric Newell, Michael Phelps, and I were joined by four of Slocan's directors: Jim Shepherd; Don Selman, a highly respected chartered accountant; Brandt Louie, an accomplished Canadian businessman who we appointed as vice-chair of the Canfor board; and Stephen Jarislowsky. Stephen appeared to consider himself a mentor to Jim Shepherd and the two of them were very close.

Unfortunately, Stephen and I had gotten off to a bad start. Many years earlier, I paid him a visit in Montreal to consider him as a pension manager for Canfor. Because we did not follow through on that plan, he seemed to develop a dislike for me. In one of his books, Peter Newman describes how when I took over as Canfor's CEO, Stephen predicted that the company would be out of business in three years. After reading that, I couldn't resist sending Stephen annual reports showing our profits of more than $100 million, three years in a row, with a note attached saying, "At least we're going broke in style."

Stephen and I were seldom on the same page, though one subject on which I agreed with him was the salaries and bonuses of the CEOs and senior officers in Canada and the United States, which were generally getting out of hand. I completely concurred with his view on compensation policy, and he brought a lot to Canadian business by being outspoken on the issue.

In 2006, another respected businessman, Paul Tellier, joined our board. I greatly admired Paul. He had served as clerk of the privy council under Brian Mulroney before heading up the Crown corporation CN Rail, which he turned into a highly successful public company.

WE HAD A RECORD YEAR after Canfor and Slocan came together, thanks mostly to good product prices, including high panelling prices for OSB and plywood. But by the fall of 2006, our management problems were becoming intolerable.

At the end of the October board meeting, we held our routine in-camera session after management was excused. The session focused on stories about key people in the company who were going to leave Canfor unless we changed top management. We were also finding that performance on capital expenditures left a lot to be desired. In short, the controllable budget numbers from Shepherd's own business plan were not being met. In the course of our discussion, we found that we had a split board: five of our members wanted a change in leadership, but five felt Shepherd should be given some time to correct the problems.

As I always did after the board's in-camera meetings, I went to the CEO to give him a report. I advised Shepherd that half of the board wanted to dismiss him, but we had not taken action. I told him that even though I was in the group that wanted to dismiss him, as chair I would give him my full support and cooperation.

It was a most disagreeable situation and unfortunate timing because as chair, I was dealing with a split board on another issue. The same directors who wanted to retain Shepherd were expressing concern about Jim Pattison's increasing shareholdings. They were more worried about who controlled Canfor than about the company's performance. My primary focus was the well-being of the company and the potential loss of our good people if we did not do something about our president.

After our meeting, Stephen Jarislowsky phoned me with his concern: "I don't understand why you don't want to protect your family's interest and why you stand by idly while Jimmy is buying more shares," he said. "If you vote with my group, we're prepared to keep you on the board and we may even consider leaving you as chair."

"Thanks for your call, but no thanks," I replied. "I won't be joining your group."

Pattison was also upset with the in-camera session and its outcome. He called me to say that he was fed up and thought we should call a shareholders' meeting to clear the air. He was going to make a written request and I asked him not to. If he did, as chair I would be obliged to call the meeting, and although I have enormous respect for Jimmy, the five dissenting board members could well have had a big following among our shareholders.

Fortunately, Jimmy complied with my request. Instead, we invited Third Avenue, a New York fund management company (which had not been represented on the board even though they had a double-digit holding in the company) to come out for a meeting. We asked Third Avenue to agree to vote their shares with the Pattison Group and our family group (Matthews Cartier) and my own shares. With this arrangement in place, we would have a minimum of 52.5 percent of all outstanding shares. Third Avenue agreed not to trade in the shares between then and our annual meeting, and to vote their shares with us in exchange for two seats on Canfor's board.

Paul Tellier, for whom I have enormous respect and who had always been a friend, was our newest director but he was unhappy with the split and he chose to resign from our board because of it. Our remaining four directors wished to continue and suggested that they would run their own slate for the annual meeting, which might have led to a lot of embarrassment both for the company and for those who would lose.

Aside from Shepherd, the four opposing directors were all prominent Canadians, and some had made valuable contributions to our board. I respected them all but saw that they were collectively locked into their position and insistent upon voting. To prevent embarrassment, we suggested that their lawyers meet with ours and confirm our voting position. I was in Palm Springs for much of this stressful time and met there with the other side's de facto leader, Michael Phelps, to continue my attempt to convince them that we did have control, and to eventually negotiate Shepherd's exit.

Only a few days before the information circular for the annual meeting went out, the dissenters backed down. They capitulated, however, only after seeing our statements showing that we had a voting control of the company, and after negotiating the severance package for Shepherd, who agreed to remain until the annual meeting and resign at its conclusion. The four dissenting board members agreed to resign and were not on the slate for election. It was an emotional day. Boards rarely have to part ways with people who are so respected.

To fill the two positions we had offered them, Third Avenue appointed Ben Duster IV, who had Ian Lapey join him on the ballot in 2007. However, there appeared to be a conflict of interest and it was too late to change the ballot, so we asked that Duster step down after the vote. He never came to a meeting and did not receive any director's fees. We immediately moved on to consider Thomas Tutsch, a former senior officer at Nesbitt Burns from Toronto, and invited him to take Duster's position.

Our board debacle had lasted from October 2006 to February 2007, and it unfortunately left me with a worsening case of myasthenia gravis, a neuromuscular condition that made it difficult to chew, swallow, and talk. It's now under control with medication. I was in hospital at the time of the 2007 AGM, so Ron Cliff kindly acted as chair and went on to replace me when I stepped down and became chair emeritus in 2009.

With the dust finally settling, Canfor needed a new CEO. We had brought in several good people who we hoped might be considered for senior management positions, but unfortunately they did not work out. Jim Shepard ("Shepard II"—a new one, spelled differently), retired CEO of Finning, was a proposed nominee to fill one of the board vacancies. Initially, we had not thought of bringing Jim in as our top executive, but he accepted our invitation to act as interim CEO while we conducted a search. When he took charge with such effective gusto in the first three months and clearly gained the full support of those reporting to him, we reconsidered and unanimously agreed to offer him a permanent position.

Jim did a wonderful job taking us through the worst downturn in our industry that I can remember. Times had changed. As he said on retiring in 2011, "It wasn't clicking then and now it is." He brought us back on track, making use of the excellent people that Canfor was fortunate enough to have retained. Thanks to his efforts, we have come through with the best balance sheet in the industry during a time when some players are still languishing. In effect, Jim "re-Canforized" the company, bringing it back to the way it used to operate and restoring the spirit and morale of our people. But he did not achieve that without a lot of pain and sacrifice. When times were rough—and they have been very rough until recently—he voluntarily took more of a salary cut than he asked our staff to take, and the board did the same. I am pleased that everyone has now been remunerated; we gave our employees back the money we had asked permission to withhold and we have restored their full salaries. We still have a distance to go, but we are well on our way.

At the 2011 AGM, Don Kayne, a long-time Canfor employee and former vice-president, marketing and sales for wood products, became Canfor's new president and CEO. One of his impressive first moves was to hire back Wayne Guthrie, who had left us for Tembec, as his successor in sales. It's obvious that Don knows our employees well, and although he has shuffled the deck, he is following the Canfor tradition of optimizing the use of the quality people who surround him.

OUR BOARD CRISIS is well behind us, but it brings to mind the importance of good governance. Boards of directors are not only necessary by law, they are essential to the success or otherwise of any public company. If the board is on top of things, you will have capable management. It's crucial that a company's directors understand their role: to create policy and formulate strategy— not to engage in the day-to-day management of the company. Canfor's current board enjoys excellent dialogue and no rifts. Our directors are by no means "yes men" and they speak their minds freely. We sort out our differences and we have a common objective in sustaining a successful business.

16

New South
Breaking Ground in the United States

IT BECAME CLEAR to us in 2006 that Canfor would benefit from more geographic diversification. The extent of our reach was British Columbia and Alberta, plus a mill in Quebec and a reman (remanufacturing) plant in Bellingham, Washington, in addition to sales offices in Brussels and Tokyo. We had also been selling product through New South, a company in Myrtle Beach, South Carolina. Eventually, we got word that some of the New South shareholders might want to sell. It was an interesting prospect.

New South had grown steadily throughout the 1900s from a collection of businesses established in the 1930s and '40s by the Wall, Sledger, Singleton, and Campbell families in the southeastern United States. Before we came along, the company had started importing white wood from Europe to supplement the servicing of big box stores such as Home Depot and Lowe's. Its main overseas supplier was a successful young Austrian by the name of Klausner who manufactured quality lumber in Austria and Germany. New South represented Klausner in the United States, with president Mack Singleton in charge. I knew Mack well and admired him for his knowledge of the industry. He played a big part in the softwood lumber debate as chair of the U.S. Coalition for Fair Lumber Imports, a group consisting of companies and landowners.

Canfor's CEO Jim Shepherd ("Shepherd I") and Klausner discussed the possibility of jointly buying New South with a plan to expand the operation. Klausner ran into financial troubles and I was not enthused with the idea of giving him an option for joint ownership. Despite his motivation and his financial situation, the plan changed in the wake of fluctuating markets and exchange rates. Our board recommended that we proceed on our own. Shepherd was ready to keep Klausner's options open, but I took a different position: either we take equity in his company instead of his payment, or we refuse to extend the period during which he had to pay up. When presented with those alternatives, Klausner did not like the equity idea, nor could he come up with the money. Thus, New South became Canfor's entirely, which made it far easier to manage.

It was a gamble, as many other ventures have been, but we were pleased with what we acquired in New South and became increasingly impressed with the organization. With New South Companies Inc. we acquired three sawmills, one remanufacturing facility, and two lumber treatment plants in North and South Carolina, a trucking company, and an international import business. The operation employed more than six hundred people and provided an excellent base for the growth of our business in the United States. In fact, since buying New South we have acquired Darlington, a fourth sawmill in South Carolina that increased our capacity.

We successfully integrated our two sales organizations with the help of Mack Singleton, who later stepped down from his position as president and CEO of New South and handed it to Doug Warstler. Mack continues to serve on the Canfor board.

The big-box stores gave us a good reason to expand New South, especially as the U.S. market fell and the currency changed. With the euro up and the dollar down, Europeans could no longer afford to ship lumber to the United States. Those conditions coincided with the collapse of the industry and, as a result, we no longer required the kind of supplement New South had previously needed from Klausner.

OUR PURCHASE of New South gave us perspective on the lumber wars from the other side of the fence. Most everyone in British Columbia knows from the media that a hot-button issue in our industry has been the softwood lumber dispute—a long, drawn-out battle that started well before my time, and has been going on in one form or another since long before the Second World War. The dispute has affected our industry perhaps more than any other influences. British Columbia accounts for 60 percent of Canada's softwood lumber exports, so the industry within our provincial boundaries is a popular target.

Without going into exhausting detail—which has been done capably by many people in and out of the industry—the issue as I see it is this: if all our logs from both provincial and private lands were exportable, then U.S. companies could bid for them if they felt they were too cheap. They then would not have an argument that the logs were subsidized.

As I have said, in the United States, timberland is owned about a third each by private companies, state governments, and the federal government. In a nutshell, what drives the issue is the U.S. private timber lot owners' opinion that, if they make it more expensive or difficult to bring in lumber from Canada, the value of their land holdings and the price for their logs will go up. In addition, they believe that the logs used to make Canadian lumber are underpriced.

U.S. trade law allows for investigations when a "subsidy" is claimed by U.S. producers, providing an importer with an advantage in the U.S. market. A number of agencies get involved in investigating these allegations. The dispute gained renewed momentum in 1986 when Canadian stumpage programs came into question in the United States and the Department of Commerce, with Canadian concurrence, levied a 15 percent tariff on lumber exported to the United States. The mistaken rationale for the tariff then and now was that our Canadian wood was subsidized by low stumpage, which it was not. What followed were many years of acrimonious argument, investigation, determinations, appeals, and challenges.

A new managed trade agreement on softwood lumber in 1996 imposed a volume quota on Canadian lumber exports to the United States, but it did not bring the five years of peace that it promised, and it particularly wounded the B.C. industry. Canada continues to try to defend its programs while facing U.S. litigation, and the dispute rages on.

The 2006 Softwood Lumber Agreement includes a price-sensitive border tax on Canadian lumber exports to the United States (the higher the price of lumber, the lower the tax). With the 2006 agreement in place, we now pay it to the Canadian government, which remits it to the provinces, although the funds cannot be used in any way to provide direct support to the Canadian industry.

An important point in this never-ending struggle is that conditions naturally differ in Canada and the United States. I remember a bad year when Canfor had a loss of $100 million and paid $300 million in stumpage, yet the United States still insisted our stumpage was subsidized.

My summary of the whole affair is this: it's a phoney debate, and one that constitutes a huge bonanza for lawyers on both sides of the border. They have persisted in accusing Canadian lumber exporters of being subsidized, which is a myth. Our government has always done a superb job of collecting optimum and fair stumpage and royalty from the forest industry. The question about whether we have done anything "wrong" in Canada has nothing to do with it.

Ken Higginbotham was well known to us as the assistant deputy minister in Alberta's Land and Forest Service and an associate professor in the forest science department at the University of Alberta, both positions earning him an impressive degree of respect. As our vice-president, forestry and environment, Ken has played an important part not only in our own forestry operations but also in the U.S. softwood lumber dispute, where he has represented Canfor extremely well with the Canadian and provincial authorities. During his term at Canfor, Ken also did a great deal to promote positive dialogue and business arrangements with the First Nations community.

Ken is now retired but will continue to act as an advisor to Canfor in the U.S. softwood lumber dispute.

THE COUNCIL of Forest Industries (COFI) is one of the biggest industry associations of its kind. It has a strong voice among international forest trade circles as an advocate for all of British Columbia's forest industry companies. The council represents the industry on everything from market access to community relations to government public policy development, and helps to coordinate anything required in the industry other than labour relations or direct selling.

A COFI president who stands out for me is Mike Apsey. A professional forester, an employee of MacMillan Bloedel, an employee of the United Nations, and then British Columbia's deputy minister of forests, Mike went on to head COFI for a number of years. Having seen our industry from every possible angle and having travelled extensively, he has a wider perspective than most on the world's forests. Mike has always said that, if we in British Columbia are not best in the world in the way we manage and protect our forests and the way we set up our parks systems, then we are pretty damn close.

Mike also devoted a good chunk of his career to fighting the Canada–U.S. lumber wars, starting in the 1980s when he was deputy minister. He saw first-hand how the United States targeted British Columbia, insisting on their mistaken conclusion that our stumpage system constituted a subsidy. In about 2008, the U.S. government, encouraged by their industry, began to look at stumpage rates paid for timber killed by the mountain pine beetle.

The U.S. Coalition is accusing British Columbia of "cheating" because of "low" stumpage paid on low-grade, beetle-killed logs. They further claim that we were intentionally mis-grading sawlogs to take advantage of low stumpage on very poor-quality logs. It's a curious accusation given that these trees are dry to the point of shattering, they throw off volumes of dust that has to be removed from the air to protect the employees, and we have to invest more in the mills that cut them. The recovery volume of beetle-kill lumber is lower and the product has a lesser value.

WHEN HE WAS British Columbia's minister of forests in the early 1990s, Andrew Petter started a Forest Advisory Committee to deal with policy issues that involved big, medium, and small companies as well as representatives of the environmental movement and First Nations groups. MacMillan Bloedel, Canfor, Weyerhaeuser, Weldwood, and Interfor were the integrated companies, and Lignum was the largest of the smaller companies on the committee.

Around the same time, the integrated companies felt they were not being properly represented on the Canadian Forest Industries Council (CFIC), and they asked me to act on their behalf by becoming vice-chair to Jake Kerr of Lignum Forest Products, one of Canada's lead negotiators on softwood lumber. I agreed but quickly became frustrated with the process of softwood lumber negotiations in Washington and I returned to my winter home in California.

After arriving in Palm Springs, I received a phone call from Washington to say the talks were in a deadlock. What I had not realized was that Dick Bennett, a sawmill owner in Idaho and vice-chair of the U.S. Coalition, had also flown back to Palm Springs because he was equally frustrated. The council asked me if Dick and I could get together and help move the discussions ahead. As members at the same golf club, we met and managed to do just that. Their hands were tied in Washington and it took our joint effort to call the two sides and suggest to them what might be possible.

Frank McKenna deserves a lot of credit for the good work he did on the lumber agreement while he was our ambassador in Washington. Michael Wilson, who succeeded him, was the one who negotiated and finalized the 2006 softwood lumber agreement. Canfor did its utmost to help them sell this deal to the Canadian industry.

Mike Apsey talks about a U.S. politician who said to him, "When are you going to understand? It's not 'do as we do,' it's 'do as we say.'" Senator Max Baucus from Montana was a particularly caustic example of this kind of thinking, and one of Canada's worst trade enemies. He famously declared that he had never met a Canadian who would look him in the eye and say that the Canadian industry is not subsidized. Well, Mike ended up being the Canadian who would do just that. With two U.S. colleagues in tow, he went to the senator's office and waited a long time for a very short meeting. When the senator finally appeared, he did not shake Mike's hand or say hello, but began to yell about the "bloody subsidy." He went on and on, and even his own assistant was starting to look worried, when Mike interrupted.

"Senator!" he shouted, and looked Baucus in the eye. "Canadian stumpage does *not* constitute a subsidy."

The senator did not reply. He turned and left.

Where do we go with this continuing problem? The lumber industry is not included under NAFTA because the softwood lumber dispute was outstanding when the trade agreement was established. They went ahead without us. I realize that under the terms of NAFTA, Canada cannot threaten to cut off the United States on energy or water as a negotiating ploy. But I hope we can find a window of political opportunity that leads to a continental policy on lumber and bring it within the free trade agreement instead of leaving it as an orphan.

The U.S. industry has changed, as has ours, and it's possible that we will find some peace now that West Fraser, Interfor, and Canfor operate on both sides of the border, as does Weyerhaeuser. I can guarantee, though, that change will not happen in Washington, where the cottage industry they have created to deal with the dispute has a life of its own.

In the end, the situation may resolve itself, given that the United States is going to need our lumber. At the moment, some U.S. timber owners put heat on the big U.S. lumber companies, saying if you want our timber, you have to support the U.S.

Coalition. This is an uncomfortable pressure play because the timber owners can always let the trees grow for another year and not cut them, but the mills need a continual supply to operate. I tried to encourage Peter Correll, the CEO of Georgia Pacific, to stop backing the Coalition, as he was one of its largest financial contributors, along with International Paper. Peter believed in free trade and understood our concern. Because of his requirement for logs, he had to continue his support, but reduced his payments. I understand that both major players have now left the Coalition. With the U.S economic recession in 2008 and 2009, the power of the timberland owners may be declining because some of them may have a need for revenue.

Whatever their views really are, the forest products companies have to play the game. British Columbia could resolve all of this if we were able to negotiate our way out of the Softwood Lumber Agreement by making our logs exportable. But our local governments want logs processed locally or provincially if possible because they do not want to "export jobs." In fact, opting out would create more jobs. In the B.C. Interior, we have some of the lowest cost mills anywhere and since the logs are landlocked (transportation to the United States being prohibitive), they would continue to be processed in British Columbia as they are now.

The coast is different. Here we aren't logging the industry's annual allowable cut because there is no significant demand for the logs. We have lost not only the mill jobs but also logging jobs, many of which could be reactivated if we allowed log exports. Exporting would be economically viable because of the great Pacific waterway, making it possible for the logs to be towed to the United States or loaded on deep-sea vessels bound for China and Japan.

As for us, Canfor is still a relatively new presence in the United States, but I expect New South to continue its expansion, providing us with a source of supply that is not subject to U.S. softwood harassment. The lumber dispute has been with us for decades, and although I would like to see it end, I fear that it may go on forever.

17

Beyond Canfor
Giving Back

MY FAMILY MIGHT have sometimes thought throughout my career that Canfor has been my first love. That was only partially true because I care very deeply about Sheila, each of my four daughters, my son, and all their growing families. Like many men of my generation, I have spent a significant portion of my life going to work. That's what I wanted and enjoyed. Even now, I value my ongoing connection with Canfor and Canfor Pulp.

Responsibilities far beyond the business have periodically drawn me away from home and from the Canfor story. In addition to the time I have spent on outside boards, I have joined many others in their efforts to improve our province and country. I developed a sense of civic responsibility from my father and Uncle John, who passed along a profound appreciation for how Canada accepted our families when we first arrived in 1938. They showed me how important it is to give back through hard work, time, and donations to organizations and causes we believed in.

One of the most interesting and rewarding endeavours I became involved with was the Business Council on National Issues (BCNI), which subsequently became the Council of Canadian Chief Executives. I had the privilege of serving on the executive committee of the council for fourteen years under the able guidance of its president, Thomas d'Aquino. That experience afforded me an opportunity to get to know and engage in dialogue with some of Canada's top business leaders as well as our federal politicians and provincial premiers. I found it most stimulating and rewarding.

It has always been challenging to get western Canadians plugged into the national scene. The BCNI wanted to find someone on the West Coast with whom they were comfortable, and they welcomed me as the first British Columbian to serve on the council's executive as vice-chair to David Culver of Alcan, Ted Newell of Nova, Jacques Lamarre of SNC-Lavalin, and David O'Brien of Canadian Pacific. Two more Westerners followed me as members of the executive—our Jim Shepard when he was still with Finning, and then David Emerson.

My involvement with Prime Minister Mulroney's Canada–Japan Forum 2000 was another wonderful experience. I learned a lot working with chair Peter Lougheed and alongside many others, including our Japanese counterparts. I chaired the Forum's Trade and Investment Committee, which included Raymond Royer from Bombardier (later the head of Domtar) and Jack Munro, then president of the IWA and subsequently co-chair of the Forest Alliance. During my tenure, our committee had access to the federal finance minister, Michael Wilson, and the external affairs minister, Barbara McDougal. We would meet with the ministers and review our discussions with our Japanese counterparts to make sure that our work was compatible with the government's thinking.

I also enjoyed working with the B.C. Business Council, an organization that liaised with the government on behalf of bigger companies in the province. The council's goal was to enhance dialogue and offer input on policies and legislation. Before my time with the council, I saw that the calibre of membership companies was slipping, with a number of mid-sized companies dominating the scene rather than the major employers who needed a consolidated voice to deal with government. I was pleased as chair to be able to get all the major players to re-engage in the work of the council.

BOARD DIRECTORSHIPS can be onerous in the time and energy they demand. I have never taken on these jobs without careful consideration. I was overloaded with directorships when we owned Versatile; I served on their board and their subsidiary boards, and had previously accepted directorships with Balco, Shell Canada, the Bank of Montreal, and the international advisory board for the Chemical Bank.

I learned a great deal from each of those experiences, especially at Shell, where I was able to watch their outstanding CEO, Bill Daniel, in action. Although the company was 78 percent-owned by parent companies, the Canadian board maintained legitimate and full input. My direct involvement with a resource company was invaluable to my experience at Canfor. I learned that at the level of their board of managing directors, Shell's vast global organization spent 25 percent of their time *on people*, identifying and monitoring all potential stars as early as possible and moving them to different countries and through different aspects of the business. The CEOs of Royal Dutch Shell and British Shell Transport were members of the Shell Canada board. The CEO of the Dutch company also served as chair of Shell in the United States, and the British Shell CEO served as chair of our Canadian board. I admired that they never, ever threw their weight around, even though it was their company. The only rule they imposed was a global one: Shell as a company did not make political contributions.

Based on that Shell directorship, I was invited to join other boards, all offers that I would have liked to accept but that I turned down because of my responsibilities as Canfor's CEO at the time. That position was my priority and I had to limit my outside responsibilities.

The Bank of Montreal was another board to which I had been committed for many years. Long ago, the Royal Bank had approached me about joining their board. I was then president of the Fort St. John Lumber Company, which we had just purchased. The lumber company had historically done business with the Royal Bank, but our plan was to consolidate with CFP, and we had always dealt with the BMO. The Toronto Dominion Bank, a 10 percent shareholder in Yorkshire Trust, was next to invite me because of our association there. And finally, W.A.C. Bennett asked me to be an initial director of the Bank of British Columbia. I declined all these invitations because of our loyalty to BMO.

In time, the BMO chair and president came to visit my dad, my uncle, and me in our office to say that they would like one of us to join their board. Uncle John accepted without hesitation and served for many years. Upon his official retirement, I was invited to replace him, and actually ended up replacing four retiring directors, reducing the membership from fifty-four to fifty-one directors, which was a ridiculous number. It had been a nice club to belong to but not very efficient. When I left, we were down to sixteen directors at BMO, and that made a lot more sense. I have particularly enjoyed my increasingly involved role on the BMO committees since retiring as Canfor's CEO in 1995.

SHORTLY AFTER JOINING BMO as a director, I received an invitation to serve on the international advisory board of the Chemical Bank. Before accepting that position, I checked with Bill Mulholland, then CEO at BMO, who encouraged me to take the post with a view to possibly helping him create a similar organization for the Bank of Montreal. When Jake Warren left public service, he joined the Bank of Montreal, and I worked with him to achieve that.

Whereas many countries had only one representative at the Chemical Bank, Canada and France had two, and the United States had several. I first served with Jean de Grandpré, then chair of Bell Canada. When the bank wanted to replace Jean, they asked me to recommend another Canadian with Quebec and bilingual experience. I recommended Brian Mulroney, who had just left his position as prime minister, and we served on the board together for several years. Brian was a good choice and he made a very useful contribution.

It was an honour to be involved with that bank along with so many top leaders from around the globe. The bank's senior executives, including Walter Shipley and David Rockefeller, served along with many highly respected individuals, such as Lord Carrington from the United Kingdom, Henry Kissinger from the United States, Ratan Naval Tata from India, and Peter Woo from Hong Kong. Over my twenty-two years as a director, I witnessed the transition when the Chemical Bank merged with Manufacturers Hanover, then purchased the Chase Bank, and finally merged with J.P. Morgan to become J.P. Morgan Chase. Another fellow Canadian on the J.P. Morgan board was Paul Desmarais.

When I finally left that position, the Carlyle Group, then the world's largest private investment fund, asked me to join their Canadian advisory board. I was pleased to work there with Peter Lougheed, Hartley Richardson, Red Linton, Laurent Beaudoin,

Paul Desmarais, Allan Gotlieb, Frank McKenna, and two other well-known names—John Major, the former British prime minister, and James Baker of the United States. Since Carlyle did not do much in Canada, after two or three years, the Canadian board was discontinued.

BEYOND CANFOR, I have sought out another venture that holds promise and allows me to collaborate with my son, Michael, who worked with Canfor for a time and has always been loyal to the company. He had just graduated from the Stanford business school when we bought Northwood, and we reluctantly let people go as we brought the two companies together. Unfortunately, we were not able to give Michael the type of advancement he was seeking at the time, and he chose to leave and go into business as an independent consultant. He was doing that successfully when I asked him to head up SierraSil, a nutraceutical company that makes a supplement comprising natural materials, as opposed to pharmaceuticals. I am grateful that Michael accepted and he's doing an excellent job growing that business, which is doing well. It's a pleasure to be involved in a company that offers people an opportunity to become pain free. We've earned two patents as a nutritional supplement for osteoarthritis and we have encouraging anecdotal evidence that the product may reduce symptoms associated with Crohn's disease. Additional research shows that it appears to protect human cells from radiation.

My commitment to health and education has carried me through decades of involvement with a number of institutions and organizations. Establishing the first hospital foundation in British Columbia at Vancouver General Hospital was an important step. I was proud to be a part of it along with so many outstanding members of our local community.

All my daughters attended York House School, where I served as chair and succeeded in consolidating the ownership of the city block where the school sits. My involvement at my old school, St. George's, which my son and several grandsons also attended, has always been rewarding.

At UBC, I served on the advisory board of the forestry faculty and the business faculty, of which I am now a "Distinguished Fellow." I was also honoured when UNBC president Chuck Jago invited me to take the position of chancellor in 2004. We are fortunate that, after his retirement from the university, Chuck joined the board of Canfor Pulp.

I have valued my long-standing association with both UBC and UNBC, each of which has granted me an Honorary Doctor of Laws degree. I have also worked with Simon Fraser University, where I was given the Distinguished Community Leadership Award long after serving on the initial committee. I am a convocation founder and was also a member on the President's Council.

I am proud to be a board member of the Canadian Institute for Advanced Research, an organization founded by Fraser Mustard, which gathers distinguished teams from around the world to conduct scientific and social research. This group is making a tremendous difference in reversing the brain drain from Canada, and it has raised the standard of education and research in Canada. For the past eleven years, Chaviva Hosek has ably led the institute.

My six years on the board of the Banff Centre meant a lot because it took me back to Banff, where I had attended business school and where Sheila had gone to the Banff Mountain School. Mary Hofstetter, the exceptional president and CEO of the Banff Centre, has made a big difference to the school's current and future viability. I greatly admire the Banff Centre. On retiring from that board, I was amused to receive the gift of an Honorary

"BA" because the Centre is not a degree-granting institution. This "BA" stood for "Bentley's Amortization," reflecting my emphasis on that topic while chairing their finance and audit committee.

For the celebration of Sheila's and my seventieth birthdays, unbeknownst to us, our five children had a room in the Banff Centre music building dedicated to us. We knew that something was up, but we had no idea that all our children and their spouses would be there for the dedication ceremony. Sheila and I were both overcome by that wonderful surprise.

I have been less involved in the arts, but I served briefly on the Vancouver Art Gallery Foundation board. My current position as a director of the Vancouver Playhouse Theatre is meaningful because my uncle, John Prentice, respected and supported the Playhouse in the early years.

ATHLETICS HAVE ALWAYS BEEN one of my passions, and I was quick to follow in my father's footsteps by working with various sports organizations. I served as president of the B.C. Golf Association and in that role opened up membership so that public course players could participate in the national handicap system. I was also involved for a long time with the Royal Canadian Golf Association (RCGA), and chaired the Canadian Open Committee for ten years. In recognition of that work, I was made an honorary director of the Canadian Professional Golf Association. My wife, Sheila, who was president of the Canadian Ladies' Golf Association before it merged with the RCGA, and I received a joint award from the RCGA for our contribution to Canadian golf.

Then came my time with the B.C. Sports Hall of Fame, where I was honoured in 1999 with the W.A.C Bennett Award, and where I served for a time as its chair, dealing with all manner of issues, some big and some small. In its early days, the Hall was located on the Pacific National Exhibition (PNE) grounds in the B.C. Building, which contained a magnificent relief map of British Columbia surrounded by the Hall of Fame exhibits. One day, I received a curious phone call from our manager there saying that we had been threatened with eviction from the PNE if we "ever interfered in their business again." When I asked what on earth he was talking about, he explained that the PNE president, Erwin Swangard (a former sports editor of the *Vancouver Sun*), had raised hell because one of our employees had changed a light bulb in one of our showcases. Swangard insisted that this was a job only for the PNE–unionized electricians and, if we didn't play by their rules, we would be evicted. I went out to see Erwin and told him that he was off base. I conceded that we would not change the light bulbs in the building itself. But because of the valuable contents in our showcases, which were locked, if bulbs had to be changed, we would be the only ones changing them. Swangard accepted that we wouldn't touch the building bulbs and they wouldn't touch the showcase bulbs.

POLDI BENTLEY and John Prentice's ambition was not based on greed or monetary progress. Rather, my father and uncle's philosophy involved playing the "Big Game of Life" with the goal of success in the most positive sense of the word. I have enjoyed my part in the same dynamic game that combines responsibility and integrity at all levels of society—and I know and am very proud that my children are already carrying this ethic forward.

18

What's Next?
My View from Here

LOOKING AHEAD, I see many great opportunities for the forest industry. One is that the B.C. coast has every chance of making a major comeback based on logging second-growth timber. We have learned a lot from the technological improvements developed for smaller timber in the Interior. This knowledge could be applied on the coast in the logging and processing of smaller second-growth hemlock, fir, and cedar. The next generation of coastal logging will require specialized equipment and slightly higher costs for steep terrain, but we will enjoy transportation savings to overseas markets. Another opportunity will be markets in the Far East, which will consume so much wood that the impact of housing starts in the United States will not have its traditional effect on prices.

The global situation has always fluctuated and it will continue to do so. When I began my career, the Atlantic coast, the United Kingdom, and continental Europe were our major export markets.

As time passed, Japan became our principal overseas market and we reduced volumes going to the U.S. eastern seaboard. When Scandinavia increased its production of dry wood that compared favourably with our rough green, the United Kingdom and Europe almost fell off our map.

The southern hemisphere, where they once used wood mainly for fuel, also has enormous growth potential and is becoming a bigger and bigger factor in the pulp equation with their plantations of fast-growing trees and low production costs in new mega-mills. The products, however, cannot compete in quality with the strong long-fibred pulp that we produce in the Interior of British Columbia.

Change is afoot in western Europe, too. Scandinavia produces excellent lumber. In the postwar era, they modernized their operations. They were serious competitors in Europe but did not ship to North America until the late 1990s. Germany has a number of up to date sawmills developed over the last few years in the wake of terrible windstorms. They knew they had to log the damaged blow-down while it was still useable, and production rose dramatically. Austria also has some fine sawmills and Romania's industry is just getting started.

Russia has enormous potential with perhaps the best, largely untapped northern fibre wood in the world. But the infrastructure there is less than adequate, and they have proven to be somewhat unreliable as producers and shippers. We may eventually develop alliances with them, and we periodically check in to evaluate that possibility. For the moment, though, it appears that Prime Minister Vladimir Putin prefers to use Russian wood for upgrading their own infrastructure instead of for export. It will take a long time, but some of the Russian producers will make the grade and become serious competitors.

Of course, exchange rates, and not just supply and demand,

play a big role in the marketplace. When the U.S. dollar was strong, the Europeans shipped quite a bit of their lumber to the East Coast of the United States and competed with our product from the Interior. But as the U.S. dollar fell relative to the euro, all of that changed.

Most people are not aware that nearly half of the lumber we sell into the U.S. market is used for renovations, remodelling, industrial purposes, or all three. The other half goes into new housing. Since this last devastating downturn, repossessions are still taking place, and the inventory of unsold houses remaining on the market will delay new construction in the United States getting back to anywhere near its historic levels.

Filling the gap, China has taken off as a major purchaser of lumber, especially in the past three years. Framed housing has been on the rise in Japan and, more recently in China, and it's the way of the future. They are currently building six-storey apartment buildings using wood-frame construction supplied by Canada. The volumes of material shipped to China have leapt past those going to Japan, with the Chinese market growing at a startling pace—so fast in fact that U.S. lumber prices have risen significantly from their low point, even though new housing construction there remains close to a record low. This surge in demand has resulted in a tightening of supply in the United States. Don Kayne, supported by both Shepherd I and Shepard II, played an important role in securing a significant opportunity for Canfor to participate in the Chinese market.

Shortly after shutting down our Quesnel sawmill because of a weak market, we found one customer in China who offered to buy the mill's total output cut to metric specifications. The mill is now up and running again and 155 people have their jobs back. This is the first time we have ever sold an entire mill's production to a single customer.

China still has tremendous growth potential, and India offers significant new growth opportunities with the rapid expansion of its middle class.

The volume of product being shipped from British Columbia's north coast to the Far East is growing, and Prince Rupert may ultimately become the major port for our shipments.

WE HAVE COME a long way in reducing our use of fossil fuels and replacing them with the industry's residuals. The greener we get by making positive contributions to the environment, the better it will be for our industry.

Our timber base is not unlike an agricultural crop except that it is slow growing and therefore its cycle is longer. We are learning to care for it, to plant and cultivate the right species, and in some cases even to fertilize to accelerate growth. The materials Canfor produces are environmentally friendly and use less energy to produce than competing products. On a pound for pound basis, lumber is stronger than steel, has more liveable characteristics than cement, and is more attractive to the eye.

Our industry is looking at major opportunities in energy production and even in fuel production for aircraft and automobiles. The energy sector's use of biomass is another major change, and one that will only gain momentum. Our industry will not only sell energy in the future but also produce new materials such as pellets to help others create energy or heat in industrial and private sectors. We are now close to producing bio-fuels, which will be a viable substitute for fossil fuels. In decreasing our use of fossil fuels, we are now achieving what has always been our ideal— total utilization. The impact of this is that we are headed for a shortage of what used to be considered waste, with competitive bidding for its different end uses.

OUR INDUSTRY has yet to see some of its best years. But that will not happen until the United States recovers from the housing surplus created by the recession. Major factors that have helped stabilize prices at the current liveable level include the growth of the Chinese market for our products; the reduction in supply brought about by reduced annual allowable cuts in Ontario and Quebec; the beetle kill in British Columbia; and a degree of additional market curtailment taken by the industry. In the B.C. Interior, where the pine beetle has ravaged the forests, we are looking at a reduced cut for the next half-century, but those forests will eventually come back to a vibrant state.

In the future, writing and printing papers (where much of our pulp once went) will require less volume because of digital technology. On the other hand, tissue is a growth industry and a global phenomenon that will be influenced by radical increases in demand in China and India.

The industry trend to form larger and fewer companies has not ended and will continue. The combination of the need for scale to serve customers as they get bigger, and the need to be able to finance major capital expenditures because the industry is so capital intensive, have forced this trend.

A great deal of ingenuity has been invested in the evolution of the B.C. forest industry. The culture of forestry is also changing. Many more women now teach and study in the UBC Faculty of Forestry and all the young students have an increasingly global perspective. I have seen changes at every level, from companies adapting to constant market fluctuations to equipment manufacturers devising new ways to produce high-quality lumber. The industry will never employ the number of people we used to, primarily because of technology; we now require fewer people to produce a 1000 FBM than ever before.

LOOKING AT the big picture, we are seeing a different phase of evolution. Mike Apsey made a speech some time ago that summed it up nicely.

"Will we have a forest?" he asked.

"Yes," he answered.

"Will it be the forest that we knew or now know?"

"No."

"Will we have an industry?"

"Yes."

"Will it be the industry that we knew or now know?"

"No."

"Will we have markets for our products?"

"Yes."

"Will they be the markets that we knew or now know?"

"No."

So many unknowns, yet we continue to evolve and find answers to difficult questions.

Canfor's strengths are many. First, we have a strong focus on our customers and enjoy close working relationships with them. Second, we have a committed board and a talented management team. Third, we have a capable work force. And forth, we have a strong balance sheet, which gives the company credibility in the market and allows us to be opportunistic when suitable candidates for acquisition become available.

Although Canfor is not yet a major international company in terms of capitalization, it is and will continue to be a supplier of SPF lumber and northern bleached kraft. In both cases, we will be among the two or three largest in the business, with an enviable reputation in the marketplace.

Despite our promising future, challenges lie ahead. We are trying to find new opportunities for acquisitions so the company can continue to grow on a sound basis. We may have to make tough decisions to close some assets that cannot compete, either because they are short of fibre or the product isn't right for the market. The U.S. softwood lumber dispute is an ongoing frustration and expense.

Naturally, my role at Canfor has changed. In one sense, I remain emotionally and intellectually part of the company. Since I gave up the top job, I have recognized that not being CEO meant that I clearly had to act as any other independent director might, even though I had intimate knowledge of the industry, the company, and our history. I am also aware that in many cases when a CEO steps down, it's best to leave the board in order to offer a clean slate to his or her successor. In my case, I was not only a former CEO, but I represent a family that is a significant shareholder in the company. As a result, I am always available to management if and when they want to consult me on an issue, and I have been conscious of not interfering in their day-to-day operations.

To survive in the forest industry for more than sixty years, it helps to be an optimist. Rather than seeing it as a sunset industry, I see a bright future. I am proud of what the industry has offered to our society and am confident it will continue to make meaningful contributions. I have enjoyed the people I have worked with in the company, in the industry and, in most cases, the government.

Now the company my father and uncle founded not only has the strongest balance sheet in the industry, but it has a positive culture. Canfor is well poised for great success in the years to come. The industry will probably continue to be difficult for some time, but ironically, that may just enhance Canfor's opportunities to move forward.

Acknowledgements

I T IS IMPOSSIBLE for me to thank, much less identify, every person who has contributed to Canfor's success. Many appear in the chapters of this book. Others I would like to honour here as significant people who hold a place in my memory, some from Canfor and others from the forest industry. If I have inadvertently left out any friends and colleagues, I am sincerely regretful. You are all very much appreciated.

First I want to thank my family for the love and support they have given me personally, and for all that they have offered Canfor. I have been extremely fortunate to have Sheila as my wife, and she has been a wonderful mother to our five children Barbie, Susie, Joanie, Michael, and Lisa. Each of them has made us proud, and the same is true for our fifteen grandchildren: Tyler, Kristy, Tory, and Scott Hislop; Christopher and Tania Kololian; Alexis, Whitney, and Grady Ball; Spencer, Nathaniel, Caleb, and Theo Bentley; and Ben and Tosh Turner.

Two members of my immediate family have worked for Canfor—my daughter Barbara Hislop, who spent twenty-eight good years with the company, and my son, Michael Bentley, who worked with us for several years before attending graduate school and moving on to other ventures.

Canfor would not have thrived as it did without our employees. From the very beginning, I was lucky to have among my colleagues remarkable individuals, a number of whom ranked among my closest friends. Many dedicated themselves, and in most cases, their business careers, to working with us at Canfor.

In addition to the chief executive officers mentioned in this memoir, the company has always been well served by highly capable people heading key departments, including corporate secretaries Rick Weinman and David Calabrigo, and corporate comptrollers such as Jeff Hart, Ray Haslam, Brian Hobson, and Alan Nicholl.

After forming Canfor's operating group, we hired Roger Dee, an MBA whom we transferred to Balco to help them get "Canforized." Roger was a versatile member of our team who also took care of the minutes of the operating group for me. Orest Novick worked with Roger at head office and moved to Panel and Fibre. Bob Macdonald was a long-standing tax expert with the company. We had many outstanding secretaries at head office, including Pat Morrison, Julie Bradbeer, Diane Gooderham, and Kathy Simmons.

At Pacific Veneer, two of our main players were Jack Zilm, on the production side, and Norm Springate, who headed up maintenance.

Our Building Materials Division often welcomed the previous owners of the companies we purchased. Morey Edwards from Huntting-Merritt shingle mill was our temporary CFO before he went on to take charge of BMD. Also at BMD were Joe Jarvis, my cousin's husband, who later moved to pulp sales; Milton Orr, one of the most knowledgeable building materials people in Canada; and Pat Philley, a tower of strength and also a star soccer player for the Westminster Royals.

Victor Whitall stands out as our man in the Shingles and Shakes Division. Known as "Mr. Shingles," he managed Huntting-Merritt and later came to sit on our board. Victor's son, Pat, later became our sales manager for shingles and cedar lumber. Stan Douglas was manager of Stave Lake Cedar until his retirement.

Eburne's memorable staff included: Jimmy Robinson, whose father, Ronnie, ran Ottawa Valley Lumber with his very good manager in the Maritimes, Laurie Black; Jack Stevens; Andy Boucher; Alf Nichol; and Les Roblin, who subsequently became superintendent of the Eburne mill. Jim McWilliams, a UBC forestry graduate and a Rhodes Scholar, worked as Eburne's manager before moving to Chetwynd. One of the four head sawyers was Oliver Krog, a good friend and a trainer of Canadian champion retrievers. Hal Smith progressed through management at Eburne and wound up as president of Balco after David Balison retired.

In Lumber Sales's early days we had Bill Strike as our manager, an old-school salesman who was also one of our initial non-family directors of the company. Bill's right-hand man was Paul Cantwell, and English ex-naval officer John Harris completed Eburne's early sales team.

Later, Jack MacMillan headed up Lumber Sales and developed the "Customer Comes First" orientation; Bill Dunbar was one of several characters on our sales force. Bill King was also in sales with Ron Holton specializing in market research. Bruce Tombe, who sadly died prematurely, headed up rail transportation and was succeeded by John Trask.

Don Kayne, Canfor's current president and CEO, succeeded Jack MacMillan as head of Wood Product Sales, and Don was followed by Wayne Guthrie, a valued employee who left us to head another company's sales department, and has returned to fill this position.

Managers at our Englewood operation included Wayne Green, who succeeded Cecil Salmon, and Jim Williams. Glen Patterson was our fire protection officer there and became a key player at our Grande Prairie operation and in the positions he held after that.

We enjoyed the contributions of John Hruby, who ran Westcoast Cellufibre after we bought the company from him. His oldest son, John, succeeded him.

In Pulp Administration, Mark Gunther, former president of Evans Products of Canada and previously of MacMillan Bloedel, managed our pulp operations in Prince George and went on to become vice-chair of the company.

Garth Decker was manager at PGPP.

Bill McMahan was in charge of Pulp Production, and Rudy Paradis was the first pulp mill manager when we started at Howe Sound.

Pulp Sales and Operations started up with Harry Macdonald, whose right-hand man and Sandhurst graduate was David Amorre. Christer Arneson replaced Harry as head of Pulp Sales until Joe Nemeth succeeded him. Mats Strandberg managed our European offices for years, in Brussels, London, and Milan. John Murphy was another of our pulp salesmen. Fraser Evans was a longtime employee and Mike Bradley still offers technical support.

Bill Hughes was a manager at Howe Sound who we moved to head up PGPP and Intercontinental. We later brought him back to Port Mellon when we undertook the major expansion with Oji. Bill was followed by Don Stewart and Mac Palmiere, who is now in charge of Port Mellon. For many years Gary Thompson was our chief accountant at the Port Mellon mill.

Joe Nemeth succeeded Paul Richards as president of the Pulp Income Fund, which became Canfor Pulp Products Inc. Nemeth heads a team that includes Brett Robinson, Sean Curran, and Terry Hodgins.

In Forestry, Roy Jewison worked closely with chief forester Tom Wright before taking charge of forestry for our Joint Ventures (Takla Forest Products and PHAs) in the early years of PGPP and Intercontinental. Doug Rickson succeeded Tom as chief forester, a position he held for many years; Ken Higginbotham was our vice-president, forestry and environment, and he also held the softwood lumber file; Ken recently retired and was succeeded by Mark Feldinger, vice-president forestry, environment, and energy, who first joined Canfor at the Chetwynd Division. Paul Wooding, Ed Mulock, Leo DeHaan, and Stan Chester were also great contributors to our forestry efforts.

Arnold Smith was the first of Canfor's human resources managers (known for yanking guys out of the pubs and putting them on a boat headed to one of our camps. It was a hell of a way to do it, but it worked for a time!). Arnold found Jake Holst, a labour leader who helped us develop our relationships with unions. Doug Edwards served the company well as manager of Industrial Relations; and Doug Daniel worked hard as head of our labour negotiations. Rob Stewart, an employee dating back to our "Better Methods" training program, was vice-president, human resources until his retirement, when Gus Butow took over.

Daryl Mawhinney headed communications and Peter Moonen later oversaw public relations.

George Herbert and Anita Spencer helped us become an industry leader in information technology, a tradition that was continued by Art Mohn.

David McCutcheon headed up centralized purchasing, a position held later by Marj Vernon.

Bob Duncan was our first corporate pilot, who stayed on as our chief pilot when we went on to have a genuine aviation department. As the fleet grew, Bob hired Carl Enzenhoffer, whose son David was our last head pilot. Carl's right-hand man was Bill Quackenbush. Keith Pickett looked after maintenance.

We are proud that so many first-, second-, and third-generation employees—a total of 3,237 as of December 2010—have become members of Canfor's 25-Year Club. Linda Featherstone organized annual celebrations until Sally Murdock took over. Attending those events was a highlight for Sheila and me every year, and I welcomed the opportunity to express my appreciation by shaking hands with these individuals who had served our company for so long. Due to the size of the company, I may not have met a number of them before these ceremonies. Glyn Jones and Brian Hobson arranged semi-annual meetings for retired salaried employees in the Vancouver area.

In my own office I would like to acknowledge the help over many years of my executive assistants: the late Louise McConville, who joined us with John Liersch from the Powell River Company; Yvette Vassal, who worked with me for many years; and Cyndi Anderson who has been my capable assistant since 2004.

The family members on our first public board included my father, Uncle John, Ron Longstaffe, Joe Jarvis, and me. In addition, we invited four outsiders: Ron Cliff, Peter Lusztig, Ron Mannix, and Lou Rasminsky. Ron Cliff is a lifelong friend and the son-in-law of Fred Brown, who had led us to our most successful timber purchases. Ron is currently the chairman of the board and his contributions have been outstanding. Peter Lusztig, dean of UBC's Faculty of Commerce and Business Administration, chaired our governance committee and later served on the board of Canfor Pulp. Ron Mannix spoke up on issues and did not hesitate to voice his views. Lou Rasminsky, the last of the first public directors, was a distinguished Canadian and a former governor of the Bank of Canada who agreed to hold a spot for Bill Daniel, CEO of Shell Canada, whose arrival on the board was delayed for a year or two. Bill went on to be a strong director; he asked all the right questions and was an excellent influence on the rest of us.

The next generation of Canfor directors carried on the degree of excellence that we had come to expect. Members included Ron Riley, a senior executive from Canadian Pacific with diversified experience; Michael Phelps from Westcoast Energy; David Emerson as Canfor's president; and Eric Newell, the knowledgeable head of Syncrude and another invaluable presence from Alberta. Carole Taylor brought us valuable insight on the environment and on media issues, and also did a stellar job chairing our environment, health, and safety committee. Carole was the third woman on our board at the time, joining my cousin, Marietta Hurst, and my daughter Barbara Hislop, both of whom were valued directors who replaced my father and John Prentice after they died. Mark Cullen came to us for a short time from RBC with sound financial advice. Jim Pattison and Michael Korenberg became directors before our acquisition of Slocan. With that acquisition, we were joined by Don Selman, Brandt Louie, Stephen Jarislowsky, and Jim Shepherd. Paul Tellier joined later.

With changes in 2007, we invited Ian Lapey from Third Avenue and Thomas Tutsch, formerly of Nesbitt Burns. Jim Shepard II came on the board before being appointed interim and then full-time CEO. Ian Lapey was later replaced by Conrad Pinette from Lignum and B.C. Forest Products. With the purchase of New South we welcomed Mack Singleton. Glen Clark, Ross Smith, and Bill Stinson are our three newest directors.

When the three pulp mills in Prince George were dividended out to Canfor Corporation shareholders, the shareholders obtained 49.8 percent of the partnership, while the company retained the remaining 50.2 percent. The company now required two boards, one consisting of three independent directors who represent the public shareholders—Charles Jago, Stan Bracken-Horrocks, and Don Campbell, who also serve on the partnership board along with David Calabrigo, Ron Cliff, Joe Nemeth, Michael Korenberg, Bill Stinson, and me.

It is not practical to mention all the bright individuals I have known throughout our industry in this book, but I would like to recognize a few that come to mind:

Seaboard, the lumber sales and shipping co-op, was originally organized by Chuck Grinell. For years it was then headed by Claude Effinger (Jimmy Robinson's father-in-law), who was then succeeded by Harry O'Hagen. Seaboard's sales manager Bob Edgett along with Neil Morrison headed the U.K. operations, where he looked after Sheila and me during our visit. Clive Roberts started with Seaboard in the United Kingdom and succeeded Vassill Forrester as head of the shipping company. Clive then became president and CEO of both sales and the shipping company.

Roy Whittle, vice-president of B.C. Forest Products, had the best insight in the industry into labour matters, and he offered a great deal of wisdom.

Scott Paper enjoyed good leadership first under the guidance of George O'Leary, Bob Stewart, and John Reed.

At Weldwood, George Richards moved ably into Tom Buell's shoes.

Duncan Davies succeeded Bill Sauder at Interfor and proved to be a competent CEO.

Some independent operators I knew well included Asa Johal, a great philanthropist and operator at Terminal Sawmills; the Andersen and Stewart families in the Interior; Ivor Killy, the first sawmiller to enter into a chip agreement with PGPP; Ivor's son, George; and Dave Ainsworth in the Cariboo.

Finally, thanks also to those who helped me complete this memoir through its many phases: I cannot say enough about Robin Fowler, my ghostwriter, for her help and research, and most of all, for her patience. Cyndi Anderson, my talented executive assistant, has provided continual support and assistance throughout this process. I would also like to thank Bob Plecas for his early advice; Mike Apsey for his input and careful reviewing; along with Gordon Armstrong, David Calabrigo, Barbara Hislop, Michael Jordan, and Ken Higginbotham. Many thanks to Sally Murdock for looking after the Canfor archives and photographs.

I would also like to extend appreciation to my publisher, Scott McIntyre, to Trena White, and to the whole team that supports them.

Index